Joyous
Living
Journal

Joyous Living Journal

Petra Weldes

Christian Sørensen

Spiritual Living Press
Golden, Colorado

Spiritual Living Press
573 Park Point Drive
Golden, Colorado 80401-7042

Printed in USA
Published November 2012

Cover photo by Susan Pahnke

ISBN 978-0-917849-06-0

Joy is the most infallible sign of the presence of God.

—Pierre Teilhard de Chardin

Foreword

You were meant to live joyously and deeply connected to Life, Spirit, Love, and Peace. This is your natural state. We all know that it is more pleasurable and fulfilling to go through life happy rather than miserable. In fact, we are designed and intended to live rich, full, blessed and prosperous lives. Taking joy from our inner being, sharing joy through our relationships, and bringing joy into the world through our meaningful contribution—this is what Spirit is trying to live and express through us, as us, in our everyday, ordinary experiences. Every moment we are invited to choose joy, love, peace, or simply the Presence of Spirit as our ground of being. When we do so, Joyous Living becomes our reality.

Yet, too many times we forget we are at choice about joyous living when life rises up to confront us with its normal "soul stretching" moments. We can, so easily, fall back into unhealthy habits, limiting ways of thinking, and false beliefs that cause us pain or convince us we should be trying to protect ourselves. Any choice that causes us to shrink, contract, or self-protect takes us further from our natural openhearted, joyous, and loving nature. Joyous Living is about choosing, over and over again, to heal and release those old ideas and behaviors, while stepping boldly into our true and essential spiritual, joyous nature.

You have all the spiritual tools within you right now to meet any of life's challenges, and the *Joyous Living Journal* will remind you how to access them. The quotes from the great thinkers will inspire you, the messages will get you thinking, and the reflective thoughts will point you to a personal exploration while the daily affirmations will lift your soul.

Just reading the title, "Joyous Living," is a great reminder for starting your day. This book has been created to be your companion for a year. It's not intended to be rushed through but savored and enjoyed over time. It will unlock one door after another, leading you into revelations about yourself and your soul patterns of behavior while empowering you to be a greater conscious co-creator of your life.

It has been fun watching our first book, *Joyous Freedom*, go into extra printings. We continue to hear all sorts of wonderful stories from across the country, from individuals as well as spiritual communities, sharing how transformative and empowering it is to be on the "same page" for richer living with other spiritual journeyers. Partners on the spiritual path as well as small groups have told us about the depths of personal insight they've experienced by going over the reflective questions with one another. We look forward to walking the Joyous Living walk with you as we continue on the path of deeper, richer living for a fuller, more meaningful life.

May your whole year be filled to the brim with Joyous Living!
Petra Weldes and Christian Sørensen

How to Use This Book

Joyous Living Journal was written directly to you with the intention to help you engage, practice, respond, and explore—daily—new ideas that invite you into a fuller experience of yourself and your ability to live joyfully.

As an individual

As you read each thought for the day, journal, doodle, draw, or comment in whatever way allows you to explore the idea presented. Where are you with it? What do you think about it? How can you engage with it? And most importantly, how can you practice freeing yourself to experience the joyous life that is the Divine Intention wanting to manifest in, through, and as you?

As a book club or small group

Each month has a theme that is broken into daily topics. Groups may meet weekly or monthly to explore the topics and themes. Meditate on the theme together. Share what you discover in your journal. Discuss deeper practices that will help you and the members of your group. Pray for each other during the meetings, and as prayer partners, between meetings.

As a Spiritual Community

Using a journal like this allows your whole community to be on the same page for the whole year. Joyous Living can be a wonderful annual theme to focus your year around. The theme for the month can also be utilized by the children and youth. Each week's lesson can be based on the topic within each month's theme. When there are five weeks in a month, this allows for an additional deepening into the overall idea being explored. The individual days provide excellent material, quotes, and ideas for weekly lessons or presentations.

Weekly or monthly study groups can be formed, as mentioned above, in support of engaging with the material and practicing it more deeply. These can take place at your community location, or in members' homes for a more intimate, community-building experience.

January

Living Your Vision

Happy New Year

Behind all the fun and flash of the New Year, there is deep spiritual significance. It's only in the last few hundred years that the Western culture has come to recognize January 1 as the start of the New Year. Up until 1752, the British Empire celebrated their new year on the 25th of March. But celebrate they did, as have people through time participated in symbolically ending a chapter in their life and beginning the next.

Many people look forward to the new year for a new start on old habits.
—Unknown

There are varying New Year's customs which could feel like superstitions … such as polar bear plunges to cleanse the old; people throwing old things out their windows in some towns; people burning effigies at midnight in others … all of which seem to come from a parallel conviction of setting things right, cleaning up messes, making amends with friends. It's about completing the old and beginning the new year in the manner you'd like it to unfold. As you sweep out the old, it's important to fill the space with what you desire; otherwise the world will fill the void with what it's got left over. In many Spanish-speaking cultures, one of the more popular New Year traditions involves buying new underwear in a certain color to determine what kind of experience you will have in the upcoming year, with each color having symbolic meaning attracting to you a specific intention. Whatever tradition you are choosing … toasting with champagne, watching fireworks in the sky, or smooching with your loved one … people around the globe are recognizing an important transition from what was and welcoming what can be through their symbolic actions. Be conscious as to what you are calling into your New Year.

Reflection: Write a list of what you are willing to leave behind in last year, and write out what intentions you want to set in motion for this year.

Affirmation: I create space in my life for the glorious good God's got in store for me!

The Gift of Life

Spirit has given you the greatest gift; it is the gift of your life. What you make of it is the gift you give back to Spirit! So, what are you doing with this gift? Are you living the life of your dreams? Look beneath the specific forms of your life, your job, car, house, or other material things to the quality and essence of your life. Is it fulfilling? Meaningful? Are you being Creative? Loving? Connected? Playful? Is your intelligence being stimulated and your passion kindled?

Capture a new vision for your life. What needs to be changed, renewed, or created so that you experience the quality of life that you've always dreamed of? What does it feel like to be you, living inside your dream life? Remember, you are free to create your life any way you choose. Then know that the strength and intelligence of the Universe is on your side!

Life is like a game of cards. The hand that is dealt you represents determinism; the way you play it is free will.

—Jawaharlal Nehru

Reflection: What kind of a life is my dream life if I were to describe it in qualities or experience, not in specific forms? How close am I to living that right now?

Affirmation: I create a rich, meaningful, and fulfilling life for myself. The Universe supports me by taking care of how it manifests in form.

Joy + Vision = The Dance

Choose One Thing

What do you want to do, have, create, or experience this year? Take some time to really think about all the things you said you'd like to have different or to work on. Now pick the ONE thing you will focus on. Picking one thing that you really intend to change or one way you intend to grow this year keeps you from scattering your energy and becoming overwhelmed by your own list. Staying focused on just ONE thing keeps you from frittering your energy away on trying to do all things all at once.

You and I are essentially infinite choice-makers. In every moment of our existence, we are in that field of all possibilities where we have access to an infinity of choices.
—Deepak Chopra

Focused intention is the most powerful force in the Universe! It's like taking the spray nozzle on the garden hose and changing it from a light gentle misty rain that sort of goes everywhere to a powerful, intense stream of water that can peel the paint off your house or clean the dirt off your deck. Focusing on ONE thing narrows your intention and your time, energy, and commitment into a powerful force for change and growth.

Reflection: What ONE thing am I willing to commit to focus on this year?

Affirmation: I stay committed and focused to ONE thing this year, creating change and growth in my life in a powerful new way!

Believe in Your Vision

Believe in yourself! You are a delivery system for Love and Life. The inner urge that is pushing you toward something is Life itself wanting to be expressed, through you, as you. You are Life, showing up as you. Your heart's desire is what is right for you. Now this isn't just the simple desire for a candy bar or a new car. This desire is the fire in your belly and the vision in your heart that you have for what you want to make of your life.

You can cocreate your dreams into reality and live the authentic, meaningful life for which you are longing. This is the very purpose of your life: to express your gift. Remember that since this is Love's urge, through you, as you, you are already supported in moving in the direction of your heart's desire. Life believes in you!

> *Believe with all of your heart that you will do what you were made to do.*
> —Orison Swett Marden

Reflection: What's on fire in your heart and mind? What burning inner urge lights up your eyes and makes you come alive?

Affirmation: I trust my heart's desire and follow my dreams. I believe in myself, and I know that Life believes in me!

Joy + Vision = The Dance

Reason for Being

When you are held down by the waves in the ocean, there is such a strong desire for air that you'll find strength you didn't know you had to get you to the surface. When you are held down by life ... going through a dark night of the soul, missing your desire to live, going through an inner crisis ... there doesn't appear much strength left to get you to the surface. You can attempt to talk yourself through it or listen to your friend telling you, "You can make it; try harder," but it falls on deaf ears and usually just doesn't work when you are down deep.

When you do things from your soul, you feel a river moving in you, a joy. When actions come from another section, the feeling disappears.
—Rumi

When you are in the depths of darkness and have lost the will to live, it's not words but the stirring of your soul that activates your strength. A reconnection, a remembering, or an awakening to your soul's purpose and meaning is the revelation that will have you finding your hidden strength to get you back into action. It's the sudden appearance of Grace, the mystical stirring within your heart ... not the intellect of your head ... that will reignite your fire to live and express again. Not only will you survive the crisis, you will rise again stronger in living your reason for being.

Reflection: What excites your soul and gives you strength—and are you doing it?

Affirmation: I am finding more and more strength from within to share myself with the world!

Joy + Vision = Your Next Dance

One of the timeless truths is the Oneness of Spirit in and through all things. Yet, have you ever struggled with two apparent opposite views in life? For example, you are to be filled with Joy for what you have—versus don't settle for less, aim for the stars, and go for your dreams. Which one is correct? Could it possibly be both? Could you live in Joy and have Vision? To experience the Joy of the moment and appreciate how Spirit is presently blessing your world in Its myriad of ways will only create a solid foundation and confirmation of the unfolding ever-present blessing there is in life.

> *If God is going to interpret Himself to man, He must interpret Himself through man. And Spirit can make no gift that we do not accept.*
> —Ernest Holmes

To have a Vision that calls forth a greater aspect of yourself is also a gift. There is Joy in creation as all artists will acknowledge. When being in the flow, there is a fresh, revitalizing experience of life. The balance of Joy and Vision is a great combination. Vision will keep you from getting stuck in life, and Joy brings the intriguing celebration and appreciative energy to the manifesting experience. It's the honoring of the Presence in the present moment while being open to the greater-yet-to-be looking to be manifested. The Vision is the Divine request for your next dance into your awaiting Good.

Reflection: Where is your present Joy? What Vision is calling you to dance with God?

Affirmation: I live my Vision and feel the Joy!

Joy + Vision = The Dance

January 7
Trusting the Law

The Universal Law of Cause and Effect is always operating in your life. Any time you set an intention, make a declaration, or claim your desire, you set a Cause into motion. In that instant, the Effect, or result, is already assured. Think of it like two sides of the same coin. You cannot imagine a coin with only one side. Every coin has both a head and a tail. The cause is the head and the effect is the tail.

Cause and effect, means and ends, seed and fruit cannot be severed; for the effect already blooms in the cause, the end preexists in the means, the fruit in the seed.
—Ralph Waldo Emerson

The good news is, then, that you do not have to make something grow from a new cause you have intended. Once you have set a new cause in motion, planted a new idea in mind, or committed to an intention, you can relax and trust this process.

Reflection: Find as many examples of the Law of Cause and Effect in Nature as you can. It works exactly the same way in your life.

Affirmation: I relax and trust that every new Cause I set into motion automatically blooms into its intended result.

Beyond Your Itinerary

So often what calls your attention is not really what's at the core. The surface catches your interest, but the real gifts await your unearthing. The mythic journey that called Gilgamesh or Arthur out into the world was a willingness to say yes to adventure and discovery beyond the reason for going. When traveling, there are great destinations and experiences waiting for you that you know nothing about. You have to step out the front door and get out of your neighborhood.

In joyous living, what's ahead of you is beyond your itinerary. The twists and turns can hurt and the insights may shock you, but the revelations will liberate you. You will come to trust a life beyond your plans.

All happenings, great and small, are parables whereby God speaks. The art of life is to get the message.
—Malcolm Muggeridge

Reflection: Where am I not willing to trust the adventure my soul wants to go on?

Affirmation: I trust my spirit's yearning to go!

Wait Until Asked

Give up the notion that it's your job to save the world. People must come to their own realization of the Truth and demonstrate God for themselves. As much as you think you have the pearl that can heal your friends' lives, unless they're looking, asking, or reaching out for it in some way, they are not ready for what you have to offer. It doesn't matter how much you think they could benefit from a little more positive approach to living, even when you know what you know can transform a life.

Do not give what is holy to the dogs; nor cast your pearls before swine, lest they trample them under their feet, and turn and tear you to pieces.

—The Bible (Matthew 7:6)

What you can do is be joyously living and have your life working for others to see. Those who are open, responsive, and receptive to a greater possibility of being can then receive a bit of light that is emanating through you. When you are asked for guidance, God's grace will give you all that is necessary to respond to the call for wisdom. It's important to remember when you say yes, it's not you who heals, but Spirit that does the work. When you know this, the Divine activity will make Itself known as results in a transformed life.

Reflection: Where am I being pushy with my spirituality? Where do I need to back off a bit and wait until asked?

Affirmation: My spiritual offerings are appropriately given!

January 10
Unique and Precious

You are whole and perfect, just as you are! You are wholly yourself, and that is the Holy made visible. There is no one just like you; there never was, or will be. You are precious to Life and infinitely loved by the Universe! Just as no two blades of grass or two snowflakes are alike, you are an absolute original.

Explore this spiritual Truth about you. Where do you feel imperfect? Whom are you comparing yourself to? Are you celebrating your uniqueness?

The roses under my window make no reference to former roses or better ones; they are what they are; they exist with God today. There is no time to them. There is simply the rose; it is perfect in every moment of its existence.
—Ralph Waldo Emerson

Reflection: What would your inner world feel like if you KNEW this truth about YOU?

Affirmation: I am a radiant, magnificent, precious being, unique and wholly myself.

Circumpunct

The circle with a dot in the center is perhaps one of the simplest and most incredible of symbols. The circumpunct has been used throughout secret societies for millennia. In the language of symbology, it has represented the sun as well as the Egyptian sun god Ra; in the world of alchemy, gold—the perfect metal. It's been associated with the wisdom of the Philosopher's Stone, the moment of creation, and even the omniscient all-seeing eye hovering atop the unfinished pyramid.

God is an infinite sphere, the center of which is everywhere, the circumference nowhere.
—Hermes Trismegistus
Book of the 24 Philosophers

The circle represents wholeness, perfection, and oneness. The circumpunct has been associated with the Orphic Egg with the seed within, or our universe within the heavens. It is the spark of the male within the cosmic womb, representing where the one becomes the many. It is the symbol of the unformed potential of the celestial realm. It is a perfect secret symbol to represent God … the circle being God in its Omni-potential and the dot as manifested you. All that you are comes from that which you are in.

Reflection: You are the point of creation, drawing from the Infinite potential. What are you calling into form?

Affirmation: I live and move and have my being within the Infinite potential!

Oneness

The Master Teacher reminded us of our oneness with the Divine when he said, "When you see me, you see the Father." And "The Kingdom of Heaven is within you." Your life is the Life of the One, Whole, Infinite Reality expressing Itself as the individualized being that is you. You are as inseparable from the ONE as your hand is inseparable from your body. Your hand is a way that you express and interact in the world, just as you are a way that the ONE expresses and interacts in the world.

Part of the human condition is this sense of separation. Our senses and our science give us lots of evidence that this is true. But it is not

We must come to believe in the invisible principle of Christ, the consciousness of immediate Oneness between man and the Spirit.
—Ernest Holmes

true! The only thing you ever need to heal is your sense of separation—from others, from yourself, from the Divine. This is your true nature and the source of peace, power, and joy in your life.

Reflection: Contemplate your oneness—with all life and with the Divine.

Affirmation: I live in Oneness with all life. All sense of separation is an illusion of the finite mind. I sense and feel my connection with the whole!

Unrepeatable You

January 13
Unrepeatable You

Life is profound, mysterious, wonderful, powerful, and sometimes deeply challenging. Life is constantly changing and growing. Everything is shifting, except one thing—Life Itself.

This is also true about you. You are mysterious, deep, and profoundly complex. You are a rich tapestry that is in the process of being woven, right now.

A human being is a single being. Unique and unrepeatable.

—Eileen Caddy

Nothing about you is fixed, except one thing—you are uniquely you and always you and only you. Stop selling yourself short and trying to be like everybody else! You are a precious bloom in Life's garden!

Reflection: What profound and mysterious truths are there about me? Where am I trying to be like someone else? What is precious and special about me?

Affirmation: I discover myself in the Heart and Truth of Life. I am a unique and precious being just as I am.

High Vibration

You are surrounded by and immersed in a field of energy that is alive with potential and creativity. This is the very energy that powers the whole Universe. Quantum scientists call it "the Field" from which all creation emerges. Your being is the essence of that energy made uniquely individual as you; thus, your innate state is to vibrate at the frequency of Life.

Have you noticed how there are some places and people that feel light and spacious whereas others may feel heavy and dark? Sometimes you may have noticed an atmosphere of Love in a room; other times it's filled with anxiety. Even the hum of mindless busyness has an energetic vibration to it. Notice which vibrations lift you and which do not.

Light is infinitely more powerful than the dark. When darkness crowds in around you, become luminous and walk in the brilliance of your soul.

—Unknown

Reflection: What vibration and energy are you living in most of the time?

Affirmation: I tune myself to my highest frequency and align my energy with the Love and Light of the Universe!

The Joy Factor

Your life is intended to be joyous! The very cells and molecules and atoms of your being are vibrating in tune with life. Your whole life is the delight of the Divine! Simply notice the spontaneous, open laughter of a little child, and you see the powerful joy that is within everyone, including you!

When you are not feeling joy, you may be depleted or depressed. First, rest! Then, plug into Spirit. Plug into what makes your heart sing. Take some time in nature or play with friends. Start a stimulating conversation or get out your art supplies. Spend time in the silence feeling your connection with the Divine.

There is a laughter of God—let's laugh it. There is a song of the Universe—let's sing it. There is a hymn of praise—let's praise it. There is a joy, a beauty; there is a deep, abiding peace; let's experience it.
—Ernest Holmes

Then, feel your joy come bursting forth!

Reflection: What is your joy factor these days? Where would you like it to be? What plugs you into Spirit and makes your heart sing?

Affirmation: Joy is my divine nature, and I allow it to sing throughout my life today!

Effort or Struggle

Anything you really want to change takes diligence and sustained effort. Focusing your attention and intention means you are disciplining your mind and actions in the direction of your dreams. It's like hiking up a mountain. You may reach the top panting and sweating because of the work it took to get there, but the path itself was lovely, and the views along the way were glorious. So there you stand at the top, vibrantly alive and proud of your achievement.

This sustained effort does not mean you must struggle over it, however. Effort and struggle are two different things. Effort means focus, discipline, and consistency in thought, word, and action. Struggle means you are in resistance to that which is causing inner pain and anguish. Struggle means you are resisting the steps it takes to climb the mountain.

The great violinist Itzhak Perlman was told by an admirer one day, "I'd give my life to be able to play like you." To which he replied, "I did."

Reflection: How do you tell the difference between effort and struggle in your life?

Affirmation: I am diligent and focused and apply sustained effort to achieve my dreams.

Overcoming Challenges and Obstacles

Out with Doubt

Doubts are like parasites that wiggle their way into your thinking. You will honor either these fears or your faith, but not both. Which one gets to stay? Whichever you entertain becomes your friend and influencer. You weren't born to struggle for a living. You were born to show forth the beauty and glory of your creator. Fear and doubt will pull you away from your joyous living. Send doubt packing so it doesn't become the predominant force in your thinking!

Our doubts are traitors and make us lose the good we might oft win, by fearing to attempt.
—Shakespeare

The negative thought will short your Divine circuitry. You are in the same kind of relationship with God as an electric gadget is to its flow of power. It may be a great gismo, but unless it's plugged in, nothing is going to happen, and it doesn't matter how long you pray over it. Fear and doubt pull the plug to your Source. Faith and conviction plug you in. You get to choose what thoughts you are going to entertain.

Reflection: Which thoughts are you entertaining that need to be escorted out?

Affirmation: I am plugged in to the Divine circuitry of Life!

Gathering Evidence

We all know the studies about students who rise or fall according to the level of the expectations of their teachers. Even those teachers who expected the best from their students didn't get perfect performances. What would have happened if they had started focusing on those things that weren't working or going right in their classes? Would their students have continued to excel?

The same thing is true in your own life. Stop gathering evidence for your negative expectations! Look for and gather evidence to support your dreams, your joy, and what is working in your life, no matter how small it may seem. Your mind will cooperate by showing you whatever images you focus on. Remember—what you pay attention to GROWS!

Dwelling on the negative simply contributes to its power.
—Shirley MacLaine

Reflection: What negative expectations do I gather evidence in support of that I now want to let go of? Where is my life living up to my expectations? What is actually working and growing?

Affirmation: I expect things to work out. I expect good things to happen. I notice and celebrate every time these expectations are fulfilled!

Overcoming Challenges and Obstacles

Examination Time

Socrates was forced to drink hemlock and was put to death for corrupting the youth. He wasn't selling them drugs but was telling people not to be drugged by blindly accepting the information others fed them as truth. Socrates encouraged the folks of his day to live in the question and not just accept information they were told as absolute truth, even if it came from authority or experts.

An unexamined life is not worth living.
—Socrates

Take time to examine what people of position have told you to see if it's relevant to you before making it a part of your information intake filter system. Just because someone said something or you read it on the Internet doesn't make it true. For example, if you sit in a draft you'll catch a cold. God sits in the sky and judges. We're in a recession, so things are tough. What you see is all there is. And the list goes on ....

Reflection: What pieces of information do you hold that could use a reexamination at this point in your life?

Affirmation: The Divine within me knows all I need to know!

Challenges and Obstacles

There are so many clichés about handling the problems and challenges of life. "If Life hands you lemons, make lemonade." "What doesn't kill you makes you stronger." "It doesn't matter how many times you fall, just that you get up one more time." The thing about clichés is that there is actually a kernel of truth in each one, even if it sounds quaint or we don't want to hear it.

You are responsible for the way you respond to obstacles and difficulties. You can fold under them or hope someone else will handle them, or you can confront the challenges in your life with confidence. You have the strength, wisdom, and intelligence of the entire Universe on your side. You are capable of making good decisions and moving forward in new ways. Trust yourself. Trust Life!

If you want to succeed in the world, you must make your own opportunities as you go on. The man who waits for some seventh wave to toss him on dry land will find that the seventh wave is a long time a-coming. You can commit no greater folly than to sit by the roadside until someone comes along and invites you to ride with him to wealth or influence.

—John B. Gough

Contemplation: How do you respond to the pressures of obstacles or challenges? Is this strategy working? Is there an obstacle or challenge you need to face and overcome?

Affirmation: Spirit as me is capable of handling and overcoming any challenge or obstacle in my life. I move confidently, with strength and wisdom, in every area of my life.

Overcoming Challenges and Obstacles

Daring to Dream

You are not calling forth your inherent gifts by refuting what others have seen as possibilities. Can you dare to take a vision to the next level? Are you the one who is willing to dream beyond what has been seen?

Daring to dream means a willingness to invite a new revelation. It will take courage to speak it in the face of what has been. But when you dare to take action for a greater way, you will find all sorts of heavenly support showing up beyond your dream to make it possible. That which gave you the dream will give you what it takes to make it so!

We must all learn to live together as brothers or we will all perish together as fools.
— Dr. Martin Luther King Jr.

Reflection: Where have you not dared to dream big enough?

Affirmation: I dare to enter my dreams!

Broken Dreams

When you are deep in thought or concentrating heavily on a project and a young child comes to you with his broken toy, what do you do? Is the first reaction one of annoyance? Do you instantly go to compassion? Whatever emotions arise in the moment are fine; it's what you do with them that makes the impression on the sensitive receptors of the child. Are you able to step from the depths of your thoughts to be present with the pain of a child?

No matter the complexity of the operations of the universe, in an instant there is responsiveness to your pain. Life responds in support of your heart. Are you truly able to let Spirit handle the concerns of your world, or do you just want the attention and to be heard? Either way is fine; it's just good to be honest with yourself.

Reflection: Where do I cry out to the universe for change, but don't really want to let go of my story and position?

As children bring their broken toys
with tears for us to mend,
I brought my broken dreams to GOD
Because He was my Friend.

But then instead of leaving Him
in Peace to work alone,
I hung around and tried to help
With ways that were my own.

At last I snatched them back and cried
"How can You be so slow?"
"My child," He said,
"What could I do?
You never did let go."
—Anonymous

Affirmation: I get out of my own way so Spirit can bring the fullness of my dream into form!

2.0

Have you ever lost your hard work on a computer? You open your saved file and find that all your time, efforts, and creation have been lost somewhere in cyberspace forever … and you want to scream! The computer gremlins have taken it away, never to be retrieved again. Stunned in disbelief with nothing you can do, you either have to start the re-creation process again or cry. At some point you have to rise above your myopic focus of disappointment that keeps you from realizing you created it in the first place, and you can do it again and even better, for there is so much more where it came from.

Once we accept our limits, we go beyond them.
—Albert Einstein

Just as in Egyptian mythology, the old phoenix builds a nest it ignites, going up in flames, and from the ashes rises a new younger phoenix—the 2.0 version. There is shock and hurt in loss, but you must never lose sight that the great within you is waiting to rise from the ashes. You must stop fixating on your pain and realize it is the birthing of something greater.

Reflection: Where are you fixating on a loss rather than looking for the greater good rising?

Affirmation: I see the good rising in my life!

No Forcing the Flash

A fearful thought can take hold of your imagination and bring a wave of anxiety over your body in an instant. On the flip side, a great idea can take hold of your imagination and in an instant raise the excitement of possibilities to a whole new vibration. Genius and creative expressers know that great ideas come in flashes. Are you a receptive spot for newness to land, catching you by surprise? You can't force inspiration; you must be an available recipient.

To receive the fruitage you want, bring yourself into a conscious alignment—then listen. Become receptive and responsive to great ideas by creating space for them. The inspiration

The quieter we become, the more we hear.
—Ram Dass

may come now or when you least expect it. Once you've made yourself available, you might be walking along the beach or waiting in a grocery store line when all of a sudden you see something that triggers the flash that you weren't even looking for in that moment, but earlier had made yourself available to.

Reflection: Remember a time an emotion instantly took over your body and changed your heart and pulse rate? Take some time today and make yourself available for an inspirational thought to do that to you.

Affirmation: I am receptive and responsive to great ideas!

Inner Guidance System

Remember when you used to play the game "hot/cold" as a kid? Remember how you were blindfolded and then had to find something in the room. Each step toward your goal, your friends yelled "warmer," then "colder" as you turned the wrong direction. Finally "warmer" would turn to frenzied yells of "hotter, hotter" until you were right on top of whatever you were seeking!

It is only when you have both divine grace and human endeavor that you can experience bliss, just as you can enjoy the breeze of a fan only when you have both a fan and the electrical energy to operate it.
—Sai Baba

Learning to listen to your inner guidance system is a lot like playing the game "hot/cold." There is the deep urge of life within you pushing you in some direction while the Universe is giving you signals that you are getting closer or farther away from your desires. Become aware of the subtle push of energy within you that is aligned with a subtle pull of vision that is larger than you. It's a dance of stepping out on your course, listening to the response, correcting your course, and listening again.

Reflection: Are you dancing with the Divine Guidance of Life? Are you equally willing to step out and then to listen and course correct? Where are you playing hot/cold with the Universe?

Affirmation: I am guided by Divine Grace as I dance boldly through life. I am comfortable stepping out toward my dreams and listening to the nudges of the Universe.

Some Questions

When you make a list of your priorities in life, does what governs your world match up with your soul's desire? If you look at your Day-Timer and schedules, do your activities validate and support what is most important to you? Are you spending your time with the people you want to, while doing the things that are nearest and dearest to your heart, or are you hanging out with people you don't want to be with while doing things your heart's not into?

When you allow your heart's vision to carry you away, where do you go? Are you living your life there? If not, what can you do to make it your reality? Are you stuck doing what's safe and has always worked in the past for you and those you feel responsible to because you're telling yourself it's the wisest choice? Is your wisest choice the best choice in honoring your heart's desires?

> *When the soul wishes to experience something, she throws an image of the experience before her and enters into her own image.*
> —Meister Eckhart

Reflection: Answer the preceding questions.

Affirmation: I am living my days concurrent with my heart's desires!

Conscious Choice

How many times have you found yourself standing in front of the refrigerator not knowing what you want to eat? How often have you felt like you didn't know what you wanted in life? Often this is a product of simply being unwilling to actually say what you want. You may worry about whether you want the right thing or what will happen when you finally choose it. You may even become paralyzed between two choices, feeling unable to decide.

We are what we repeatedly do. Excellence, therefore, is not an act but a habit.
—Aristotle

Yet, you cannot live a choiceless life. Even not choosing is a choice. More often your choices are completely unconscious, made out of the habit of other previous choices. Your job is to become aware of what you are choosing and then decide if that's what you consciously WANT to choose. Practice consciously choosing. Cultivate the ability and the willingness to choose, and it will become your most valuable habit.

Contemplate: What am I not willing to make a choice about right now in my life? What is holding me back? What conscious choice would move me forward?

Affirmation: I am comfortable and confident making choices in my life for myself. I am consciously choosing to create the habit of making conscious choices.

The Dentist

Visiting the dentist may not make your top ten list of fun things to be doing in your spare time, but somehow that visitation keeps coming up. Paying someone to stick his big hands inside your mouth to go poking, scrubbing, and drilling while you remain calm under the bright lights is not the most dignified experience in one's calendar year. Yet as uncomfortable as this appointment is, you schedule the next one on the way out of the office.

Some tortures are physical
And some are mental,
But the one that is both
Is dental.
—Ogden Nash

Isn't it interesting to note your willingness to submit to some discomfort when you know it is for your greater good and health? Imagine if you could have a brighter smile, greater twinkle, peace of mind when thinking about it, a healthier body, not have to pay for it, and have a good feeling while doing it? Resisting meditation as if you were going to the dentist doesn't make sense. When the loving hands of Spirit reach inside your heart, your soul sparkles after its cleaning, and the experience does make your top ten list of things to do.

Reflection: In what way do you resist meditation? List your excuses. Now commit to a regular daily appointment with Spirit.

Affirmation: I make my time with God a priority!

Choices and Practices That Support My Unfolding

Balance

Think of the willow tree. It sways so softly and gently in the breeze. Yet at its core, there is a mighty and strong trunk that is rooted deeply in the earth. Imagine the lovely stream as it bubbles merrily along its way, flowing around obstacles in its path. Yet over time it can round off the largest boulders or cut through layers of rock to create a deep gorge.

If you have built castles in the air, your work need not be lost; that is where they should be. Now put foundations under them.
—Henry David Thoreau

Spirituality is as strong as it is soft. There is a place for power and for surrender in your spirituality. Do not be fooled. Strength is required to say YES to our dreams and NO to our dysfunction. Unleash the power of Spirit as you! Let it flow through you and be the core of strength within you.

Contemplation: Where do you need to stand strong and firm in your life? Where do you need to practice flowing and yielding?

Affirmation: I am strong and gentle. I balance power and allowing in the pursuit of my dreams.

From Idea to Manifestation

You can't change anything in your life with intention only. Like maybe you'll get around to it if the stars line up just right; your goal is to start regular spiritual practices; your aim is to get back to working out? A target without action is only a dream. Are you really ready to live a conscious life?

Learn to enjoy the discipline it takes to get you from idea to manifestation. Conscious action from prayer and contemplation is a terrific way to transmit the inner vision to the outer world of form. Your trek in life is what builds your confidence in the strength of your spirit and your ability to access it.

Pray to the Great Spirit and row your boat away from the rocks.
—Native American saying

Reflection: Where are you not congruent with your inner vision and your outer trek through Life?

Affirmation: I am enjoying my spiritual practices.

Healthy Body

Your body is the physical temple of your spirit. It operates according to a divine blueprint of wholeness. This blueprint is for a vibrant, powerful, healthy vehicle in which your spirit is housed. This blueprint is inherent in your being and informs every aspect of your body.

Your body is continuously seeking realignment with its own inherent wholeness. Your job is to provide a healing and wholesome environment so your body can achieve this realignment. This environment includes what we say to and think about our bodies as well as how we eat, exercise, sleep, and take care of ourselves.

Every one is the builder of a temple, called our body, to the god we worship, after a style purely our own.... We are all sculptors and painters, and our material is our own flesh and blood and bones.

—Henry David Thoreau

Reflection: How do I treat my body as a temple of Spirit? When am I not?

Affirmation: I provide a healthy and loving environment for my body to flourish and align itself to its perfect divine blueprint.

February

Living In Love

Being Peace

Have you ever walked along the beach and sensed the abundant joy of nature just singing all around you or walked a path through the woods and felt the blessings of your surroundings?

Sometimes you can forget you are also an expression of nature. Just as all of nature sings with the Divine vibrations, you do, too. You just might have let your smog-covered thoughts cloud your remembrance of who you truly are. You are just as much a blessing as the trees in the forest or the abundant joy of the ocean. Let yourself so emanate nature's life force that when others walk by you they feel as if they have been in the presence of the Divine vibrations of nature.

Real strength is not in power, money, or weapons, but deep inner peace.
—Thich Nhat Hanh

Reflection: What, in your thoughts and world, is keeping you from feeling the inner peace you feel when strolling through nature? And what can you do to experience that Divine vibration again?

Affirmation: I walk in Peace!

Groundhog Day

An early American reference to Groundhog Day can be found in a diary entry dated February 4, 1841, of Berks County, Pennsylvania, shopkeeper James Morris: "Last Tuesday, the 2nd, was Candlemas Day, the day on which, according to the Germans, the Groundhog peeps out of his winter quarters and if he sees his shadow he pops back for another six weeks nap, but if the day be cloudy he remains out, as the weather is to be moderate."

If Candlemas be fair and bright,
Winter has another flight.
If Candlemas brings clouds and rain,
Winter will not come again.
—An English poem

There was a festival, Imbolc or St. Brigid's Day, which is the seasonal turning point of the Celtic Calendar which was celebrated on February 1 and also involves weather prognostication. The holiday was, and for many still is, a festival of the hearth and home and a celebration of the lengthening days and the early signs of spring. Celebrations often involved hearth fires, special foods, divination or watching for omens, and candles or a bonfire if the weather permitted. How powerful it is to look for signs from nature in support of your direction and celebrate what you see.

Reflection: Where do you look for omens or signs from nature to help support your direction?

Affirmation: I see the subtle messages of wisdom all around me!

Love Yourself

Every teenager tries on different hairstyles and clothes to try to discover who she is. It's amazing how much alike each teenager looks while trying to become uniquely herself. Everyone goes through this stage of exploration. The important thing is not to get stuck in trying on other people's ideas of who or what you are.

I love myself, the way I am. There's nothing I need to change. I'll always be the perfect me, there's nothing to rearrange. I'm beautiful and capable of being the best me I can. And I love myself, just the way I am.
—Alliance

You are uniquely you. Don't try to be someone or something else. Just be you. Wholly you. Holy you. They both sound the same because they mean the same. Being wholly yourself, not trying to be perfect, reveals the precious, unique being that you are. This is the Divine, as you—and therefore holy! You are already holy and perfect as you are wholly yourself, Spirit incarnated as You!

Contemplate: What is unique about you? What is precious and funny and lovable about you? What do you most like about yourself?

Affirmation: I am a unique and precious expression of life. I am a radiant, magnificent being of Light. I am the Divine incarnated as Me!

Coming Alive

Doesn't it sometimes feel like you're supposed to be like Mother Teresa, Gandhi, or Jesus? They're the people who are usually held up as examples of someone who has made a difference and changed the world. You, however, are not meant to be just like one of them. You are meant to be just like you. Become clear about who you are and the gifts and talents you have to offer. Listen to what makes your heart sing when you think about changing the world.

One person can make a difference! Give of your time, talent, and treasure in ways that support, empower, and grow people. Find causes and communities that are working

Don't ask what the world needs. Ask what makes you come alive, and go do it. Because what the world needs is people who have come alive.
—Howard Thurman

for something you believe in. Lend your helping hand, your loving heart, your clear voice, or your strong faith to another. If you touch only one person's life, you will have made a difference.

Contemplate: When I am most alive, what gift or talent is most alive in me? How could I give it to make a difference in the world?

Affirmation: I have a unique gift to give. I have a necessary and needed talent to share. I make a difference.

Self-Love

February 5
Live from Being

Who would you be if you weren't so busy doing? Do you feel like you have to keep doing to prove your worth and value? You do not actually earn love, get points in heaven, or impress God with everything you are doing. Acting and doing are a normal part of life, but not when they alone become the source of your value and worth.

Start each day in peace and stillness, then you can go forth and face whatever the day may bring in perfect peace and joy.
—Eileen Caddy

Let go of your need to "do." Your "doing" is actually supposed to be the way you express your "being." This means you have to actually BE—"be" you—so you know how you want to "do." Practice "being." Let the "doing" naturally arise from that.

Contemplation: What are you doing because you think you need to in order to be valuable and worthwhile? What is your worth simply being you?

Affirmation: I am a human being, allowing the action and doing of my life to flow easily and effortlessly from the being that I am.

Self-Love

Learning to love yourself is the beginning of being able to love others. Stop listening to and saying the things you were told as a child. They are simply NOT true. You are a miracle of love, light, life, and joy—no matter what anyone has ever told you!

Imagine holding yourself in your own arms as a small child. Look deeply into your own child eyes. See your smile. Hear your own gurgling laughter. See just how precious you are. You are just as precious and beautiful and have the same potential for joy, love, and happiness as any child you have ever met and fallen in love with.

How could anyone ever tell you, you were anything less than beautiful? How could anyone ever tell you, you were less than whole? How could anyone fail to notice, that your loving is a miracle...
—Libby Roderick

Contemplate: Do you speak to yourself and think of yourself with the same love as you would give to any other child you might meet or see? What would you change if you did?

Affirmation: I love myself just the way I am. I know I will continue to grow and learn, but who I am is already precious and beautiful.

Evolving from Love

Evolution has taken the world as far it can by evolving consciousness to the place where self-consciousness has emerged. It's as if Gaia (Mother Earth) has evolved a creature that can leave the planet, float out in space, and look back at her. This evolution has been impelled by love, by Spirit giving Itself into creation, so that self-consciousness could emerge, as it has in you.

The most telling and profound way of describing the evolution of the universe would undoubtedly be to trace the evolution of love.
—Pierre Teilhard de Chardin

So now you are part of what will evolve the planet and all of life to the next level. What can you do today to express your love for the world and all creation so that they may continue to evolve toward beauty and joy? You can love and enjoy the beauty that is already here. Love it enough to help protect it; clean it up; nourish its thriving. Value this world as your home and handle it with love.

Contemplate: Which choices express your love for the world and which are in conflict with it? Pay attention to what you are choosing!

Affirmation: I choose to love and support this planet, my home, by making choices that are healthy for me and for all creation.

Joyous Loving

Joyous Loving is an open-hearted embrace of life with laughter, enthusiasm, and a positive regard toward all people. Explore those people, places, and situations in which you feel and act freely and joyfully, without the need for any intoxicating substance. As you notice where and when you are more open, anchor the feeling in your heart. Now seek to be that same way in other situations and with other people.

Withholding this love doesn't do anything to anyone else. It's like a beautiful rose refusing to bloom simply because it's withholding its light and lovely perfume. You can't be only partially shut down, just like the rose can't refuse to open only one half of its bloom. Withholding love closes all of you down and keeps you shut off from your own experience of Joyous Loving!

> *Love doesn't make the world go round, love is what makes the ride worthwhile.*
> —Elizabeth Barrett Browning

Contemplation: When are you most openly loving and free? Where and when are you not able to be that way? What would it be like if you could?

Affirmation: I am open-hearted and free—joyfully and lovingly engaged in life and with the people in my life.

Love in Action

Relationships are our soul assignments. They are our life course to deeper self-awareness if we choose to pay attention. They create optimal opportunities for personal growth. There are no accidental encounters. There is a soul agreement before we ever got here, putting us on a path for a casual crossing or a lifelong journey of togetherness; there is no mistake.

Love has no meaning if it isn't shared. Love has to be put into action.
—Mother Teresa

Relationships are eternal … they are of the soul. The bodies may pass but the energetic exchange resonates in the energetic field of who you are. Remember, just because someone has a lot to reveal to us doesn't always mean we enjoy being with him/her. The encounters on the path are there to support our evolution, calling us out of our familiar world so we are free to know the ecstasy of the Divine.

Reflection: Who is calling you out of your familiar world?

Affirmation: I express Love in all I do!

Relationship as Spiritual Practice

Relationships are an amazing spiritual practice. Relationships offer one of the most profound and challenging ways to spiritually grow. Each relationship offers the opportunity to learn about yourself, another, and Life. In relationships, you are confronted with all the ways that your past, your negative beliefs, and your subconscious patterns are still playing themselves out in your life. You get to see where you are unable to be unconditional love, where you harbor resentment and judgment, or when you actually withhold love.

Each relationship offers you an opportunity to practice the way you want to see the world and be in the world. Are you acting from integrity, speaking the truth, seeing with love, and looking for the good? You get to practice living out of the spiritual truths and principles you believe.

The highest form of spiritual practice, for those of us who aspire to create Heaven on Earth, is our relationships with one another.
—Andrew Cohen

Contemplation: Are you using your relationships as spiritual practice? Are you learning about yourself and practicing living from your spiritual ideals?

Affirmation: I allow my relationships to be my teachers. I am open to learning about myself. In every relationship, I practice living from my spiritual values and principles.

Gratitude for Love

Celebrate all the love in your life, whether you are in a primary relationship or not. Celebrate your partner, your family, your friends. Celebrate your willingness to be open, to trust, and to give of yourself. Celebrate how amazingly lovable people are!

Someday, after mastering the winds, the waves,
the tides and gravity, we shall harness for God
the energies of love, and then, for a second
time in the history of the world, man will
have discovered fire.
—Pierre Teilhard de Chardin

Contemplation: List every person you have ever loved in any way you have ever loved him or her. Then say a prayer of gratitude for all the love in your life.

Affirmation: I easily love others and accept being loved by others. Love is the connection between hearts and the bridge between souls. I open myself to love.

Intimacy

Marriage is a gift to the world when it's a place where two healthy individuals unite to be more than they would have ever been by going solo. You can't play a duet until you have learned how to play the instrument, and you definitely can't play it by yourself. Bringing your Wholeness to the relationship intensifies joy and increases your sensitivity while creating music together. When you give yourself completely in an honest, transparent, self-exposed, and vulnerable way, it awakens and enlivens every cell of your being, opening the window of your soul so you may be truly seen. Love is caring about another and, when the other cares about you, this felt communion and weaving of lives dissolves loneliness and fear.

The minute I heard my first love story,
I started looking for you, not knowing
How blind that was.
Lovers don't finally meet somewhere.
They're in each other all along.
—Rumi

Intimacy in relationship comes when you let go of any manipulative strings, knowing you and your partner love each other no matter what. Your marriage is a safe sanctuary to go through whatever spectrum of emotions and mishaps arise from the depth of your being or the actions in life, because no one is leaving. Intimacy is the revealing and offering of the essence of who you are to a sacred partner. When you live from trusting your relationship, you fully surrender to your sensitive, sensual, and intuitive feelings, by clearly seeing with the eyes of love. Passionate people are lovers of life who create a sweetness and harmony, filling the eternal moment with a grateful stroll through a world of joyful living.

Reflection: How can I be a safer place for truth to be shared? How can I reveal more of my soul to my partner?

Affirmation: I am intimately honest and passionate with my soul partner!

Sexuality and Spirituality

Not making a big deal out of sexuality is to deny the presence of one of the most natural forces in our lives. Your body's ability to feel pleasure is one of the great blessings of having a body. When you open your soul to loving another human being, you can transcend the boundaries of bodies, uniting in a transitory experience that is out of this world, which you can get to only when two unite. To be able to connect with the essence of another's soul and see the Divinity within will move you beyond all your old attitudes and conflicts around lovemaking.

Real love is the love that sometimes arises after sensual pleasure: if it does, it is immortal; the other kind inevitably goes stale, for it lies in mere fantasy.
—Giacomo Casanova

When you are brave enough to have the heart to take the time to look deep into the soul and essence of your partner, you are mingling with more than just a body. It's in the tenderness of this vulnerable space that you can allow yourself to open and be seen, intensifying everything. Your spiritual life is elevated as you learn to trust your vulnerability to take you places the mind and body cannot go. Your sexuality can be a sacred part of your spiritual life.

Reflection: What old beliefs around making love still keep you from fully letting go?

Affirmation: I soar to new heights as I am with the perfect person to entrust with my vulnerability!

The smallest movement of the lips can ignite a flood of emotions opening the closed sanctuary of the soul—uniting two into one breath. Whether it's as soft as a feather or as strong as a god, it can send the body quivering in anticipation, yet create the paradoxical desire to delay gratification. Make sure you indulge yourself this Valentine's Day with one of those magical memorable kisses.

*'Twas not my lips you kissed
But my soul*
—Judy Garland

*Kisses are a far better fate
than wisdom....*
—E.E. Cummings

*People who throw kisses are mighty hopelessly
lazy.*
—Bob Hope

Reflection: What do you feel that allows you to trust a moment to intimacy?

Affirmation: I love to love!

The Power of Love

Hearing your sick child moan in discomfort is not a comfortable place for a parent. You are willing to try all your metaphysical tools and conventional approaches to alleviate his pain and discomfort. You are even willing to swap your well-being for his aches. Without knowing how to make your child feel instantly better, you sit by, watching and waiting, which can be a heartbreaking sense of helplessness; but somehow it turns into an outpouring of deep love.

The soul is healed by being with children.
—Fyodor Dostoevsky

You find yourself pulling from something more than you knew you had. You pray your touch brings comfort and relief. There is a calling in of a transformative power, you don't know where from, but with all your being you believe there could be Divine Intervention. You look for positive signs of emerging Good. When you feel the fever break, see a bit of a smile and color return, you are reminded, once again, of the real power of love and the influence of your caring presence, which does make a difference.

Reflection: Have you found yourself holding a sick child, calling upon something greater than yourself to help with the healing? Did you feel a stronger love fill your soul?

Affirmation: I know a greater expression of love is always available to me!

Love as Spiritual Practice

There are so many ways to understand and define love. Many of these definitions revolve around romantic love. But this just isn't enough. Love is actually a spiritual principle that is at the heart of Life itself. Love is the impulsion of Life to express and become more through everyone and all of creation. Therefore everything is already in Love and worthy of Love.

The spiritual practice of Love is having a positive regard for another. Love is a decision to act and behave toward another in a positive and consistent way. Love is the desire to know another as much as you know yourself. Love is the ability to care, deeply and fully. Love is vulnerable, accepting, yet strong. Love is not afraid to tell the truth. Love is the most powerful force in the world.

In real love you want the other person's good. In romantic love you want the other person.
—Margaret Anderson

Contemplation: How do you live the spiritual practice of Love in your life? How do you practice being Love when you don't feel loving?

Affirmation: I am love in expression. I bring love to every situation. Every person deserves Love from me through my words, actions, and positive regard for him or her.

The Transformative Power of Love

The Transformative Power of Love

Love is the transformative force in the universe. Love and giving are inseparable, just as the scent comes naturally from the rose. God loves to love. Love is not complicated; it's caring, accepting, and kind. Relationships are the laboratories of life where you have the opportunity to move from conceptual love to the experience of love by unconditionally sharing of your heart.

Perhaps love is the process of my gently leading you back to yourself.
—Antoine de Saint-Exupery

You cannot force another to love. You can be a loving expression, and what will manifest in your life is love. It may not be with whom you want, but, if they are incapable of returning love, it's not your job to make them into something they are not. Your responsibility is to be love and what does not nourish that will fade away. Love yourself enough to let go, and trust love to continue to transform your world.

Reflection: Where are you using love to attempt to get what you want rather than trusting the natural expression of who you are to attract more love into your world?

Affirmation: I am trusting the transformative power of Love in my life!

Attraction

Remember playing with magnets in science class as a kid? All those metal shavings on the paper could be shaped and formed by moving the magnet around. The positive pole attracted the shavings and the negative pole repelled them. This same principle is operating in your life, only it's your positive and negative thoughts and attitudes that are shaping your life around you.

Remember, you are a magnet! Your attitude, beliefs, and words are attractors. Choosing to focus on what you do want rather than what you don't want, makes you a magnetic attractor for your positive desire. Attract more good/love/joy/ abundance into your life by focusing on how those things are already in your life. Notice positive things, speak about positive things, and be grateful for the positive things in your life.

Like attracts like. Whatever the conscious mind thinks and believes, the subconscious identically creates.
—Brian Adams

Contemplation: What pole of your magnet are you generally living from? Do you see the good in every situation or do you often point out what's not working or not right?

Affirmation: I am a magnet for the positive life I want. I release any negativity and old patterns. I look for the good in everything and praise it!

Understanding Before Reacting

Early one morning, a man got into his rowboat and paddled out into the thick tule fog on San Francisco Bay. As he was quietly gliding along at the break of dawn, he saw another small boat coming toward him. He started to shout at the other guy to change direction, but the other boat kept coming straight toward him until he was broadsided, almost knocking him into the cold morning water. He became angry and started yelling at the other person, when he noticed there was no other person on board the other boat. Apparently it had become unmoored from its dock and floated downstream.

It is one of the commonest of mistakes to consider that the limit of our power of perception is also the limit of all there is to perceive.

—C. W. Leadbeater

Instantly his rage dissipated; he laughed at himself. It's interesting to note that even when your perceptions and beliefs are not correct, they still can get you all fired up and into upset. If you can remember to seek understanding before reacting, it just might save you a heartache and give you a good laugh.

Reflection: Where in your life could being open to understanding some of your emotionally charged perceptions differently help you resolve confliction between some of your reacting and how you actually want to be in the world?

Affirmation: I see clearly before responding to life's calls!

Intention

Your intention is the most powerful tool you have! This is the only act of will you will ever need. It's not the power of willing something to happen, but rather the power to keep your will, your intention, focused on your desired outcome. It is an inner movement in consciousness that is the will to be and become whatever you have chosen.

Set your intention on the quality of experience you seek. Decide what you want to express. Become clear about the outcome you want to have, not only in form, but also in texture and quality. Then your intention, your disciplined will, will lead you through the twists and turns of

There are three kinds of people in the world, the wills, the won'ts, and the can'ts. The first accomplish everything; the second oppose everything; the third fail in everything.
—Eclectic Magazine

"how" it will all happen. You do not need to be concerned about "how" it will come to be. Just stay focused on your intention.

Contemplation: What is the difference between "willing something to happen" and using your will to stay focused on your intention? How do you stop doing the first and start doing the second?

Affirmation: I am focused on my desired outcome. I set my intention and use my will to hold it steady. From this intention, I cannot be moved.

Action

Intention, without action, is not enough. Decide, act, move in the world with confidence, knowing you are moving from and toward your intention. Do not allow your fear, doubt, or uncertainty keep you from doing, acting, or moving in the direction of your dreams. Trust your intention to guide and support your actions.

Don't fear failure so much that you refuse to try new things. The saddest summary of a life contains three descriptions: could have, might have, and should have.
—Louis E. Boone

Don't think that just having an intention is enough. You actually have to move out from your intention into activity in the world. This activity can be confident and without stress, however, because you know you are moving in the direction set by your intention.

Contemplate: What intention have you set that you are not acting from? Either let go of the intention or start acting like it is true.

Affirmation: I act easily and boldly in alignment with my intentions. I let my intention lead me, acting and doing without stress or worry.

The Nuclear Force for Change

Have you ever found yourself locked into an extended state of being powerless within an unjust circumstance or caught in despair and depression you can't seem to shake? When you have begun a search for the way out, you are opening an avenue beyond what you know. This invitation invites a Grace greater than you, capable of lifting you to higher ground.

If your present thoughts and behavior have allowed this shroud to engulf you, then there must be a piercing of this seeming injustice that is beyond your present consciousness. As a seemingly powerless traveler through the darkness who has been caught in uncontrollable circumstances, a higher power has to help you out. If you can't find your way out on your own, a life crisis will help you by having you evaluate, reevaluate, and reprioritize so the healing revelation can enter. The nuclear force for healing is allowing love, forgiveness, Grace, and gratitude from within your heart.

> *When we are no longer able to change a situation, we are challenged to change ourselves.*
> —Viktor Frankl

These mystical stirrings are available to access within you at all times, even in the darkest of moments. The key to accessing them is remembering you can't make those moments happen no matter how much you beg; rather you must make yourself available for the Light to lift you from the darkness by letting go of your grip on where you are. The transformational force for change will come. And when it does, there is no experiencing it without change, which is why so many won't let go of their grip of the known.

Reflection: What pain are you willing to release your grip on and trust where you will be lifted?

Affirmation: I am lifted by Grace into joyous living!

Self-Forgiveness

Love is an amazingly important part of growing your prosperity. Unforgiveness, anger, and judgment all close down your heart and your consciousness. This restricts the flow of all good into your life. It also becomes the filter through which you see yourself, others, and every situation in your life.

Use the amazing, prospering power of Love to bless your life and the lives of those around you. Practice loving and forgiving those who have hurt you. Most importantly, forgive yourself for all the things you blame yourself for. Spirit can give to you only what it can give through your own inner acceptance. If you do not accept yourself,

Only happy sights and sounds can reach the mind that has forgiven itself.
—A Course in Miracles

love yourself, then God has a very small and narrow opening through which to shower you with joy and prosperity.

Contemplation: Where are you holding anger and unforgiveness in your heart toward another or toward yourself? What do you need to do to bring love and light to this state of mind?

Affirmation: I allow my anger and unforgiveness to melt in the Light of Life. I am loved and lovable. I see that others are, too!

Mystical Act of Forgiveness

You cannot be cynical or resentful and be an avenue for love. You must give up your old hurts and pains. Forgiveness is the transformative power that will disengage a righteous mind looking for justice and retribution to justify its less-than-loving behavior. The mystical act of forgiveness calls back your anger and pride from the combat zone.

Forgiveness will challenge the injured rational mind to trust love. It will invite caring and understanding beyond the walls of your walled protection. Mystical activity transcends reason and welcomes Divine revelations. Forgiveness is your transcendent passage to the freedom of joyous living.

We either make ourselves happy or miserable. The amount of work is the same.
—Carlos Castaneda

Do you prefer that you be right, or that you be happy?
—A Course in Miracles

Reflection: Whom have you previously barred from your heart are you being guided to now love? What old wounds and stories do you need to let go of so your heart can open to love again?

Affirmation: I follow my loving heart!

The Mystical Act of Forgiveness

Forgiveness

Forgiveness isn't going to change the past, but you have to let the past go if you want a brighter future. Forgiveness doesn't make sense to the reasoning mind that wants retribution. There is an inherent archetype that seeks justice and fairness. When a debilitating poison of anger has been released within your field of thinking, it will affect your body and world of affairs until it gets what it wants or you release it from its duty of revenge. The rationale of release doesn't always win out in pain-veiled circumstances. You somehow have to remember forgiveness is a spiritual choice, not usually the logical one.

Forgiveness is the fragrance that the violet sheds on the heel that crushed it.
—Mark Twain

Mahatma Gandhi said, "The weak can never forgive. Forgiveness is the attribute of the strong." No matter how atrocious childhood wounds might have been or how horrific adult experiences were, you must stop living in a tomb if you want the gifts of today. Let your story be heard by a trusted friend or worthy counselor to honor your pain, which is an important cathartic process of healing. Forgiveness will help unbury you from the grave where you've taken residency. You'll find inner peace only when you choose forgiveness over maliciousness. Forgiveness is the key to healing, freedom, and joyous living.

Reflection: Find an area in your life where you feel you've been violated, where there is internal conflict about forgiving someone, and list the logical reasons for not forgiving. Witness and honor those reasons, but then make the illogical spiritual choice to bring inner peace into this situation and journal how this choice can heal and free you.

Affirmation: I am free to be me in all areas of my life!

Given to Give

John says, "God is Love." If Spirit is what you were created from, then your true nature is love. Yet it gets covered up by the various experiences of life. When you begin to feel fear as a natural state and love as an unnatural state, it's an indication that it's time to do some shifting in your thought world. What you put out is what you get back; you don't get a karmic reprieve. Every thought you have takes you to either heaven or hell.

Whenever you choose love over fear, it is a blessing to you and the world you live in. Fear will contract you while love will expand you. You are here to share your gifts with the

God is love.
—1John 4:6, 16

world, which so desperately needs what you have been given to give. When you love something, it becomes more beautiful. God isn't looking for victims of fear but lovers of life. Your world has given you the perfect environment for awakening to new levels of love by loving what's in your world now. You will have in life whatever you are willing to be.

Reflection: Where is fear wiping out your love experience in life? How can you return to love?

Affirmation: I am now choosing to express my true nature of love!

The Mystical Act of Forgiveness

Sympathetic Vibration

Do you have any friends who see you in a different way than you feel you really are? Maybe they see you as one who is always late or someone who says the wrong thing at the wrong time or whatever your faux pas may be. The strange part is that your behavior begins to be a bit awkward, and you end up fulfilling their perception. Could you actually be tuning in to their thoughts and living them in their presence? When you refuse to accept another's perspective of you by maintaining your true identity, there will be a present shift for both of you.

When you offer a vibration, the Universal forces are working in concert with each other in order to satisfy you. You really are the center of the Universe.
—Esther Hicks

On the flip side of that, it feels good to be around people who unconditionally love you and are blessing you with their thoughts of praise and calling out your greatness. Sympathetic vibrations occur when you resonate to a particular vibrational frequency. Be the one to see Spirit and greatness within all those you interact with, and they can't help but see it in you.

Reflection: Are there some people you feel a bit awkward with? Could it actually be their thoughts you're picking up on? Reclaim your composure by seeing the loving presence within them.

Affirmation: I live within the Divine Frequency!

The New Gift of Now

Having the money and time to ski twenty to forty times a year might make you take the experience for granted. You'd ski the first tracks on the mountain until lunchtime, then wait a couple of days until the next powder snow.

But as lifestyle changes and responsiveness to nature's promptings are curbed by the demands of other responsibilities, it is amazing how just getting out on the mountain and skiing, whatever the conditions may be, becomes exhilarating and enjoyable once again. It no longer needs to be an epic day to be filled with enthusiasm. Just being out in nature with the wind on your face traversing through the trees down the mountain is wonderful.

Life is never boring, but some people choose to be bored.
—Wayne Dyer

Some children have so many toys that they are no longer impressed with a new one. Be careful not to become so full and blasé that there is no longer room to experience, without comparison, the new gift of the now.

Reflection: Where have you become so blasé that you are unable to feel the joy of a gift without comparing it to a prior experience?

Affirmation: I feel the joy that comes with this day!

A Gift of 24 Hours

So many people are wishing for more time in their life. Well it just so happens every four years you are given an extra day—a full twenty-four hours—for the calendar to catch up with the sun and for you to catch up with … your emails? Is that what you really want to do with your gift of an extra day? Some folks feel it's a gift to the corporate world because it gets the extra day of your life. But that is true only if you choose not to spend this day differently.

When you're young, your whole life is about the pursuit of fun. Then, you grow up and learn to be cautious. You could break a bone or a heart. You look before you leap and sometimes you don't leap at all because there's not always someone there to catch you. And in life, there's no safety net. When did it stop being fun and start being scary?.
— Sex in the City

Imagine if everyone around the world took control of this day as a holiday—to live in joy, to leap from the common day to an extraordinary twenty-four hours. Don't waste this precious gift by just doing another day like yesterday. This is a magical moment where time has expanded for those who seize it. How are you going to make this gift memorable and different? .

Reflection: Ask someone who is near the end of his life what he would do if he were given an extra health-filled day of life? Then realize you don't have to come to the end of your life for this realization, because today is the day you've been given the gift of an extra health-filled twenty-four hours. Are you going to do what you did yesterday or honor the gift?

Affirmation: I step away from my routine and take hold of my free day!

March

Choosing to Live

March 1-6
Enjoy Your Self

March 7-14
The Garden of Thought

March 15-21
The Third Way

March 22-27
Chaos = Crisis + Opportunity

March 28-31
You!

Sit, Breathe

Learning to still your mind keeps your emotions from running amok. Taking charge of your thinking means you can focus your attention on the good rather than on what's not working. Listening in the silence allows you to hear your intuition.

If you want to find God, hang out in the space between your thoughts.
—Alan Cohen

Sit.
Be still.
Listen.
Be Quiet.
Breathe.
Contemplate the silence.

Affirmation: I am comfortable with silence and with being still.

Timeless Moments of Peace

As stress escalates, it becomes harder to hear Spirit's voice because the one inside your head keeps raising its voice. Imagine, while you are surfing, a giant set of waves comes rolling in. You realize you are not in a good place and get caught inside looking up at a thunderous moving mountain of foam crashing down on your head. It's important to stay calm and breathe as long as you can.

After going through what seems like a washing machine with no light, only to have your surfboard ripped from your hands, you finally find your way to the surface gasping for air, only to see yet another larger wave crashing down on top of you. You use your last bit of strength to fight your way back to the surface, only to see your life pass before you, while gasping for at least a sip of air while being taken down another time. Somewhere, you find the strength in your muscles to fight your way through the turbulent commotion around you to get to the air. In a five-wave knock-down set, it's easy to lose your ability to hear your inner voice that's saying, "Stay calm, everything is going to be all right."

It's all about where your mind's at.
—Kelly Slater,
11-time World Surfing Champion

Life has the ability to amplify what appears to be a relentless onslaught of terror, whether from doctors, lawyers, economy, or relationships. But no matter how loud, distracting, or painful the facts of this world can be in knocking you down, consuming you amidst the turbulence, remember, the voice of Spirit can always be heard if you can enter the timeless moment of peace. You will find the strength to rise triumphant to ride the waves of life again.

Reflection: Where are you being relentlessly taken down? Pause in this commotion and feel the peace, then journal your insights from there.

Affirmation: Wherever I am, God is!

Enjoy Your Self

Enjoy Yourself

Thich Nhat Hanh suggests that meditation is as easy as simply sitting and enjoying being with yourself. What if it really were as simple as that? No elaborate rituals or techniques. No extraordinary discipline required, simply relaxing into the idea of enjoying your own company, being with yourself!

Meditation brings wisdom; lack of meditation leaves ignorance. Know well what leads you forward and what holds you back, and choose the path that leads to wisdom.
—Buddha

Contemplate: Who is this you whose company you are enjoying?

Affirmation: Every day I easily sit and enjoy the company of my Self.

Beyond the Nets

It can be tough leaving your sense of Good for the unknown possibility of something greater. But that is exactly what Jesus did when he told his prospective disciples to leave their nets. Those nets were those men's careers. They were their source of income. They were their reputation. If more fish is what they were seeking, then it might not have been the wisest move to leave the nets behind.

If you are fishing for more fish, more supply, more health, more employment, you just might be forgetting the greater Good waiting once you leave your nets for your desires of the material universe behind. You

It is our choices ... that show what we truly are, far more than our abilities.
—J. K. Rowling

are a multidimensional being who, when you leave the attachment of producing in the old way, can open up to the fuller aspect of the universe with all the richness that comes from knowing the Life Source. What lies beyond your present ways of doing and knowing fills all voids and then some.

Reflection: Where am I holding on to my less-than-spiritual ways of doing things? What might happen if I bring a great realization of Spirit into these practices?

Affirmation: I leave my known ways for Spirit's ways!

Enjoy Your Self

Hurry, Busy, Rush

Hurry, busy, rush, rush, rush … this seems to be the pace of life these days. Even with all this hurrying, the inbox is still full, the emails keep coming, and the time feels shorter and shorter. The product of all the busyness is a tendency to feel isolated, out of balance, and off center. So what do you need to do about it?

Whatever the method, the purpose of quieting the mind is always the same ... to step out of your own way and touch a Universal Oneness with all things.
—Susan Jeffers

You must make time for God. What is more important than knowing and experiencing the Ultimate Reality of the Universe? Set time aside to be with the One—as you, as others, as the Whole, as the Mystery, even if it's only for five minutes to start out with. The more often you take these five minutes, the more of this sort of time you will crave. And the more you indulge yourself and let five minutes grow to ten and then to twenty you will discover that the space/time continuum is much more flexible than you believed. You will effortlessly discover that you really do have all the time you need.

Contemplation: Simply sit in silence and contemplate Oneness. Do this every day.

Affirmation: I have all the time I need because there is an infinite eternity in God!

It's Not Real

Growing up, I'd sometimes go to the studio and watch my dad, who was an actor, shoot a scene. By an early age, I had seen my dad beaten up and shot in the Westerns, hanged in *Hang 'Em High*, crushed by trucks, blown to smithereens in *Star Trek*, and, at the end of the day, he would wash away all his wounds. What I realized was that not all the bad I saw was true. I realized a lot of what I saw was an illusion. How can I see through that which isn't based in Truth so as not to be fooled by the appearance others create?

Of course, the studios are for fun and entertainment. When you are in contact with the Divine script,

A person does not have to be behind bars to be a prisoner. People can be prisoners of their own concepts and ideas. They can be slaves to their own selves.

—Maharaji

then your world unfolds accordingly, which is to help bring heaven to earth for all to see. It will be a blockbuster. If all you want is to be used by Spirit, then the trickery of this world will hold no power over your reality. If you do not connect with the Divine Producer who has all the support lined up for your success, then the illusions of this world will appear real, and you'll find it tough to wash away your wounds.

Reflection: Where in your world are you being fooled by something that is not real?

Affirmation: I see through to God in all things!

Whose Story Is It?

When doing some people-watching, whether intentionally or just natural observance, it's easy to slip into interpreting what's seen. The image of someone with a limp or torn jeans or a child in tow will often arrive to the brain with a perceived story to support the image. When you have your perspective of what you see or hear, it becomes more difficult to have a neutral space to hear the true story.

Some people complain that roses have thorns, but I'm excited that thorns have roses.
—Unknown

It's easy to determine what you think you know from what you've seen, when you don't give others the opportunity to share their story. The loss of not hearing their truth becomes your loss. Are you able to step back from your opinion of your observation to create the space in your perception to ask them, "Can you tell me about yourself?" Are you willing to have someone else speak his/her story without slipping into adding your assessments?

Reflection: Have someone tell you his/her story and listen to hear that person's experience.

Affirmation: I am open and able to hear others' truths!

The Script of Your Life

Pay attention to your thoughts, for they are running your life's movie. Do you like the script? If not, it's time to sit down and write a new one. Throw away the thoughts of limitation, resentment, victim, and projection. Write a new story—your story—and start telling it to yourself every day!

> *You are today where your thoughts have brought you. You will be tomorrow where your thoughts take you.*
> —James Allen

> *It has been proven now scientifically that an affirmative thought is hundreds of times more powerful than a negative thought.*
> —Michael Beckwith

> *Change your thinking, Change your life.*
> —Ernest Holmes

Contemplate: What new story do you want to write with your thoughts?

Affirmation: Today I write a new story. I think affirmative positive thoughts. I think about Spiritual principles and how they are working in my life. I think about God.

The Garden of Thought

Yes

Walking through a rainforest, I find it's easy to notice that nature doesn't choose what seeds she's going to grow. She uses whatever has fallen on the rich soil. Some orchids actually grow from air, hanging in trees. You can watch these plants develop, but you can't see what causes them to become full-grown lush expressions of what was coded in the life of the seeds. Our thoughts are those seeds sown in the fertile soil of consciousness. There is a force of nature that doesn't get to choose, it only produces. Like the soil, the universal principle of Mind in Its Infinite Wisdom knows how to produce.

By faith we understand that the worlds were fashioned by the word of God, and the things that are seen came into being out of those things which are unseen.
—The Bible (Hebrews 11:3)

Just as no one has ever seen the law that operates upon the intellect of a seed, no one has seen the producing principle that says yes to the thought-seeds you've released. What you do get to see are the results. By the fruits, you'll know whether you've been casting negative life-strangling vines or delicious juicy fruit that is the nectar of the gods. The point is, the universe says yes, and it is your responsibility to seed your field and stay aware of what's growing in your life.

Reflection: What life-constricting thoughts are you sowing? Where can you be sowing some more delicious and juicy life-producing seeds?

Affirmation: I am conscious of the thoughts I sow!

The Garden of Thought

Your life is like a garden in which the fruits of your beliefs are growing. You can learn to tend to the garden of your life by tending to the garden of your mind. With your intention and attention, plant what you want to harvest. Keep your thought firmly fixed on ideas that are powerful, memories that are lovely, beliefs that are wholesome, and thoughts that are in alignment with what you want to experience and live. Keep planting seeds of joy and watering them with gratitude.

Pull out the weeds of anger, shame, blame, or lack and limitation with spiritual principles and the power of love. Do not rent space in your mind

One Joy uproots a hundred griefs.
—Chinese proverb

to people and situations from the past. Root them out and toss them in the compost heap! The work you do every day in the garden of your mind will determine the quality of the harvest in your life.

Contemplate: What seeds are growing in your garden? What weeds need to be pulled? What will you plant instead?

Affirmation: I plant the garden of my life with the seeds of joy, plenty, and love. My life is a bountiful harvest of peace, fulfillment, and connection.

See What Is

The Journey to Cosmic Consciousness starts with an ability to see what is. Take a good, long look at your life. Where are you taking the material world as Reality and finding yourself stuck with conditions you don't like? By first seeing what is, you can discover what you believe. Once you understand what you believe, you can begin to create new beliefs based on your new understanding about Spirit, the Divine, the Universe, and how it all works.

It is done unto you, as you believe.
—Jesus of Nazareth

Wherever you are experiencing limitation, you can start believing in possibility and abundance. Wherever you are experiencing struggle or anxiety, you can start believing in the Power and Presence of an Infinite Reality capable of accomplishing anything. Wherever you are experiencing anything that is not in alignment with the Truth of who you are, start believing in that Truth.

Contemplate: Look at your life and admit to yourself what beliefs you see operating.

Affirmation: I look clear-eyed at my life and uncover hidden false beliefs I no longer need. I release these beliefs easily and effortlessly because they are not true.

Self-Talk

Become aware of your self-talk. How much judgment, sarcasm, comparison, or self-pity goes on in your thinking? Listen to some of the things you say to yourself. Are you repeating the very things that were said to you as a child? How often do you call yourself stupid or say something unkind to yourself? How often do you bemoan, "I just knew something like this would happen. It always does."

You would be appalled if someone else said these same things to someone you loved! If you had a friend who spoke to you the way you speak to you, he would probably no longer be your friend. Speak as kindly, supportively, and truthfully to yourself as you would want another to speak to you. Use your self-talk as simply another place to be positive and affirm what you want to experience in life.

> *You may find the worst enemy or best friend in yourself.*
> —English Proverb

Contemplate: What is the nature of your self-talk? What are you ready to change in the way you speak to yourself?

Affirmation: I speak lovingly and with kindness to myself. I speak positively and compassionately about myself and others.

Geometric Patterns of Spirit

Watching a frozen lake you've walked and skated on defrost is a powerful reminder of the impermanence of life. The beauty of the geometric patterns emerging, giving way to expanding layers of warming water as the sound of cracking races across the ice is an indication that everything changes. Non-attachment to the creative brilliance of nature brings the realization of the infinite possibilities of its expressions. Noticing the underwater currents revealing their location by streaks, cracks, channels of water, and ice islands is a hint as to the goings-on of something below the surface.

The road to success is always under construction.
—Lily Tomlin

There is also a force of nature stirring below the surface of your world looking to present itself in your world. You are a brilliant outlet for the new patterns of life to emerge. It doesn't matter how hardened you've become, and whatever the reason, there is still a moving current of Spirit below, revealing patterns of possibility. What is below the surface will be revealed and prevail. Surrender to your emergence.

Reflection: Where do you notice yourself softening to something moving below the surface of your world?

Affirmation: The emerging patterns of my life are beautiful!

Adventure

On my kitchen wall, I have a lovely picture with Helen Keller's saying, "Life is an adventure or it is nothing." Can you imagine being deaf, blind, and unable to speak? Can you imagine the overwhelming excitement mingled with fear when you discover a world of possibilities you never knew existed? Talk about leaving your comfort zone! I had a dear blind friend many years ago. Each time she ventured into something new, the possibilities of expanding her life were enormous, but she would have to learn to completely reorient herself in this new place. Everything was different, and she would talk about being completely out of her comfort zone. Yet this was the only way she could break out of the shell of an otherwise boring routine.

We are all inventors, each sailing out on a voyage of discovery, guided each by a private chart, of which there is no duplicate. The world is all gates, all opportunities.
—Ralph Waldo Emerson

Stand at the edge of your comfort zone and look out into the possibilities that are calling to you. Stepping out of your comfort zone is by definition "uncomfortable." Yet it is here that the new opportunities for growth, awareness, and self-expression abound!

Contemplate: What opportunities are calling to you? What new adventure awaits? Where are you holding back and clinging to your comfort zone?

Affirmation: New opportunities invite me out of my comfort zone. I welcome the adventure and embrace the new possibilities!

Part of Nature

Preparing to return home after an idyllic stay in nature where the experience has been otherworldly can be a shock to your system. You were out among the towering pines looking upon magnificent snow-capped mountain peaks; you watched eagles soaring in the pristine blue sky and the fish jumping through the glassy surface of the blue lake; you breathed in the crispy clean fresh air as you listened to the thunder of silence and wondered, "How am I going to deal with the tumultuous energies back home?"

We do not see things are they are. We see them as we are.

—The Talmud

Realizing it's not the time in your life to make this location your new permanent residence, you attempt to take it all in. You attempt to get one last impress upon your subjective—a mental photograph. But you can't seem to get it all in your mental memory … there is always something more to capture. Close your eyes and surrender to the silence and you'll hear nature inviting you into her scene. You'll realize you are as much a part of nature as the trees and the animals. When you stop trying to take it with you and allow yourself to become part of the Infinite, you will always have access to every aspect of God's beautiful territory.

Reflection: What have you been attempting to shrink down to your size?

Affirmation: I am in Heaven now!

Internal Review

When on the spiritual path, pause to take a look at the events in your world for their significance. What in you has attracted them into your life ... the positive or soul-stretching ones? If it's one of those soul-stretching times challenging the very fabric of your faith, you start looking at the different behaviors or attitudes that might have contributed to the energy-depleting experience you find yourself in.

What's interesting, if you are doing an honest internal check, is that you may find there are a number of places your attitudes and actions were less than clean. What is valuable about this review, whether any of those sensitive points played into what's going on or not, is that they are points of concern that come up for you from your subjective. Since they are coming up for you, it would be a good idea to clear up those areas if you can. It will make your joyous living journey forward less bumpy and more fun.

I am a woman in process. I'm just trying like everybody else. I try to take every conflict, every experience, and learn from it. Life is never dull.
—Oprah Winfrey

Reflection: Make a list of the points of concern that come to your awareness as possible causes when deep challenges hit your world. What adjustments can you make to clean up some of those areas without creating total chaos?

Affirmation: I courageously look at all points of concern my subjective reveals to me!

The Third Way

The Third Way

Learn to disagree with ideas, not people. This will allow you to find a place for authentic dialogue, without creating attack or defense. Keeping disagreements from becoming polarized is the only way to find the third, greater solution—which is always better than anyone's individual idea. William Ury calls this the "Third Side."

Conflict, in itself, is not a bad thing. Conflict is a natural and healthy process, necessary for making progress and dealing with injustice… the goal is not to end or eliminate conflict but simply to transform the way it is expressed.
—William Ury

To find the Third Side of a conflict, you must expand your view beyond the two opposing sides to the view from the whole group, whether that group is a relationship, a family, a work group, a community, a nation, or the planet. The Third Side looks at the conflict from the point of view of what's best for the whole, and that emerges from the collective rather than simply choosing one side or the other.

Contemplate: Where have you allowed yourself to become polarized into seeing only one side of an issue? Try imagining it from the view of the other side. Now try imagining it from the view of the Whole.

Affirmation: I am no longer frightened by conflict. I know it is a natural part of life and relationships. I practice healthy, mature communication and conflict resolution.

Spirit Prevails

Some of the issues facing humanity today are beyond human means for solution. They are beyond the grasp of political leaders and their "think tanks." If there were solutions, they would have been implemented by now. These are the times that challenge one's beliefs, and one can give way to doubt and fear. Is your faith in God bigger than your faith in this world's challenges?

The world's issues will be solved spiritually, not by taking sides or through dominance. You must rise above thinking in human terms and be open to Grace revealing a new revelation of what is possible. Yes, vote for whoever you feel represents the wisest form of leadership, but the world will be lifted by the people who believe Spirit does prevail. As you come to experience the peace and clarity of this inner kingdom that already exists parallel to the human world of doubt and concern, you'll know it's just waiting to be tapped.

As above, so below. As within, so without.
—Hermes

You cannot solve a problem from the same consciousness that created it. You must learn to see the world anew.
—Albert Einstein

Those individuals who have come to experience their own trials and somehow came through to return to joyous living become the great contributors to the emerging collective consciousness that is now changing our world.

Reflection: Is your faith in God bigger than your faith in this world's challenges? When have you been caught in the trials and tribulations of the human world, thinking there was no human answer, and then touched that spiritual place where you saw with new eyes and your world was transformed?

Affirmation: Spirit prevails in all my affairs!

Change from Within

"If only she would act differently, then I'd be happy." "If only he wouldn't behave that way, then things would work out!" How often have you found yourself busily trying to change others to suit your view of how things ought to be? How often has this actually worked in your life? Gandhi reminds us that we must "be the change we want to see in the world."

Seek not to change the world, but choose to change your mind about the world.
What you see reflects your thinking. And your thinking but reflects your choice of what you want to see.
—A Course In Miracles

Positive change in your relationship with others comes about when you are willing to change yourself. You must learn to ask for what you want, give what you want to receive, and see the other with loving and compassionate eyes. Trying to change others for your life to be better simply doesn't work in the long run. Changing your life requires changing your own thoughts, attitudes, conversation, and perspective. Practice making these changes, and you'll be amazed at how others around you "mysteriously" change!

Contemplation: Who are you trying to change so your life will be happier or better? How could you see this differently? What do you need to change?

Affirmation: I change my thinking by releasing judgment and need about how another should be. I change my life by choosing whom I want to be with and how I want to behave and be treated.

Benevolent Presence

How many times have you sat in a group of people and cringed because of what was happening? How often have you noticed tensions rise or felt that things were getting seriously off track? If you notice it, then you are the one who is in the position to bring it up and help get things back on track.

It's so easy to assume that you are not the leader, especially if someone else has that title or role. However, this is not true. You are a leader anytime you are willing to bring conscious-ness into a group or conversation. It may not always be comfortable, but in the long run it is always better. Do not simply sit back, let others take over, and then complain about where things are going! Invite others to see what you see, hear what you hear, and notice what's going on. Practice doing this in a calm manner, without shame or blame. Simply bring it to the awareness of the group. Then offer a new way to proceed. Lo and behold, you discover that you are, in fact, a leader!

> *If your actions inspire others to dream more, learn more, do more, and become more, you are a leader.*
> —John Quincy Adams

Contemplate: In what situations do you hold back and not speak until you finally either leave or shout? How might you do this more constructively?

Affirmation: I am a benevolent and constructive presence in any group. I am willing to say what needs to be said without making anyone else wrong. I am a leader.

Present in the Present

What you listen to is what you become, and what you become is the world you'll be living in. Every place you take a stance for your higher self, the lower sense of self fades away. The visionary is able to see the innocence beyond the mistakes. No matter what has happened, you can always return to the greatness of your heart. Forgiveness is a worthy tribute to your heart's magnificence.

Always forgive your enemies —nothing annoys them so much.
—Oscar Wilde

Without forgiveness, life would be intolerable. You'd be shackled to the pains of the past while the perpetrators of the pain are off enjoying themselves. Forgiveness is usually contrary to the thinking mind, but necessary for your soul's healing. Forgiveness is not something that usually happens in a flash, but tends to be an unfolding process of releasing from grief and pain. Forgiveness doesn't mean you have to befriend those who hurt you or have a conversation with them. It does mean you will be free to be present in the present moment where the new and exciting possibilities can once again be heard and touch your soul.

Reflection: Where could you use some forgiveness work so you can be released from the pain of the past?

Affirmation: I forgive and move forward in my life!

Contentment

In the beginning, God created all of creation, heaven and earth and all its creatures, and at each moment, it is written, God found that it was good. There is the implication from the ancient mystics and prophets who wrote this story that the Divine was somehow content with each stage of the work of evolution. Every bit of progress was greeted with pleasure and joy and was pronounced good!

When was the last time you sat back, looked over your life, all your efforts, growth, and spiritual practice, and saw that it was good? Contentment is a rare state, since we are usually living in the past or the future.

Health is the greatest gift, contentment the greatest wealth, faithfulness the best relationship.
—Buddha

While learning from the past and dreaming about the future, it's important to actually live in the present. See what has already manifested in your life. Enjoy the great and small ways that Life, Love, and Joy are already showing up. Be content with what you have, where you are, and how far you've come.

Contemplation: Savor the moment of right now in your life. Appreciate where you are and what you have. Discover an inner contentment with yourself and your life.

Affirmation: I look at my life and pronounce it good! I am content with myself and with my life!

Chaos = Crisis + Opportunity

Move Your Body

Sitting is the new smoking, studies have revealed. You sit in the car, sit in front of the computer, then sit in front of the TV. You sit to send a text, get on Facebook, and look at your email. This constant sitting causes your whole body to slow down. Even if you walk two to three times a week, if you don't move during the day, it's simply not enough.

If you don't move your body, your brain thinks you're dead. Movement of the body will not only clear out the "sludge," but will also give you more energy.
—Sylvia Brown

GET MOVING! Move your body and release the sluggishness of your life. Dance, walk, ride a bike, do yoga, stretch—anything, just start moving! Walk to get water every hour at work. Park farther away and walk to the door. Text standing up and spend time in the yard rather than in front of the TV. As you move your body, you will be amazed at how your life starts moving and how much better you feel!

Contemplate: How much time do you spend sitting every day? How could you move more often and more regularly?

Affirmation: I love to move and walk. I dance and strut down the hall and down the street. My whole life is refreshed, and I have renewed energy!

Chaos = Crisis and Opportunity

My son was born in a cabin in the mountains, and I had planned to raise him there, close to nature. As a single parent, I discovered that I could not support myself living thirty miles outside of a town of six hundred people. I sold my beloved cabin and moved to the South with my parents, where my son was raised. For years I railed against God and was angry about what had happened.

Yet when I look back now, I see how beautifully my life has unfolded since then. My son's relationship to his grandparents was made possible by living near them. I found extraordinarily meaningful work and my circle of friends is more dear to me than ever. My spiritual practice was strengthened, and my faith knows no bounds.

Everywhere we see adversity, the soul sees opportunity for our healing, expansion and enlightenment.
—Unknown

Every crisis is an opportunity in disguise. Begin by accepting what is. Then look clearly at what was. Look boldly at the worst scenario and imagine what might have been. Between the poles, there is a world of possibilities. Trust that Good will come of every crisis and that you are strong enough to meet the challenge.

Contemplate: What is the opportunity in this crisis for you to do, be, think, act, or live differently?

Affirmation: I know that I face this challenge with Spirit at my side. I accept it as an opportunity to go deeper, build more faith, and become even stronger in who I am and what I know.

Chaos = Crisis + Opportunity

Persistence

Remember when you first learned how to ride a bike? At first it was wobbly and challenging, but with diligent effort and consistent practice, the next thing you knew, you were riding free-hand down that great big hill in your neighborhood. Perhaps you had this same kind of experience when learning to play an instrument in school or tennis after school. Each activity started out with an idea and then came the hours of practice. Did you quit along the way and now wish you had kept it up?

It is with many enterprises as with striking fire; we do not meet with success except by reiterated efforts, and often at the instant when we despaired of success.
—Françoise de Maintenon

Every dream or goal is a bit like that. You must believe that you are never given a dream or a goal without the means to make it happen. You may have to work at it. Your dream may involve real effort (not struggle!) on your part. It may require diligent practice, constant improvement, and sustained effort. Life will not be made manifest by cowards or complainers. You can do it and the Universe supports you!

Contemplate: What dream or goal are you willing to practice or put sustained effort toward? What does that practice or sustained effort look like?

Affirmation: I move consistently toward my dream, without complaint. I am not a quitter. I practice every day, and every day I get better and closer to my goal!

The Passover

A powerful story of freedom is when God helped the children of Israel escape slavery by inflicting ten plagues upon the Egyptians, the worst being the last one, which was the death of the firstborn. The Israelites were instructed to mark the doorposts of their homes with the blood of the spring lamb so the Spirit of the Lord would know the firstborn in those homes were not Egyptians and pass over them. When the Pharaoh freed the people after losing his son, it's said they left so fast their bread hadn't a chance to rise. Passover is observed beginning at the sunset of the previous day on the night of the full moon after the northern vernal equinox.

Let me tell you the one thing I have against Moses. He took us forty years into the desert in order to bring us to the one place in the Middle East that has no oil!
—Golda Meir

This story is a reminder that no matter what the oppression may be in your life, there is always a higher power ready to intervene. The pharaoh of your consciousness that has you enslaved in limited self-expression must acquiesce to Divine intervention. No matter how strong the hold may be, Spirit will start tapping and, if need be, will get louder and stronger until your earthbound mind gives free passage to the emerging possibility of the awaiting "promised land."

Reflection: Where in your life have you been enslaved and, by some miraculous unfoldment, were freed from the painful grips of that situation? Where, now in your life, do you feel trapped? Can you return to the feeling you had when you were freed? Allow that spirit to fill you again, giving you the strength, courage, and confidence to claim your freedom, even if you don't quite yet know where the "promised land" may be.

Affirmation: I claim my freedom in all areas of my life!

Chaos = Crisis + Opportunity

Choosing Gruesome Images

Thinking twice before submitting yourself to cinematic emotionally charged gruesome images is a wise pause before choosing a movie. When you surrender to the journey the director takes you on in those scenes, remember that what you see and experience is as real to your psyche as if you had the experience on the streets.

The thing always happens that you really believe in; and the belief in a thing makes it happen.
—Frank Lloyd Wright

If you are working on being more receptive to the subtleties of life, developing your intuitive side, honing your abilities to hear the inner voice and to see with the inner eye, why give your emotional body more crud to process than it's already getting from living life? You have all that it takes to see Spirit in the physical world or cinematic one, so why consciously choose to fill your field of vision with violence?

Reflection: Pause before you submit yourself to screen time and ask, "Are these images that I'm about to give my power of influence away to worthy of my time?"

Affirmation: I wisely choose what I fill my field of vision with!

Buzzards, Bats, & Bumblebees

There are some fun analogies reminding us of our freedom: if you see a caged buzzard at the zoo, the top will be open in a pen that's no larger than eight feet because buzzards need about twelve feet to run for launching themselves into flight. So the bird won't ever attempt to escape. A bat on flat ground is stuck until it crawls to something with a bit of elevation so it can finally launch himself into flight. A bumblebee in a clear, tall, open drinking glass will attempt to get out through the sides at the bottom until it dies of exhaustion, never attempting to fly out the open top.

Every wall is a door.
—Ralph Waldo Emerson

Don't be like the buzzard, bat, or bumblebee, forgetting to look up and remember you are now free. Prayer is an attitude that can lift your vision higher and remind you of the way out. Whenever faced with a dilemma in your life, always stop, look up, and keep in mind the option of the opening at the top.

Reflection: Where in my life do I need to stop and look up?

Affirmation: I am now free!

You!

I Get It

One of Jesus's final statements when he was on the cross was "Eli Eli lama sabachthani," which in his language of Aramaic means "My God, My God, for this I was kept." In a flash, he realized this was his destiny. In the extremeness of the moment, he was exalted to a greater state of revelation and he got it … he saw, he understood fully what he had intuitively known, worked toward his whole life and sacrificed. There are some interpretations that state he said, "Why has God forsaken me?" which only lends credence to the success of his enemies. It would seem strange that Jesus would be doubting God. In Aramaic, *sabachthani* means to keep, to preserve. In that transcendent final moment, Jesus faithfully pronounced the fulfilling of his destiny and the prophecy.

The willing, Destiny guides them; the unwilling, Destiny drags them.
—Seneca

Reflection: Is there an aspect of your life about which you are so clear that it is yours to do that nothing anyone can say or do will stop you from fulfilling as your destiny?

Affirmation: I am clear as to what is mine to do in this world!

Expectations

Take a look at the size of your expectations of life. Are you going to the river of life with a thimble, a dipper, a bucket, a barrel, or a pickup truck? How big can you dream? How much can you imagine? How much are you willing to claim by expecting and accepting your good? Are you still limiting yourself by your parents' standards, or based on a previous experience in your life, before you were spiritually awake?

Make "outrageous" demands on the Universe! Expect to be happy! Expect to be financially free! Expect to be surrounded by love and filled with joy! Expect to be in healthy relationships. Expect things to work! Then anticipate the miraculous ways ALL these things show up! Collect this as evidence that life does support you!

The whole mystery and meaning of the teaching of Jesus is bound up in this word believe—to act as though the good were true; to expect it to happen, to have faith, to trust, to be as a little child whose enthusiasm is unbounded.

—Ernest Holmes

We should confidently expect a greater good than we have ever experienced, or than we have ever known of anyone experiencing.

—Ernest Holmes

Contemplation: What is the size of your expectation? Where are you going to the river of life with a thimble and where with a barrel? Why the difference?

Affirmation: I expect great things. I expect miracles. I expect things to work out. I expect Love and Joy and Happiness in my life!

You!

March 31
You

In life, while there are few guarantees you can use as a reliable reference, death is one those knowns you can depend on. Yet there is such fear around the subject that people deny taking a look at and getting comfortable with it until it's in their face. This transition, this transformation, is as natural and common as birth. When you step from one side to the other side, what you know for sure is that it will be different.

I am not afraid of death, I just don't want to be there when it happens.
—Woody Allen

When you spend time knowing your life force through meditation or contemplation, then you come to know you without form. If you've ever traveled out of your body or done some lucid dreaming, you realize you are more than your physical appearance. Don't wait until the last minute to make friends with the inevitable. Embrace the you that is animating your body this go-round, and know that you are more than your body.

Reflection: Remember a time when you saw the lifeless body of a loved one after his/her spirit had moved on. Didn't you know that body was not him/her and the spirit that was, was no longer in residency? Can you open your heart and still feel his/her presence and love now?

Affirmation: I know who I am is more than my body!

April

Living from a Higher Vibration

April 1
Your Healing Chant

As strange as it may sound, one of the powerful ways to assist in your joyous living is to look death in the face and become comfortable with it. When you are no longer afraid to die, you are freer to live. Many cultures prepare their people in advance, because it is as natural to step into the other side as it was to step into this world. Nature has made provisions for both entries. There is the Egyptian Book of the Dead; there is the Tibetan Book of Living and Dying; the Native Americans have their death chant; and there are many others.

At the time of death, whatever you have focused on the most will determine your next life.
—Tibetan Book of Living and Dying

The Native Americans learned their chant from their vision quests or it was passed on to them by their grandfathers. It was a powerful statement of their Wholeness that connected them to the ancestors, bringing a sense of peace. It was a chant they repeated many times throughout their lives, in times of challenge and difficulty, allowing them to reclaim presence and awareness from the adversity of the moment. At the time of death, without thinking, this well-used chant would come to mind, bringing comfort during the transition, allowing them to remain consciously aware, rather than being consumed and losing control to fear ... then following their chant through the threshold.

Reflection: It may be more comfortable to call it a healing chant, but find yours. What spiritually comforting phrase does your heart want to sing out that connects you with all life? What words bring you a sense that all is well? Put them together and chant them over and over. When a time of challenge comes to your world, remember to call on this healing chant and follow it to your peace.

Affirmation: In times of challenge, I follow my healing chant to peace!

Beginner's Mind

In Zen Buddhism, there is a notion called "beginner's mind." This is the mind you have when you approach something completely new for the very first time. It is a mind open to discovering this new thing, unburdened by judgment, comparisons, or preconceived ideas. It is a mind open to possibilities and receptive to to what is immediate and current reality in the present moment. This mind is capable of anything.

To move more easily and openly in your life, to discover new possibilities and to be available to intuition and Divine Guidance, you must learn to let go of your preconceived ideas about "how it should be." Release your need to be in control! Let judgment, comparisons, resentments, and unforgiveness die from lack of attention. This is the tomb of the dark night of the soul. Rest here a moment and revel in the freedom.

The mind that dies every day to the memories of yesterday, to all the joys and sorrows of the past—such a mind is fresh, innocent, it has no age; and without that innocence, whether you are ten or sixty, you will not find God.
—J. Krishnamurti

Contemplate: What situation in your life is calling for you to have "beginner's mind"? What needs to die in you today so your life can blossom into the beauty it's meant to be?

Affirmation: Today I approach my life with an open beginner's mind. I release and let die any old hurts, judgments, and expectations. I embrace my life, fresh and new.

Now What?

April 3

Abracadabra

Have you ever seen a magician have someone step into a box and, while he is standing there, slice him into quarters by slipping a sheet of metal at his neck, hips, knees? Then even more amazing, the magician pushes the boxes apart from each other to the right and to the left. And if that wasn't enough, he opens the different covers of each of the four boxes exposing the various body parts detached, then talks to the head, tickles the moving feet, and shakes hands. With one big abracadabra, he brings the various boxes back together and out steps the subject ... whole once again.

We do not need magic to change the world. We carry all the power we need inside ourselves already: we have the power to imagine better.
—J. K. Rowling

Occasionally life can look like someone or something has sliced and diced your world to pieces, leaving you feeling like you have been dismembered. The abracadabra of it all is returning to your mindful awareness of your inner source and strength. Realigning is about remembering to stop giving the power away to the pieces and remembering your Wholeness. The Infinite Wisdom of the universe, which holds all the parts of the cosmos together as one living organism on a galactic scale, can by all means bring your awareness back into an understanding of how all the pieces of your life are fitting together perfectly if you remember to ask for understanding and clarity.

Reflection: Sit quietly and take a look at the pieces of your life that seem out of alignment with who you are. Then ask your Higher Wisdom Self for understanding and clarity about the disconnect and what, if anything, you might do about it.

Affirmation: I return to recognizing my Wholeness!

The Banquet Table of Life

Life is a banquet of love, joy, and abundance. This reminds me of the book *Auntie Mame*, in which the feisty heroine exclaims, "Life's a banquet, but most poor suckers are starving to death." The feast of life has been provided for each and every person. You are constantly offered limitless possibilities for self-expression, creativity, love, and joy.

Open your arms and your heart wide! Embrace the bounty and the beauty! Partake of the life that Spirit means for you to live. Don't settle for anything less!

We must set up a receiving center. No matter how abundantly the horn of plenty may pour out its universal gifts, we must hold up our bowl of acceptance or the gift cannot be complete. Life is ready to give us all that we desire, but we must first cast from us everything that hinders Its complete expression through us; let go of all struggle and strife, and accept the Divine bounty.
—Ernest Holmes

Contemplate: Imagine the banquet table of life. Are you feasting or starving?

Affirmation: I stand at the banquet table of life and enjoy the rich and bountiful feast Spirit is continuously serving. I take all that I need at this moment, knowing I can always go back and get more.

Now What?

April 5
Good or Bad?

There's an old Chinese story about a farmer whose only horse ran away, and all his friends said that's too bad. Then when the horse returned, followed by a string of mares, they all declared in amazement how good this was. But then the farmer's son tried to break one of the new mares and fell off and broke his leg instead. Wasn't that too bad? The next day when the army came marching through to take all the young men off to war, the farmer's son wasn't taken because his leg was broken. And so there was great good that came from the horse running away!

Trials, temptations, disappointments—all these are helps instead of hindrances, if one uses them rightly. They not only test the fiber of character but strengthen it. Every conquering temptation represents a new fund of moral energy. Every trial endured and weathered in the right spirit makes a soul nobler and stronger than it was before.
—James Buckham

There is a silver lining to every cloud and good must come of everything you call "bad." This is true because you declare and demand it from the Universal Law of Life! So, good is made of something that starts out as bad, even if you don't know what that good is ... today, or next week, or next month. Simply trust that it is so!

Contemplate: When have you had something that you thought was bad turn out to be a blessing or a great good? Is there something going on right now in your life that is calling for this perspective?

Affirmation: I trust that everything turns out for the best for myself and for everyone involved.

Courage to Change

The only thing permanent is change. Everything about life is constantly changing. You can see the rhythm of change through the season and cycles of all life. Notice how effortlessly the trees shed their leaves, the bird flies from the nest, and the moon waxes and wanes. The problem is only that sometimes you want to cling to what you have and what you know, even when you want things to be different than they are.

Celebrate changes, as the new unfolds in your life. It may be just what you have been affirming, even if it doesn't look exactly like you pictured. A wise person once said, "Breakdown has to come before

The courage to change is the measure of a real man/woman for only through change can one be enlightened and only through enlightenment can one enter the gates of heaven.

—Micheal Teal

breakthrough." Let things change, invite the changes, so that the new can enter into your life. Trust the process and declare that good will come of it!

Contemplate: What needs to change in you and in your life for things to really change?

Affirmation: I embrace change. I release what no longer serves, letting go of the familiar. I eagerly anticipate the new, knowing this change is for the better.

Now What?

Now What?

What can be life-altering is delving into deeper states of consciousness and watching your thinking mind quiet and perceptions dissolve while slipping into the joy vibration. Moving beyond your ordinary self into the limitless is freeing, to say the least. The ever-changing, shifting, thinking mind becomes stable, balanced, and mindful. Your laser perception sees the expanded and detailed version of what you are looking at because you are fully present. You feel the pulse of sound resonating through you; you see the molecular structure of what catches your attention. Then desire beyond the five senses calls you deeper, beyond identification to merge with awareness itself. All sense of self is gone. You are nothing and yet you are everything. The amazing part of this is that it's as if you wake up from a dream and wonder now what? Be kind, and give yourself a little time for re-entry.

Creation is eternally going on; change is always taking place within that which is changeless.
—Ernest Holmes

Reflection: If you were to experience this inseparable Oneness with all life, what relevance would it have in your daily walk through this world?

Affirmation: My spiritual experiences integrate smoothly into my daily life!

Joy Lives Here

Many people spend their lives chasing happiness, trying to buy it from the store, find it in a new relationship, or look for it in the approval of others. Any one of these things may make you happy for a moment, but then it fades, and the search is on again. Joy, on the other hand, is the natural state of your inner being because it is the Natural State of the Divine. The Divine Love experiences only Joy in its expression of creation and in its own Beingness.

Joy sneaks into your life when you are least expecting it. Joy creeps in when you are busy living life to the fullest, being happy with whom you are becoming, and finding the good in the people and situations around you. Make space for Joy to find its way into your lap, like a contented cat!

We are shaped by our thoughts; we become what we think. When the mind is pure, joy follows like a shadow that never leaves.
—Buddha

Contemplate: What is the difference between chasing happiness and discovering joy? What is your joy quotient today?

Affirmation: Joy wells up from the center of my being. It is the natural state of my soul. Everything in my life conspires toward greater joy.

Mind as a Calm Mountain Lake

Having spent any time by a calm mountain lake, you will have noticed it is a watering hole for all sorts of God's magnificent creatures to swing by for a drink. You will witness all sorts of activity just by remaining still.

When you can calm your mind and just sit as a witness to all the Divine expressions stopping by, you'll be amazed at the diversity of what you see. Remember not to judge the expressions as good or bad. Just notice what stops by and then moves on. There is more out there than you could ever conjure up.

In every walk with nature, one receives far more than he seeks.

—John Muir

Reflection: Quiet yourself, find a peaceful place to sit, and just watch what comes wandering up to your calm, inviting space.

Affirmation: I am a calm place for Divine Expressions to visit!

Accept Your Good

Your life can never be too good. Your happiness does not take anything from anyone else. You do actually deserve to have a wonderful, fulfilling, and meaningful life. You don't have to earn it by being perfect nor do you have to worry about there not being enough to go around.

Sometimes you may feel you have to pay a tax for your wonderful life. You may pay your tax in worry, control, waiting for the other shoe to drop, or simply an inability to accept your good. However, there is NO tax to pay for Spirit's bounty, joy, love, and presence. Simply practice enjoying it!

Give thanks, and praise the Spirit of God for the law of the self-increasing potency of every substance....There is good in the Universe, and I ought to have it.

—Emma Curtis Hopkins

Contemplation: Are you enjoying and accepting the bounties, joy, love, and meaning in your life? Where is worry draining your joy away?

Affirmation: I accept my good. I accept my good. I accept my good!

The God Field

When you have a regular practice of being consciously aware of God, you become aware of what the Presence feels like. This is extremely valuable in a confrontational moment when your spiritual practice of "It's all good" is challenged. If you find yourself walking down a dark alley alone at night and a sleazy-looking character decides you'd be the perfect one for some interaction, are you familiar enough with what the Presence of God feels like—no matter what? When you are in that Divine field, there is no space for anything but God to reciprocate.

It's only with the heart one can see rightly: what is essential is invisible to the eye.
—Antoine de Saint-Exupéry

You probably aren't going to be walking down dark alleys alone anytime soon, at least not in the physical world, but some of the places you might allow yourself to wander in the realms of your mind could have terrifying consequences. If, for some reason, you find yourself lost in the dark recesses of your fear-based thinking, are you connected enough to remember and believe the God-perceptive over the debilitating, demented dilemmas of fright-based thinking? When you merge with the familiar feelings of Spirit, you will be lifted and transported above the shadow world and will no longer be a participant in the lurkings of the low life.

Reflection: How can I find more time each day to familiarize myself with God? Where in my life do I need to re-enter the God Field and feel it again?

Affirmation: I feel the Divine Presence always!

No Transference Necessary

When you pray for another, don't try to send him/her your thoughts. You would only be validating a sense of separation. If a loved one asks you to send God to their friend, remember, it doesn't work that way. Nor does God come to you to send something out. There are not three different entities there. Never be fooled into thinking there could ever be more than The One.

In prayer, you are not dealing with people or situations. You are realizing God's Infinity expressed in and through all things, which includes people and places. Your responsibility in prayer is not to heal a situation but to find the Truth at your center. Leave the problem wherever it is; do not operate at the level of concern. Allow your awareness to be receptive to a knowingness of the spiritual Truth of the situation. Keep your mind on Spirit and your relationship with the One. You must realize there is nothing you need to heal in the mind of God. The material world doesn't have the final say because it's not the Truth. When you know the spiritual Truth and feel the release in the situation because it has been met, so will your loved one, because there is only one mind and that is the mind of God. No transference of thought is necessary, because there is only one consciousness; yours and theirs are already one in the mind of God, and when the Truth is known in one place, it is known in all places.

Most people do not pray, they only beg.
—George Bernard Shaw

Reflection: Pray.

Affirmation: Right where I am, God is!

April 13
Your Inner Companion

There is something so inviting about the idea of the Garden of Eden, a magical place where humans walked and talked openly with God. This myth speaks powerfully of the longing to return to an innocent, ideal state of Oneness with the Divine. This longing is often captured in a nostalgia for an innocence of childhood, of the "good old days" of our youth.

Deep within us all there is an amazing inner sanctuary of the soul, a holy place, a Divine Centre, a speaking voice, to which we may continuously return. Eternity is at our hearts, pressing upon our time-torn lives, warming us with intimations of an astounding destiny, calling us home unto itself.
—Thomas R. Kelly

This intuition of your childhood innocence and sense of oneness is the very thing driving your Spiritual Quest. But you cannot go back. You can never unlearn your own self-awareness. You can only go forward. Do not try to re-live or re-create the "good ole' days." Seek a deeper oneness and a conscious innocence within your life today. Then you will discover God as your constant companion. You will discover a conscious, mature communion with the Divine, knowing you have chosen Oneness over everything else.

Contemplate: Imagine what it would be like if you knew and experienced that you already walk and talk with Spirit and live in the Oneness every day, right now. Now contemplate that this is actually true.

Affirmation: I walk in oneness with the Divine. Spirit is my constant companion.

Prayer Made Simple

When praying, a powerful position to hold is that there is only One Life, the One Spirit in and through all things. When you know there is no power apart from this One Life, which is your life, there is nothing to overcome. The power of prayer lies in the embodiment of this Truth.

You may believe there could be a power apart from the Infinite (think about it … that won't make sense), but there is still no need for you to convince God of your problem-prompting prayer. All you need to do is come into alignment in your knowingness of the One Infinite Life Force and feel your true Essence, the part of you that has never been violated. This understanding will reveal the inherent Wholeness that has been there the whole time as easily as light dissipates the darkness to show what is already in the room. Rest in the knowingness of your true nature, which is Spirit expressing, until a sense of release comes and peace settles in. Healing can be this simple!

> *The eyes upturned to Heaven are an act of creation.*
> —Victor Hugo

Reflection: Repeat Psalm 46:10: "Be still and know that I am God."

Affirmation: Spirit expresses as me!

Remembering Spiritual Truth

The most powerful spiritual practice is more than simply sitting on your meditation cushion in the morning and seeking the Presence of God. It is taking that experience of the Presence with you into your daily life. This means that you know that Spirit is in every situation or circumstance. All you have to do is notice it and call it forth.

It is ideas of God which, if you shepherd well, will get you into that state of mind called heaven, when you have health, judgment, prosperity.... To say that "My Good is supply, God is my Good, therefore God is my supply" is to stir the mountains and the seas to bring us our new provisions.

—Emma Curtis Hopkins

So this means that whenever you are uncertain about what is going on, bring a spiritual principle into the process. Find a quality of God that could be revealed. Seek a healing thought within yourself. Remind yourself of a spiritual truth that is applicable to the situation and watch everything turn around.

Contemplation: What are some of your favorite spiritual principles/truths?

Affirmation: Spirit is all there is, in every situation, person, or event. I remember a spiritual truth in any moment of concern, worry, or doubt.

Coming Back Down

Your spiritual practice isn't for the purpose of getting spiritually high. Those moments of seeing beyond the mental realm with luminous clarity can be quite addicting. While the emancipation from time opens you to your true nature, you still have to come back down.

Spirituality is about bringing the higher perspective into your real-life happenings. Can you remain connected when you go home or when a life situation challenges you or when your dark side starts to stir? Spirituality is no longer escaping the physical world for some elevated plane of existence and partitioning off the good and bad sections. It is about the integration of your spirituality where no aspect of your life has any less potential for the Divine vibration to be lived.

Great men are they who see that the spiritual is stronger than any material force.
—Ralph Waldo Emerson

Reflection: When have you been so high on Spirit that you didn't want to come back down? Where have you taken the elevated perspective into a dark situation, and how was it transformed?

Affirmation: I am integrating my spiritual highs into my daily life!

Facing Doubt

How many times have you been confronted by doubt? Each time you set out to grow, deepen, or leap into a new possibility, and something inside you wonders if it's real or true or even possible, you have the opportunity to root out your own unbelief, face your doubt, and reveal a deeper faith.

When doubt creeps in, reach out for help. When your belief is faint, find someone whose belief is strong. When you forget Truth, seek out spiritual reminders. When you do not know what else to do, remember to pray, and have others pray with you. Yea, though you walk through the very Valley of Death, do not let your fear run away with you. You do not walk alone.

Here we may meet difficulties, uncertainties and doubts, barriers walling our passage. But we must not be discouraged when so confronted. We must climb over the rocks of unbelief, pass around the barriers of doubt, and plunge into the stream with faith. The stream will ever widen; the barriers will gradually disappear; though we walk through the plains and valleys of indecision and doubt, the stream will still carry us back to the ocean of our being.

—Ernest Holmes

Contemplate: When was the last time you reached out for help, support, and prayer? Are you comfortable and willing to ask for help?

Affirmation: I courageously face my doubt with the conviction of my faith. I rely on the faith of those around me until my own faith is strong.

Transform the Transgression

Mistakes and miscalculations that you or others have made most often come from lack, fear, or poor awareness. They are not calling for reprimand, but are calls for love and compassion. Mentally abusing yourself for a dumb move doesn't make anything better. Try loving yourself if you want to transform the transgression. If at the time you had known better, you would have done better. Everyone who has lived has committed his/her share of blunders.

You can keep beating yourself up until you are no longer living joyously and your health comes into question, or you can forgive yourself or another and be free of internal

You never lose by loving. You always lose by holding back.

—Barbara De Angelis

conflict. It's not your job to be the judge of the universe. Everyone has a past. What is important is what lies before you and what you are going to do today to brighten the world. Learning from your living is a good thing. Dragging the heavy mental memories from yesterday into the bright, new day being offered to you may no longer be your wisest choice. You are a child of God, forgiven and loved. Find the Peace that passes understanding.

Reflection: What past blunders still haunt your memory? Love yourself, look at it from that Love and let this Love transform it, and you'll find the Peace that passes understanding.

Affirmation: I am free!

Positive Thinking

Pay attention to the way you are thinking about things. Do you make negative assumptions, take things personally, or sometimes feel like life is against you? Are you thinking from fear, unforgiveness, worry, or anger? Unfortunately, this kind of thinking simply perpetuates these kinds of experiences in your life.

Through affirmative thinking, you are able to clear your mind of negative thoughts, fears, and doubts. This you must come to do if you are to become aware of the Presence, Peace, and Harmony of God that is within and around you. All the good that you desire awaits your acceptance of it. But you cannot experience it while you deny it. The key to right thinking and right living is the steady affirmative pattern of thought that only God's Good enters your life.

—Ernest Holmes

Turn around and think about things from a Spiritual perspective. Look for the Good and praise it. Affirm that Spirit is Present. That Love is available. That prosperity and abundance are your divine birthright. That no matter what you may be currently experiencing, these spiritual truths are what you are going to dwell on instead. You will immediately see and feel about it differently!

Contemplate: Rate your overall thinking and self-talk—one being completely negative all the time and ten being completely positive all the time. Notice if there are any times and places during the day that your rating significantly changes.

Affirmation: I keep my thoughts positive and keep my attention fixed on God's Good.

Energetic Patterns

Looking out from the fiftieth story of a high-rise, you can see for miles. You are able to see the energy of the day begin and unfold as more and more people appear and fill the streets. If you pay attention, you'll feel the sense of the collective energy of the masses. You will be able to see any hot spots where an incident may be occurring, whether an accident, parade, or a flash mob scene.

What's interesting about this perspective is that from this elevated view you can see the unfoldment of the collective energies, but you are not part of them. If you were to drive out of the city, you could choose a route away from the traffic, yet if the parade was something you wanted to be part of, you could enter into that particular scene.

Change before you have to.
—Jack Welch

You are also given the opportunity to step above the world you live in and observe the different energetic patterns that are emerging or receding. When you are on the ground level, caught in the collective congestion, it's easy to believe the experience is the only option. Your peace lies in remembering you always have the ability to step inside and rise above the pull of the crowd to observe your options. You always have a conscious choice to the route you are going to take.

Reflection: Take a few deep breaths, ride the inhalations to a higher state of personal observance, and look out upon your world from an emotionally detached height. Are there any hot spots you may no longer want to be a part of? Is there a new route out of that situation you can take?

Affirmation: I rise above the pull of the collective to live my choices.

April 21
Planting Seeds of Peace

It's easy to pretend there aren't any environmental issues on the planet. You don't need to go on a rampage of trying to change others—unless that's your calling. It's through simple awareness and subtle tweaks to behaviors that will make a difference, impacting all of us sharing this earth. When you don't know better, you can't act better.

When we plant trees, we plant the seeds of peace and seeds of hope. We also secure the future for our children.
—Wangari Maathai

As you walk lighter on this earth, our children will be blessed. Work on becoming conscious of some unconscious, negatively impactful expressions of yours. This will help you stop the destruction, thus beginning the planting of seeds of Peace and blessing future generations to come.

Reflection: Do yourself a favor and find out what wasteful activities are going on in your home. There may be a couple of simple things you can do to make a difference.

Affirmation: I plant blessings all around me!

A Lighter Footprint

So many people want to make a difference on this planet, but they get so overwhelmed by the number of environmental issues plaguing Mother Earth that they quit before ever starting. It's simple to start ... it begins in the head and heart. As you expand your awareness, the sparks become a blaze of passion of the soul, making you conscious of the effects of your choices and actions upon the whole.

When you make yourself aware, you'll know what is yours to do, the least of which is to start in your home and your life. That lighter footprint will make a difference for all of humanity.

We must learn to live with Mother Nature and put it deep in our hearts that whatever she gives we must take as blessings.
—Nader Khalili

Reflection: How can I live differently in a way that would be less impactful and more loving to the planet?

Affirmation: My footprint upon the planet is kind!

What Now

You may have heard the expression … after ecstasy, the laundry; after enlightenment, then what? There is an old story of a monk who had spent many years doing his spiritual practices in the monastery when he got to the point where all he wanted was enlightenment, which hadn't come. He went to the master teacher and asked for permission to go to the top of the mountain, because he wanted enlightenment so badly he would stay there until he received it or die trying. The master teacher, knowing his student had spent many years preparing and was ready, granted him permission to go.

Knowing others is wisdom; Knowing yourself is Enlightenment.
—Lao Tzu

On his way up the mountain, the student ran into an old man coming down the path with a bundle on his back. The old guy asked him where he was going, and the student told him he was heading to the mountaintop and was going to stay there until he received enlightenment or died. When the student saw a gleam of wisdom in the old fella's eyes, he asked him if he knew anything about enlightenment. The old man smiled and dropped his bundle. In that moment, the student got it and said, "It's that simple—you just let go of everything you are holding on to?" The wise one replied, "But it's not always that easy to let go of what you have attached your thoughts, feelings, and beliefs to." As the now-enlightened monk began to head happily off, he paused, asking, "And now what?" To which the sage bent over, picked up his bundle, threw it over his shoulder again and headed into the village with his wares.

Reflection: How would you approach your life differently if you were enlightened? Why don't you try it that way now?

Affirmation: I am approaching my life as if God is expressing through every interaction!

God's Address

Think about God for a moment—where did you first go to have this encounter? If you are honest with yourself and don't intellectualize it but notice your first intuitive response, it is an interesting exercise in revealing where the address of God is for you. Do you look up? Do you push Spirit into you somewhere so you can say God is within and point to your chest as if it's a physical location? Maybe it's the idyllic landscape that takes your breath away. It's good to watch your subjective beliefs around the God subject that all too often are so sacred that review is out of the question.

I would rather live my life as if there is a God and die to find out there isn't than live my life as if there isn't and die to find out there is.
—Albert Camus

Spirit makes all things new. This includes an emerging understanding of the Presence Itself. When you begin to acknowledge Spirit in all your undertakings, you become the activity of God. The mystics see Spirit everywhere and live in constant contact with the Divine.

Reflection: Where is God for you?

Affirmation: I am one with Spirit!

April 25
Light Brought to Awareness

Have you ever walked into a room and said something to someone and found they were so lost in thought or what they were doing that they didn't even see you or hear you? It's not that they were incapable; it's just their awareness was somewhere else. When you got their awareness, of course they could see you and hear you.

There are two ways of spreading the light: to be the candle or the mirror that reflects it.
—Edith Wharton

As the light from the sun moves through the darkness of space, it is virtually unseen until it touches something like the moon, a planet, or an asteroid; otherwise it virtually goes unnoticed. What if the Absolute Intelligence, the undifferentiated Essence of All Life, God, was infinite possibilities where all took place, but didn't take form until there was awareness brought into the equation for It to reflect and show form?

It is through your awareness that Spirit touches and brings to light the thought. When you think about your aching body or difficult world of affairs, that is what becomes real. The challenge comes when you think you are your body or your world of affairs and forget you are really the Light. But what if the purpose here is to experience joy and love that otherwise cannot be experienced in the absolute, unseparated state of pure consciousness? What if this world is Eden, and your awareness is the necessary piece for the infinite potential of God to be reflecting and experiencing love and joy?

Reflection: Think about the light beam of creative consciousness that is reflecting off your awareness ... is it revealing love and joy or something else? Are you identifying so much with the experience that you feel this is who you are rather than the Light that is reflecting off consciousness?

Affirmation: I am the Light that reflects all things in my world!

The Power

So much has been said about positive thinking, but it's important to realize the power isn't in the thinking; your thinking is the avenue. Isn't it good to know that you don't have to leave home to find this power? The days of leaving all behind and running off to live the ascetic, cloistered life is no longer necessary. You don't have to renounce your family or your home to find God and, thank goodness, you don't have to take vows of poverty or chastity. We are in a kinder time for God-realization.

Yet, your spiritual practices must be practiced! Talking about the unfathomable concepts of God over brie and Chardonnay is sweet, but

What lies in our power to do, lies in our power not to do.
—Aristotle

the depths you must go to are more than an occasional casual conversation. Getting intimate with the Divine will lead you to understanding the One Power. The revelations will show you passages to accessing the Life Forces. Some will get caught thinking it's their power, but never fall prey to this false concept. You are never the Power; you are the conduit through which It flows. With this understanding, you will never be depleted nor will you ever meet a situation that you think you need to overpower.

Reflection: Have you ever fantasized about removing yourself from the activities of your daily life that have consumed your mental and emotional space? What about that sounded good, and what kind of feelings were you thinking you might find elsewhere that would get you closer to God? Recommit today to deepen your spiritual practices, knowing all you seek is right where you are.

Affirmation: I find more God today, right where I am, than I ever knew was possible!

April 27

Stop Waiting

Remember doing puzzles as a kid? You dumped out the whole box, turned all the pieces over, and then wondered where to start. First you created the border with all the flat-edged pieces, which was easy. But what do you do next? Finding a place to start within the picture was always the most challenging thing. Sometimes life feels the same way. Unfortunately, it doesn't seem to have a lot of straight-edged pieces to begin with, but simply a lot of possibilities with nothing but the picture in our minds for a clue.

Begin somewhere; you cannot build a reputation on what you intend to do.
—Liz Smith

Do not wait for ideal circumstances, nor the best opportunities; they will never come.
—Janet E. Stuart

Don't wait to find all the edge pieces and have a nice neat border completed! Start today! There will never be a "perfect" time to begin because you will never be finished with your current to-do list. If you keep doing what you've been doing, nothing will change. Remember, Spirit is available only in the eternal Here and Now, not in some future time when you're ready or things are different.

Contemplation: Imagine that the patterns and pieces of your life are like the pieces of a puzzle spread out on the table. Look for something that catches your eye. That's a good place to start.

Affirmation: I am no longer waiting for everything to be perfect. I begin today!

Frequencies of Consciousness

Television sets used to have antennas. Some actually had them on the television box itself and were affectionately called "rabbit ears." To make things even stranger, if the reception was poor, you'd get up and adjust the "ears" and sometimes the picture came through best when you were still holding the antennae! Depending on how you stood, you could actually impact the signal received.

If your body could be a channel through which an unseen picture could be seen, imagine what else you could pick up if you knew how to tune in to the station of your choosing. There are so many unseen pos-

If everyone demanded peace instead of another television set, then there'd be peace.
—John Lennon

sible images available at the different frequencies of consciousness. When you dial into fear, where do those images come from that fill your mind? When you dial into joy, where do all those images that fill your awareness come from? You are a Divine conduit who is able to catch the higher vision for your life anytime, anywhere. Turn off what's playing, and adjust your receiver to the frequency of your choosing.

Reflection: When your awareness caught images that seem to emerge from some place other than your previous thoughts and experiences, what was your frame of mind? What was your emotional state? How were you in a different receptive mood? Can you put yourself back into a receptive frequency?

Affirmation: As a Divine conduit, I can dial into my higher vision anytime I choose!

Open Channel

There is no barrier between you and God! Life is a continuum from the infinite to the finite, from energy to matter, from spirit to form, from the Divine to the human. As with any continuum, there is no switch or door that marks the passage from one side to the other; somewhere in the middle, things simply shift. Right at the point where the one turns into the other—where spirit becomes form and energy becomes matter—right there is where you live.

As there is no screen or ceiling between our heads and the infinite heavens, so there is no bar or wall in the soul where we, the effect, cease, and God, the cause begins.
—Ralph Waldo Emerson

You are the place where heaven and earth meet. This is what makes you a cocreator of your life. You can use the Laws of Spirit to create in the realm of your human experience. This means you can bring about heaven on earth.

Contemplate: Become consciously aware of this open channel between the human and the Divine. Can you tell where one starts and the other leaves off?

Affirmation: There is no place where I stop and God starts. I am not all of God, but God is all that I am.

Divine Perception

Healing happens when you realize God as your consciousness and not something to be reached, but rather to be expressed. Your purpose is the unfoldment of this revelation. You'll no longer be attempting to change anyone or anything because your conception of the situation has changed to a Divine Perception.

In healing, people are usually asking for the opposite of the challenge they find themselves or a loved one in … like fear, lack, or pain … in their attempt to remove the difficulty. When you rise above your attempt to change conditions with

A mystic is one who intuitively perceives Truth and, without mental process, arrives at Spiritual realization.

—Ernest Holmes

your thoughts, you will no longer be bound by your thinking. You become more available to a higher realization of Spirit than you can conjure up in your mind. When God fills your consciousness, results naturally appear. This isn't because of your direction, but because you are demonstrating a spiritual freedom in all areas of your life that is beyond your thoughts. When you behold the Divine as opposed to seeing a problem to overcome, Grace enters, and you will be proclaiming your Wholeness.

Reflection: What situations are you attempting to change by attempting to think the opposite rather than knowing the Truth?

Affirmation: I look upon my life and see as Spirit sees!

May

Living from the Intuitive Side

May 1-7
In the Wilderness of Intuition

May 8-15
Wired for Love

May 16-22
Trusting Optimism

May 23-31
Dream Big

May 1
In the Silence

Silence is necessary for the soul's nourishment. Silence is the place in which our souls can grow and expand. It is room for our spirits to breathe, our minds to rest, and our emotions to become still.

There is a difference between being quiet and being in the silence. Cultivating silence in your inner life is helped by bringing silence to your outer world. Silence confronts us with all the ways we keep ourselves from being present. We use noise to cover our mental chatter, keep ourselves from being lonely, and pretend that we are connected. Turn off everything making noise—the radio, TV, car stereo, computer, and phone—no matter how important they may seem. Turn off your meditation music, affirmations, and the bells in the background, no matter how spiritual they seem. Spend time in the silence. Discover your own company. Simply enjoy being with yourself.

In the attitude of silence, the soul finds the path in a clearer light, and what is elusive and deceptive resolves itself into crystal clearness. Our life is a long and arduous quest after Truth.

—Mahatma Gandhi

Reflection: What noise do I use to drown out the silence? Am I comfortable in the silence, being with myself?

Affirmation: I rest in the silence, enjoying my own company. In the Silence, I nourish my soul, rest my mind, and find myself.

May 2
Chaos or Calm

Getting lost while driving downtown is not a low-energy kind of experience ... it can raise the intensity in the car very rapidly. But getting lost in a foreign city with very narrow, highly congested one-way streets, on a hot, humid, smoggy day with all sorts of noises and not being able to speak the language—this has even greater potential for knocking you off your centeredness.

When attempting to listen to your inner guidance for direction, oppressive street honking from every direction can definitely numb the inner communication link. Yet no matter how loud the outer world gets with all its commotion, you still have *Tough times never last, but tough people do.* —Robert H. Schuller

the power to choose whether you are going to be impacted by the outside or stay tuned in to your inner calm. If you can catch a glimpse of yourself making the choice, you can detach in the midst of the commotion. When you are the observer of yourself making choices, you become free to go with chaos or calm.

Reflection: Where in your life is there so much commotion that you've given up your calm?

Affirmation: I am going with the calm in the midst of chaos!

In the Wilderness of Intuition

May 3
Listen

I have lain awake at night, wishing I could sleep, while my brain goes on, and on, and on about something I can't figure out or don't know what to do about. Hasn't this happened to you? This monkey-mind chatter is seldom able to come up with anything new or even likely to help us move through whatever we are facing. All it does is stir up more fear, confusion, and uncertainty, which causes us to want to control, figure it out, or just plain give up.

One part of the mind is already in heaven, for there is a place in you and in me that is above confusion and fear, no matter how disturbed our thoughts may be. If we get quiet long enough and listen deeply enough, we shall hear.
—Ernest Holmes

But there is a part of us that does know. The God Presence, Spirit within, It knows. That knowing is available to us when we get quiet and LISTEN to the still, small voice within. Everyone hears that still, small voice differently. It comes as an urge, a nudge, a knowing. It comes as a snatch of a song, a fleeting thought, or a word from a friend. You can intend to get an answer and open a book, magazine, or newspaper. You can even notice the street signs along your way. Pay attention. Don't wait for the neon sign or the flashing arrow—you may not get one! But your intuition is always trying to break through. You just need to get quiet and LISTEN.

Reflection: What has my intuition been trying to tell me?

Affirmation: I pay attention to my intuition. I notice the signs. Even if I think I don't know, something within me does know. I get quiet and listen.

Inner Guidance

Guidance is always available to you wherever you are, no matter the concern. You must stop and turn within, realizing that the most insightful spiritual adviser there is for you is you. Stop running around looking outside yourself for someone else to know you better than you. Your still, small voice is on a different frequency than another can hear.

A good spiritual counselor will help you tune in to your own vibration of the Truth, not hers. When you live from a Divine connection, there is nothing too big or too small for you to be guided though. The guidance may come through what another may say, what you might be reading or seeing in the world as well as your inner activity. Be open, because Spirit is omnipresent and is communicating to you from everywhere.

No man is great enough or wise enough for any of us to surrender our destiny to. The only way in which anyone can lead us is to restore to us the belief in our own guidance.
—Henry Miller

The next message you need is always right where you are.
—Ram Dass

We need to be willing to let our intuition guide us, and then be willing to follow that guidance directly and fearlessly.
—Shakti Gawain

Reflection: Where do you need to trust your inner guidance more?

Affirmation: I am trusting my inner guidance!

Into the Wilderness of Intuition

Everyone has intuition because everyone is connected to Spirit. Intuition is knowing, without knowing how you know. Intuition is the ability to know, sense, or feel something without figuring it out or having a logical, rational explanation for it. Intuition knows from the whole to the parts, rather than the other way around. Another way of saying this is that intuition is like Spirit because Spirit is the wholeness, the Oneness, and it always knows how to create from the oneness all the many amazing and wonderful things we have, like babies and quasars, hummingbirds and galaxies. So intuition is about knowing the whole of anything, including knowing the "whole" of you.

You have to leave the city of your comfort and go into the wilderness of your intuition. What you'll discover will be wonderful. What you'll discover is yourself.
—Alan Alda

You have intuition; you know, because Spirit knows. You know your own "wholeness," your own being and reality, because you are Spirit, and Spirit always knows from the whole. So when you have confusion or uncertainty, your intuition speaks from that place of knowing, or already seeing the whole, and knowing which part you should focus on right now. Learn to hear and trust your intuition—it's an amazing way to listen to what Spirit is trying to be—as you.

Reflection: How does my intuition communicate with me? What do I sense from my intuition about the "whole" of me?

Affirmation: I trust that I know myself, wholly. I know what's good for me. I know what's best for me to do. I listen to and trust my intuition.

Cosmic GPS

How do birds know to fly south in the winter? How do the monarchs know which specific trees in Mexico and on the Monterey Peninsula are right for the end of their great migration? In animals, this inner knowing is called instinct. You, too, have an inner knowing, a cosmic GPS. Somewhere within you, you "know"—what to do, what is right, how to proceed. This inner knowing is called intuition, and it is your ability to know as God knows, see as God sees, without the need for rational thought or explanation.

This inner knowing may conflict with how you have it figured out, or with what is prudent and accept-

> *By learning to trust your intuition, miracles seem to happen. Intuitive thoughts are gifts from the higher self.*
> —Susan Jeffers

able. Sometimes intuition takes you on a wild journey across the landscape of your life. Listen to yourself. Learn to act on your "knowing." You will be surprised by the amazing way you reach your destination and how wonderfully Spirit supports you along the way!

Contemplate: What does your intuition sound like, feel like, seem like? How do you know when it is your intuition and not some fear or rationalization talking?

Affirmation: My intuition is the voice of Spirit in me. I listen to my intuition and trust it to be my guide.

My Present Spiritual Practice

Accepting whatever is before you as your spiritual practice is a solid spiritual approach for joyous living. If you are complaining that life isn't fair or blaming others for the situations you must face, you are missing out on the present gifts your world is offering you. Parents have griped about not being able to go on a spiritual trip because there are children at home to raise. When they realize parenting is their spiritual practice and getting a child through school and on the right track for life is as spiritual as building wells in an impoverished desert village, then peace and satisfaction can fill the desiring space.

Your duty is to Be, not be this or be that.
—Ramana Maharshi

Be present where you are, whether washing dishes, cleaning the house, raising children, doing business, or vacationing. The present moment is your perfect curriculum in which you will find the gifts of God.

Reflection: Where do you need to embrace what's in your world as your present spiritual practice? What can you learn from being fully present with this situation?

Affirmation: I accept what is before me as mine to do as my spiritual practice!

Corridors of Consciousness

When you step out the door of your hotel room and walk down the corridor, you haven't arrived anywhere yet. You are in the in-between stage where you aren't where you were and you aren't where you are going. In life, sometimes where you are is no longer stimulating or fulfilling. You've lost your interest in what used to entice you. The old activities don't call to you, the desire to be with some of the old friends has waned, and your daily routine no longer excites you. Yet, you don't quite know where it is you are going.

Consciousness is only possible through change; change is only possible through movement.

—Aldous Huxley

This is not an unusual corridor on the spiritual path. There is something stirring in your soul that has not birthed itself, but is growing and nudging you from the inside. The old has lost its appeal, and the new is yet to be revealed. It's a positive indicator you've completed a part of your journey. Trust what's coming forth from your consciousness, the emerging vision of that which feels right and good in your life now. Keep the faith during this transitional time until the new becomes your world.

Reflection: Is there any aspect of your life that feels as if you are in one of these transitional corridors? How can you clarify what's stirring in your soul, which can help you keep the faith as you ease on down the corridor of consciousness?

Affirmation: I am trusting this point of transition in my life!

Either-Or Thinking

In an infinite Universe, there is so much more creativity and possibility than "either-or." Black-and-white thinking limits the Limitless. Seek other alternatives by thinking outside the box. In addition to something in-between, or something completely new, there may actually be the third way that "transcends and includes," as Ken Wilbur describes it, the two seemingly opposite sides.

A false dilemma (also called false dichotomy, the either-or fallacy, fallacy of false choice, black-and-white thinking, or the fallacy of exhaustive hypotheses) is a type of logical fallacy that involves a situation in which only two alternatives are considered, when in fact there is at least one additional option. The options may be a position that is between the two extremes (such as when there are shades of grey) or may be a completely different alternative.
—Wikipedia

Reflection: Where in my life do I see only two options or alternatives? What might be some alternative ways of seeing or doing this? List them here, no matter how silly or stupid they seem to you.

Affirmation: Spirit is infinite, so there are never only "either-or" choices. There is always a third, fourth, or fifth alternative. I am creative and open enough to see these other options.

The Invisible Wall

On a cold, winter day in the midst of a snowstorm, it is kind of a magical experience to be sitting in an outdoor hot spring. There is the wonderful therapeutic warmth of the waters, then nature draws a line where the hot water ends and the cold water begins. It's as if you can put your hand through an invisible wall where just on the other side is freezing cold water. Literally, your wrist can be in the hot water and your fingers in the cold!

Stepping across the spiritual threshold can be just as dramatic. You can be stuck, feeling like you are moving in molasses; then, when you break on through to the other side,

Break on through to the other side.
—Jim Morrison

you're living in ease and fluidity. The invisible wall can't be seen, but the difference is quantum in its expression. You can be caught on this slow-moving vibrational side of reality or you can follow your consciousness through the invisible wall to the finer vibration, where concerns loosen up and revelations are manifested. Take the quantum leap to the intuitive side!

Reflection: What's keeping you stuck on the difficult side of life? Where is the edge of this reality and the beginning of the finer, more fluid way of being? Let your consciousness take you through to the other side.

Affirmation: I step on through to the graceful side!

Beyond the Comfort Zone

When you decide to make a change in your life, you are inviting yourself to step out of your comfort zone. By definition, being out of your comfort zone means you are uncomfortable. The discomfort usually takes the forms of resistance, excuses, or denial. We resist what is needed to bring about the change. We make excuses for not doing it or following through on what we need to do or stop doing. Sometimes we simply outright deny the need for a change because it makes us so uncomfortable. How many times have you allowed this discomfort to keep you from moving forward?

Resistance to change is proportional to how much the future might be altered by any given act.
—Stephen King

Resistance, excuses, or denial are important signposts that you are close to something very important in your life that has been keeping you stuck in the rut of your comfort zone. Don't be afraid. Look at your resistance. Notice your excuses. Acknowledge your denials. Examine your rut. This is the first step. Now that you know these are simply ways you experience pushing outside your comfort zone, you can move in spite of them, or you can dissolve them with your intention to live your change.

Reflection: Where am I in resistance, making excuses, or in denial about something I have really decided I want to have changed in my life? How is this about my being outside my comfort zone?

Affirmation: I boldly step beyond the edge into the new in my life. I move confidently and easily toward my transformation. I am strong enough to face the changes.

Wired for Love

Mom is the name for God in the mouths of children, yet there are no words that express the power and courage for describing her love. Mothers take care of what they can and somehow have learned to trust a higher power to work and guide their children where they can't.

Maternal love, somehow, is the catalyst to believe one can do something beyond what has been done before, because every child who comes into this world is a new expression of God with infinite possibilities. And moms are entrusted to be the first visionary of what's possible for our lives!

God can't be everywhere, so he made mothers.
—Arab proverb

Reflection: Take some quiet time to contemplate your mother's love and write her a thank-you note, whether she is in this world or the next.

Affirmation: My life is touched by Love!

Remembering to Remember

Coming back through the Houston airport after a month of hanging out on the blissful beaches of soul-stirring solitude in the sparsely populated parts of Costa Rica can be a cultural shock. And it can be even more challenging when, in your next flight, you find yourself seated in the back of a full plane surrounded by what appears to be a kids' nursery with two very expressive expressions of life. With constant crying and shouts of elation, noisy toys, loud babysitting DVDs and things rolling under your seat—this can really catch your peaceful attention and throw you off guard!

Wherever you are is the access point.
—Rumi

Remembering to remember who you are in the midst of forgetting is an important trait to cultivate. You are a Divine expression of nature. Because of your oneness with God, you are the access point to the Infinite nature of God's abundant blessings. You are that individualization which is indivisible. So pour out your gifts of peace right where you are. Don't go seeking whom to give it to … the beach or the forest doesn't care who's walking in it and definitely doesn't go looking for the right person to share its gifts. Somehow, wherever you are, you can still hear their celestial songs singing in your soul. Let those around you, no matter where you may be, appreciate the song of nature they'll feel from the rhythm of your joyous living.

Reflection: Where are your most wonderful spots of nature, and what's keeping you from being in that peaceful expression?

Affirmation: I let my soul be heard!

Magnet for More

The Law of Attraction works like a magnet. What you are on the inside, who you feel yourself to be, and how much life you can imagine yourself experiencing, this is what your magnet is made of. Since like attracts like, your magnet attracts to itself exactly that from which it is made.

Know that you can attract a beautiful, meaningful, fulfilling life. You begin by becoming on the inside what you want on the outside. Become the Love you want. Become the Joy you desire. Sense on the inside what a generous, prosperous person would feel like and imagine yourself living from that place. Start expecting to experience these things. Start imagining yourself in this beautiful, meaningful, fulfilling life. By creating the space in your consciousness to BE it, it will be attracted to you like a butterfly to a glorious flower!

> *We do not take what we wish, but we do attract to ourselves that which is like our thought.* MAN MUST BECOME MORE IF HE WISHES TO DRAW A GREATER GOOD INTO HIS LIFE.
> —Ernest Holmes

Reflection: What kind of a magnet am I? What have I been attracting?

Affirmation: I am a magnet for love, joy, prosperity, and blessing. I attract only good to me, because only good pours out from me!

Fully Present

Have you ever had your body show up, but you forgot to bring your aware-ness? Maybe you were strolling with a loved one in beautiful surroundings, but your mind was on finances. Or, you were sitting in a meeting, and your thoughts were in the Bahamas. It's one thing to get your body somewhere, and it's another to be present. Have you ever known the frustration of talking to someone and it was if nobody was home? Try watching a TV show and doing work on your laptop at the same time … it can be done, but you miss out on the full experience of both.

Mr. Duffy lived a short distance from his body.
  —James Joyce

There is so much more joy to the present moment when you are fully present with what you are doing or who you are with. The gifts of God are not available when you are not available to them. The depth of love, the magic of the moment, and the serendipitous occurrences will be missed if your mind is not traveling with your body.

Reflection: Recall a time you were physically with a loved one, yet your mind was somewhere else. Was what you were thinking more valuable than what you missed by not being present?

Affirmation: I am fully present for those I am with and where I am!

Not Now

There is this beautiful, secluded, white sand cove with warm, waveless, turquoise water. To get there, you just have to time the tide right and make sure it's going out when driving on the sand and over the river to get there. Well, one day I misjudged the tide. After spending the day in the sand, sun, and surf—sticky, salty, sunburned, and ready to go home—I drove back through the jungle to the river's edge only to discover it had swollen and gotten deeper with the incoming tide. There was a big part of me that felt I should push and attempt the crossing, particularly since it was a rental car.

God, grant me the serenity to accept the things I cannot change,
Courage to change the things I can,
And wisdom to know the difference.
—Reinhold Niebuhr

Do you ever find the better part of your wisdom has to duke it out with your impatience and what you want now only to find, by forcing the issue, you would create greater problems for yourself? Sometimes life is saying *not now* and you get all amped out demanding explanation. Maybe it can be more productive to surrender to the moment, knowing your good is coming and this is just not the time.

It would have been easy to get mad and yell at the river, but it wouldn't have changed anything and would have looked pretty silly. So I turned around, went back to the cove, and enjoyed a glorious couple of more hours and a spectacular sunset. I returned to the river, only to find another truck had tried crossing earlier and had become stuck as I crossed what was, by then, a small stream.

Reflection: Where in your life is it not right for you to push?

Affirmation: I trust Life's timing for me!

Trusting Optimism

Smile

Joy is your natural and native state! Your being is always trying to return to Joy. Resolve to be Joyful. You do this by getting out of bed with a smile and finding moments throughout the day that make you smile. You do it by contemplating the Joy you take in your home, family, loved ones, and nature. Invite Joy into your heart by imagining yourself filled with Joy! Let your life become a smile.

Sometimes your joy is the source of your smile, but sometimes your smile can be the source of your joy.
—Thich Nhat Hanh

Reflection: When are you most joyful in your ordinary day? How can you invite joy into your heart and your life?

Affirmation: I am a joy-filled, playful, open, laughing, loving being!

Openness

Openness is an essential ingredient for joyous living. You can learn something new and exciting every day if you are paying attention. Many parents enjoy the evening questions with their children … "What did you learn today?" Have you slipped into the habit of allowing your day to tire you out so much that you have lost the energy for a day's-end review for insights and inspirations?

You may know a lot, but when you are with another person, there is always an opportunity for something new to emerge and present itself. If you are humble enough not to place yourself above another, s/he can be the bringer of fresh prospects for an inspired life.

Creative experience can be produced regularly, consistently, almost daily in people's lives. It requires enormous personal security and openness and a spirit of adventure.
—Stephen Covey

Reflection: Do the end-of-the-day review to see what you learned. What insights and inspiration are waiting for you?

Affirmation: I am open to life's gifts!

Trusting Optimism

May 19

Trusting Optimism

Quantum physics teaches that we live in a Universe that is influenced by the observer. In experiment after experiment, it has been shown that what the observer expects to see influences the way the material in the experiment behaves. Who is the observer in the experiment of your life? You are. What you expect to see influences the way your life unfolds.

Optimism is the faith that leads to achievement. Nothing can be done without hope and confidence.
—Helen Keller

So stop looking for what doesn't work. Stop trying to find the weak point. Every time you focus on these things, you help make them appear in your reality. Start looking for the greater good. Start looking for the possibility. Start imagining how it might be true or might work. With your optimism, you are now positively influencing the very fabric of creation to conspire for your great good. Now, go out and expect your good to unfold in your life!

Reflection: Where are you looking for what's wrong or focusing on what's not working? What positive thing can you focus on instead?

Affirmation: I focus on my life with optimism and enthusiasm. I look for those places where things are working and where I am fulfilled and happy.

Loving Myself

Taking care of yourself is critical to your ability to give to your passion and to others. When you are depleted and unhealthy, you simply cannot give your gift nor can you enjoy your life. Lack of sleep, improper nutrition, not enough exercise, and stress all contribute to negative feelings, an inability to cope with change, and an unwillingness to see possibility. Simply trying to take care of your mental state may not be enough if your physical state is worn out and tired.

Take care of your body, your health, your spirit, and your soul with the proper nourishment and rest that each one of them needs. Your body needs sleep and regular breaks. Your health needs proper nutrition and reduced stress. Your spirit needs the expansive places in nature and the silence of meditation. Your soul needs creativity, love, self-expression, and the freedom to be.

Eight hours of sleep is equal to one hour of therapy.
—Edward Viljoen

Silence gives rest to the mind...and this means giving rest to the body. Sometimes rest is the only medicine needed.
—Unknown

Contemplation: In what ways are you really good at taking care of yourself? In what ways do you need to take better care of yourself?

Affirmation: I easily care for my body in healthy ways. I regularly nourish my spirit and soul. I lovingly care for myself.

Trusting Optimism

May 21

Loving Your Temple

Remember that amazing scene in *What the Bleep* when she starts to draw lovingly on her body, caressing and blessing every single part of herself? You must stop disparaging, blaming, condemning, and disliking your body. Your body is the vehicle for your Spirit in this life. This vehicle needs care and maintenance to keep it functioning smoothly. It also needs love to keep it glowing and healthy. Make friends with your body. It's the only one you get this time around!

I finally realized that being grateful to my body was key to giving more love to myself.
—Oprah Winfrey

Your body is a temple, but only if you treat it as one.
—Astrid Alauda

Health is the result of relinquishing all attempts to use the body lovelessly.
—A Course In Miracles

Contemplation: Shower your body with love—every single bit of it.

Affirmation: I love my body. It is the house of my soul, the temple of Spirit.

Out with the Old and In with the New

A realtor once said, "Every house or condo is basically an empty box; it's what you put in it that makes the difference." What you fill the space with will be entirely different from what someone else would put in it. What is interesting is that all too often when people move, they haul all their old stuff and fill the new space with the old couches and furniture, just re-creating what they had.

Don't you think if you are making a move it's time to start anew? Get some new energy going ... buy new dishes, tables, beds, linens, and sofas.

Nature abhors a vacuum.
—Ernest Holmes

Spirit tells us It makes all things new. What are you schlepping through life that's just taking up space? What patterns are you carrying forward, making it impossible for new experiences to show up? You know what things are taking up space in your life that you need to let go of. Treat yourself to the Good you deserve. Complete the old, stop talking about how you used to do it or how it used to be, and move into your new estate with how you want your life to look, and live it now!

Reflection: Look around your house and office. Is there anything that is outdated that you would like to replace? Look at your life and see if there are some old patterns you are dragging forward into your behaviors that it's time to dump.

Affirmation: I decorate my new estate with my new state of Being!

Seeing Clearly

Never be afraid to look at what is happening. Pretending it's not happening doesn't make it disappear; that's simply called denial. For example, not balancing your checkbook, so you don't have to see whether or not you have the money you want, doesn't change how much money is in your checking account. It simply keeps you from being able to respond to your money in appropriate ways, and it may cause you to spend money you don't even have. Now your denial has created an even bigger problem.

It is what it is, it is what you make it.
—James Durbin

What you must do learn to do, become willing to do, is to look at whatever is going on clearly and without reactionary emotions. That means to look—simply look—without judgment or criticism, without feeling like a victim or seeking blame. By simply looking at things as they are, you have a much better chance of doing something about them. You can start creating the life you choose because you will not have given your power away to the situation, and you won't have created additional issues. Now you have the power within yourself to choose how you would like it to be instead and to start moving in that direction.

Reflection: What am I afraid to look at in my life? What am I unwilling to see? What would happen if I did look at it, clear-eyed and without reaction?

Affirmation: I see clearly what is, knowing that it doesn't describe what will be. I take "what is" as my starting point and build what I want from there.

Responsibility

One of the greatest challenges on the spiritual path is to realize that you are responsible for your life and your choices. At first, this can feel like a heavy burden if you assume you are to blame for everything in your life. The best way to understand responsibility is to realize that by taking responsibility for something, you are giving yourself the ability to respond to it. You can't actually do anything about something for which you are not willing to take responsibility, not for creating it, but for responding to it.

Responsibility is to keep the ability to respond.
—Robert Duncan

When something happens in your life, blaming yourself or looking for who's at fault simply keeps you stuck in being a victim. Taking responsibility means looking at the choices that you now have before you. What is the healthiest, sanest, most wholesome choice you can make, from where you are right now? Which choice makes the greatest contribution or makes a difference? Now you aren't a victim nor are you stuck. Now you are taking responsibility for your life!

Reflection: Is there some part of my life for which I don't want to take responsibility? How could I engage my ability to respond? What new choice does that give me?

Affirmation: I am willing and capable of taking responsibility for my life. I have the ability to respond to any situation or circumstance because I have the help and support of Spirit!!

Dream Big

May 25

Stuck in Time

Your past pains need to be fed to be kept alive. This type of attachment will drain your energy and keep you stuck in time. When the wound requires today's energy supply to pass it forward, you will eventually be depleted. If you don't neutralize the negative debt, the energetic requirement grows, and its consumption will eventually bankrupt your fresh, daily life flow and start eating your body to keep it alive.

Each person who gets stuck in time gets stuck alone.
—Alan Lightman

With less and less daily power to manage the requirements of your world … like physical well-being, self-expression, and relationships … you miss today's investment from joyous living that charges you up and replenishes your life force, adding to your savings. Don't allow your history and its wounds to drain the richness of your present life. Your identity is more than your story; your healing doesn't need to take any more time. Let your healing be now, and let it be complete.

Reflection: What wounds from the past are energetic consumers of your fresh energy of today? Can you be done with this energetic debt that is keeping you bound in time?

Affirmation: I no longer feed the past with today's energy!

Dream Big

When President Kennedy declared that the U.S. would land a man on the moon within the next decade, he had no idea how that was going to happen. What he knew is that unless we are willing to dream big, we will never become the greatness we are meant to be. Along the way to achieving that dream, so many amazing things were created and invented that our lives were completely altered because of that dream. You have big dreams, too. These dreams are Spirit's impulsion to live and love, to grow and give, as YOU, through a full, rich life that contributes in a meaningful and powerful way to all life.

Only as high as I reach can I grow, only as far as I seek can I go, only as deep as I look can I see, only as much as I dream can I be.
—Karen Ryan

So go ahead, dream big—you cannot out-dream God! Live fully—it's never too much for Spirit. Explore new things; it's how Life is evolving. Love extravagantly—it's really the only game worth playing! Every time you embrace something more—greater, deeper, richer, or higher in your life—you are expanding how much of life you can express and experience.

Reflection: What is your big dream? Where are you living life to the fullest and loving the most extravagantly? And where are you holding back?

Affirmation: I dream big, live large, love fully, reach deeper, and soar higher on the wings of Spirit.

Without Form

As you move into a fourth-dimensional awareness, you come to realize your prayers are without form or words. You've gone from the wants to being the word of God. Your prayers have moved from your tongue to your inner ear. You are in the receiving mode rather than the "help me" place. A spiritual essence fills your experience, and you realize this Grace is sufficient. There is no longer separation, but a merging with all there is.

Out beyond the ideas of wrong doing and right doing there is a field. I'll meet you there.
—Rumi

You lose all sense of power over any situation because there is only One Power and that is what has emerged as your awareness in every circumstance you see. Healing happens not because you direct anything from the human perspective, but rather because you are the place for the Creative Intelligence that guides the universe to be expressed as your life. And there is no otherness that can deny Its manifestation.

Reflection: Which one of your prayers can you change from attempting to direct the Infinite Intelligence about what to do for you to becoming more receptive to the Divine Realization about the situation?

Affirmation: The Divine emerges as me!

Beyond Sight and Sound

When you can stop thinking about demonstrating things and move into the consciousness of demonstrating God's Presence, amazing good begins to happen beyond what you thought you wanted. It's your entanglement in stories that keeps you attached to your small sense of self, the one you think you need to keep helping. The mind is insufficient and feelings are too emotional to comprehend the magnitude of Spirit.

There is a universal belief in two powers, which is what causes every bit of discord in this world. It's your recognition of the Truth of Oneness that dissolves all discord. Words can be steps pointing you in the direction

Language isn't an adequate tool for expressing something that can't be perceived with our five physical senses.
—Anita Moorjani

to a true sense of communion with the Absolute, but they are not the Truth. It's only as you quiet the mind that your soul can reveal what it hears beyond words and sees beyond sight and feels beyond the senses … the good that Spirit has in store for you.

Reflection: Close your eyes and remember a time you felt so good and connected with nature, yet you couldn't put it into words. If there is a pending challenge, rather than praying for your desired outcome, reenter that good feeling and connected sense you had without attempting to get it to do anything specific. Then notice what Good emerges.

Affirmation: I am aware of more than language can define!

Dream Big

Are They Watching?

How many times have you been in a room full of people and wondered if they were staring at you? Or were watching and judging you? How often have you spoken up in a group only to be consumed with the concern about whether you said or did something stupid? Or if what you said even made sense? This is being self-conscious in a negative way, allowing your concern over whether someone is watching, listening, judging, or critiquing you, rather than simply showing up as who you are to give the gift you have to give.

> *What you think of me is none of my business.*
> —Terry Cole-Whittaker

You are the only person who can live your life. Stop worrying about what other people think. If someone does think or talk about you, they will spend only five minutes on you and then they will go on to talk about someone else, and someone else, and then someone else again. You, however, have to live with yourself 24/7, so don't let someone else's five minutes dictate who you are and how you feel about yourself for the other 1,435 minutes of that day. Be who you are, no matter how different or self-conscious you may feel. No one else can be you but you! And you are absolutely beautiful, precious, never-to-be-repeated, unique!

Reflection: When have I allowed my fear of what someone else might think keep me from doing something or being myself?

Affirmation: I am a unique, precious, never-to-be-repeated expression of the Divine. I am absolutely capable of being myself! I am proud and confident of who I am.

Cooperation and Collaboration

Competition comes from a scarcity mentality. In a soccer game, there may be only one winner, but this is seldom true in almost every other area of life. In business there is certainly many more than one customer; in creating or inventing, there is more than one idea. For resources of people, money, or energy, there is always more than one source; and for recognition, there are so many opportunities to go around.

In truth, there is no competition, unless it exists in your own mind. Spirit is infinite, so how can there be competition for resources, recognition, or success? In an Infinite Universe, there is enough to go around.

If you want to be incrementally better: Be competitive. If you want to be exponentially better: Be cooperative.
—Unknown

Try moving from competition to collaboration. You'll be amazed at how much more relaxed life can be.

Reflection: Where does my belief in scarcity show up as a sense of competition? How could I cooperate instead?

Affirmation: I know there is more than enough of everything I need for my success. I no longer fear or engage in competition. I cooperate with the Universe for my, and others', highest good.

Dream Big

Seeing the Light in Others

A friend once said, "People—you can't live with them, and you can't live without 'em!" People can be challenging and frustrating to work with and relate to. They are also a source of compassion, connection, and downright fun in our lives. The world is full of amazing, committed, powerful, and sensitive people. The world is full of flawed, challenging, and troublesome people. It just so happens that they are the same people. Which ones are you focusing on?

People are like stained-glass windows. They sparkle and shine when the sun is out, but when the darkness sets in, their true beauty is revealed only if there is a light from within.
—Elisabeth Kubler-Ross

The thing is, you can't see in others what you don't have in yourself. Often you project onto others what you don't want to see in yourself. In this way, the people in our lives become a mirror in which we can more accurately see how we are feeling about ourselves. And as you change what you focus on in others, you will change the focus within you, too!

Reflection: How are you experiencing the people in your life, in general? Are you finding yourself irritated by many folks or do you constantly run into the helpful sort? How is this a reflection of where you are right now?

Affirmation: Everyone I meet is a radiant child of God. I shine my light and love by focusing on their light and inner beauty.

June

Living on Purpose

Reveal Your Purpose

Joy and happiness are not experiences you find or create. These are the products of a soul in tune with itself and in alignment with Life. What calls to your soul? What is your life about? These are questions that reveal your purpose, your reason for being in the world, on the planet, at this particular time. Answering these questions will help you discover your purpose.

Find me one person who can get his own littleness out of the way, and he shall reveal to me the immeasurable magnitude of the universe in which I live.

—Ernest Holmes

Then, seek to be about the purpose that is unfolding in your life, and you will find joy and happiness where you least expect them. Go looking to live your purpose, be about what you are here for, and joy will sneak into your life and your heart. Happiness will no longer be something you want or look for. It will be the place you live from, every day.

Reflection: Explore how you are chasing happiness. Notice when you are living your purpose and see if happiness is already there.

Affirmation: I am aligned with my true purpose. This fills my life with Joy and Happiness.

Your Life's Purpose

Your life has a purpose. It's not to be a certain thing like an actor or accountant, nor to do only a certain thing, like sing or love. So often, your purpose has been made too small by trying to be fit into a box or a label. Your purpose is to be an inlet and outlet for Life, for Consciousness, for the Divine. Without you, there is a piece of God missing.

Life's desire is to express Itself through all creation. Spirit's desire is to experience Itself through Creation. Your purpose is for Life and Spirit to be expressed AS YOU! Your purpose is to be the Divine experiencing life. Your truest purpose—to express and experience all the qualities of God, through you, as your very life! Enjoy!

> *It seems that man exists for the purpose of self-expression. There appears to be no other reason or excuse for his being.*
> —Ernest Holmes

Reflection: What is your purpose? How are you expressing and experiencing the Divine through EVERY aspect of your life?

Affirmation: My life's purpose is to be Spirit AS me—to love, give, grow, and express as much of the Divine as I possibly can, every moment, through every action, in every relationship.

Live on Purpose

The universal power is one of creation and it operates through the Law of Cause and Effect. Whatever you focus on becomes "cause" in your life, producing the "effect," which is the life you are living today. Are you using this power for good in your life and for the good of others?

You use this power for good by focusing your intention on, and paying attention to, the good you want to create. Focus your consciousness. Intend to be loving, generous, and purposeful. The power of your intention is that it sets a new "cause," a new course, in the Law, which automatically produces a new "effect." The power of the Universe is always responding by growing and multiplying what you focus upon.

There is a power in the Universe, and you can use it for good.
—Ernest Holmes

Reflection: How consciously are you using your intention to use the power of the Universe for good?

Affirmation: I intend to live on purpose, in a fulfilled and meaningful life. My intention is the focusing lens through which I look and act.

Priorities

What are your personal priorities? Your set of priorities is yours. Others may not understand or agree with them, but when you start to go against them, you will lose a sense of self. Teaching those around you what your priorities are and your adhering to them makes for a more honest life. It will help to keep resentment from brewing. Do you work too hard at being nice and considerate at the expense of what's valuable to you?

Do you believe you have to take care of the wants and needs of your loved ones before yourself? Maybe if you tried saying "no" once in a while and stopped pouring all your energy out, there might be some left for you and your soul's yearning to express in this world. Being clear on your priorities will clarify your energetic expenditures.

Things which matter most must never be at the mercy of things which matter least.
—Johann Wolfgang von Goethe

Reflection: Write out your priorities.

Affirmation: I honor my priorities!

Go Confidently Toward Your Dream

Everyone has dreams, no matter how big or how small they may seem to you. You may dream of starting a garden, building a business, or saving the world. You call yourself into your greater life through the power of these dreams, but you may wonder how to start.

Following your dreams is like getting into a cool pool on a hot summer day. You can dive in headfirst or you can slowly ease yourself in, step by step. Standing at the edge in fear or uncertainty will never get you into the pool or moving in the direction of your dreams!

Go confidently in the direction of your dreams. Live the life you have imagined.
—Henry David Thoreau

Reflection: How do you like to start something—ease into it or take the plunge? What dream is calling you to start?

Affirmation: I go confidently in the direction of my dream. I live the life I have always imagined.

What, Not How

Always focus on the "what," not the "how." Your job in cocreating your life with God is to focus on the end result. What do you want to manifest or experience? What is your highest idea or your biggest dream for your life? Stay focused on that; that is your job in cocreation.

God's job in the cocreation process is the how. Don't you worry about it. There is an infinite wisdom and intelligence in the Universe called the Law of Cause and Effect that knows how to create anything. It created the whole Universe, so surely it knows "how" to create the way to your goal. Even when you doubt or are afraid and want to control things, it is so much better if you do not meddle in the how. Stay focused on the what. This is called Faith!

> *We can never know in advance whether we are going to succeed with something new. That's why doubt is a condition of the process. But when we experience the doubt and keep going anyway, our trust in our capacity to find our way through the unknown grows exponentially.*
> —M. J. Ryan

Reflection: What do I want? Where am I letting the "how" keep me from moving in the direction of my dreams?

Affirmation: I focus only on the end result. I leave the "how" up to God. I take each step as it appears before me, trusting in the process.

The Realm of Becoming

There's an old story of a young apprentice who once asked his spiritual teacher how long it was going to take to reach enlightenment. The master teacher told him it would take about ten years. The student then asked what if he devoted more energy to practicing twice as hard and put in twice as much time into the spiritual practices, to which the master replied that it would then take twenty years. Instant gratification is good, but it doesn't seem to work that way in the realm of becoming.

Knowing is not enough; we must apply.
Willing is not enough; we must do.
—Johann Wolfgang von Goethe

Your spirituality is in evolution. It takes time to integrate awareness into what life gives you to practice with. Your relationships, work, finances, and global concerns are only a few of life's curriculum for integration. Joyous living is based on the spiritual truth of how you are applied to your life and not the intellectual understanding of passed-along truth of the world. It takes time to develop consciousness and have it emerge in your life. Your real and relative world, with all its hot spots, is the perfect processer to develop your trust in Spirit as you.

Reflection: Where have you tried to rush the process, only to pay a higher price later?

Affirmation: I trust my life's process!

The Lure of the Physical

It's easy to get sidetracked with your worldly responsibilities, addictions, or things that just aren't in alignment with your soul purpose. What lies within you is greater than the lures of the physical. If you aren't living a life that turns your heart on, if each day isn't filled with passion and joyous living—why not? What are you waiting for? Why would you resist the gifts of God awaiting your acceptance? Pierce the veil of illusion that projects the lure of the physical. What lies before you will no longer be a reflection of the projection of the lure of the physical, but a revelation of the manifestation of what's been hidden behind the very thin veil.

'Tis one thing to be tempted, another thing to fall.

—William Shakespeare

Once you have cleared the screen for the new projections to play on and made room for the Divine, you'll come to realize the Divine is already there and always has been. Your greater good has just been waiting for the space and acknowledgement to come forth into your life. Whether you know it or not, some new alignment takes place when you move the finite self out of the way and invite the Infinite to fill the space you've made available for your viewing.

Reflection: Where and when have you discovered greater good behind your struggles? What struggles have caught your recent attention, and what possible good could be waiting for you to make space for it to emerge?

Affirmation: I am in Divine alignment!

Power of Choice

Remember that you are never stuck; it only feels that way. You are always free to change your mind. You are free to take a new road, make a new decision, make a new choice. This does not mean that there won't be consequences for making a new choice, but you already know that. It is only your fear or your unwillingness to be uncomfortable that keeps you stuck.

We cannot live a choiceless life. Every day, every moment, every second, there is choice. If it were not so, we would not be individuals.
—Ernest Holmes

You are free to express your life as uniquely as you choose. There is no prize for staying and no reward to going. In either case, you will learn and grow and have the opportunity to become more of yourself. The joy is in being true to who you are, no matter where your choices lead you.

Reflection: Where are you stuck? What choices are you unwilling to contemplate because you don't like the consequences?

Affirmation: I exercise the power of my choice and walk confidently through the changes in my life.

What Fills Your Space?

Humility is the particular attribute that allows God into your experience. People attack life as if it's their strength, power, and wisdom that will conquer their world. Before Spirit can fill your field of awareness with the Divine realization that is relevant to your situation, you've got to be clear to receive it. You can't fill space that is already full of longings and desires. The storage unit business is a lucrative business because people can't get rid of their stuff, so they pay dearly to keep it. Life is not withholding your good; it's that your container you already have is occupied with other worldly perspectives.

The truth you believe and cling to makes you unavailable to hear anything new.
—Pema Chödrön

God doesn't exist to please you and fulfill your wants. You must yield to the Divine Expression. How could you love God if you believed It was intentionally withholding your good, waiting for you to wheel and deal? That which created the universe didn't omit anything in creating you. Believe things will always work out well in your world by ultimately putting your faith not in the material world but by surrendering your will and wishes. You'll find Divine Grace filling the space with Its way of love and joyous living. Who knows what treasures Spirit has in store for you—it could just be your heart's desires and more!

Reflection: What's taking up God's space in my awareness that would be beneficial to clear out?

Affirmation: Grace fills me now!

Earth School

You are enrolled in Earth School. One of the major courses in this school is the education of your power of choice. You are learning about the freedom you have to choose and, then, to take responsibility for your choices. Every choice you make teaches you something about you, and life, and the Divine. Your choices show you what happens when you choose in alignment with yourself and your true nature, or when you don't.

The world is your exercise-book, the pages on which you do your sums. It is not reality, although you can express reality there if you wish. You are also free to write nonsense, or lies, or to tear the pages.
—Richard Bach

Not every choice is the right one, or works out the way you think it will. Don't be afraid of making mistakes; just remember to learn from them. Learning which choices support your joy, love, growth, expression, happiness, and connection, and which don't, is what it's all about.

Reflection: What choices are you making these days? What are your choices teaching you?

Affirmation: I am confident and capable of making choices that are in alignment with my highest truth. I learn from every choice and every mistake.

Mental Beasts

Doubts are normal. What is essential is not to let them take over. They will have you thinking in circles that can drive you crazy. As you feed them your energy, they will grow into mental beasts. As you just observe them, you'll notice you are not the doubter … it's your mind that is doing the mental gymnastics.

Instead of being the mental zookeeper of all the wild beasts in your mind, demanding your attention to be fed, just witness the doubts rising and fading away from lack of attention. No longer being drawn in by the tempting stories of fear, you will free yourself by seeing the natural rhythm of thoughts coming and going.

Many people think they are thinking when they are merely rearranging their prejudices.
—William James

Reflection: What doubts are you feeding? Stop giving your power away to them— just observe and let them pass from your awareness.

Affirmation: I trust the natural rhythm of thoughts coming and going through my field of awareness!

Appreciate Where You Are

Horses often stick their noses through fences so they can nibble on ... the exact same grass already on their side of the fence. How often does the grass appear greener on the other side to you? Whenever you are feeling that you'll be happier, healthier, wealthier if you just were someplace else, you are suffering from the greener grass syndrome.

Bloom where you are planted.
—Bishop of Geneva,
Saint Francis de Sales

It's important, first, to take the time to appreciate where you are and what you already have. You may already be living your bliss and not recognize it. What do you really need to change to be who you are and give your gift? It may be your situation or it may simply be your perspective. You might try nibbling a bit more consciously on the grass you're already standing in, and see if it doesn't taste just the same.

Reflection: Is there someplace in my life where I have been using the phrase "When I...then I'll...?" Can I have, get, do, or experience that thing right here and right now?

Affirmation: I notice how my life currently supports me. I make conscious choices and changes.

More of You

A drama coach once said to stop trying to be something else and give me more of you. A homiletics teacher once said to stop trying to be somebody else and give me more of you. A relationship once said, "Stop looking back and give me more of you." What your world wants is more of you. That is who you've come here to be. Don't allow yourself to be pulled into attempting to be something you are not. Look into your heart and soul to pull out more of who you are. That is all this world wants ... more of you.

The real Self is God-given and cannot be denied.
—Unknown

Reflection: Where have you attempted to be someone or something you weren't, and how did that feel? When have you dug further into your heart and soul to bring forth more of you into life, and how did that feel?

Affirmation: I trust who I am and who I am becoming!

Inner Strength

Inner strength is the product of being comfortable in your own skin, and knowing what you can and cannot do, and being willing to admit what you do and do not know. When do you masquerade behind a facade of bravado, simply pretending to be strong? How often are you afraid to be found out?

Having inner strength means you are willing to put effort into whatever you are doing, even if it seems difficult. Moving from your inner strength means you can ask for help when you need it. Living out of true inner strength means you can say, "I cannot do this," without feeling diminished or simply giving up.

What lies behind us and what lies before us are tiny matters compared to what lies within us.

—Ralph Waldo Emerson

Reflection: Are you comfortable with asking for help or saying "I don't know?" Where are you pretending to be strong?

Affirmation: My inner strength comes from the Truth of Spirit within me. I lean on Spirit, knowing it is strong enough for anything.

A Father's Strength

A child's bond with his father is special. Remember to stay interested in whatever your child may be interested in, because your child is always watching and noticing where your energy goes. Display his artwork and praise him often … it means more to him than you'll ever know. Boys are like lion cubs that show their affection by hanging, hugging, wrestling, and rolling around on top of each other. When children are young, their purpose for sports and games is to play and have fun. Remember, when children are grumpy, it's often because they are either hungry or tired, so don't take it so personally because they'll get over it and you should, too.

You know the only people who are always sure about the proper way to raise children? Those who've never had any.

—Bill Cosby

Human beings are the only creatures on earth that allow their children to come back home.

—Bill Cosby

Moms are often the matriarchs who carry a lot of the practical wisdom, but, through time and traditions, the transference of spirituality has rested with the fathers and grandfathers of the clan. Teach your children about God … if you can't talk to your child about a higher power, then you can't really talk to your child. Teach them about God while they are young so they are comfortable talking about spiritual things when they are older. Pray together as a family so they are able to pray when they are alone. Don't miss the specialness of nighttime prayers before they go to sleep. Let them know God can be trusted and is a loving Presence that will be with them throughout their lives. And, most of all, it's most important for dads to be around and present—no one can do that for you.

Reflection: No matter what age, how can you be more present and available for your children? Spend some time being in a pleasant memory of a blessed moment with your father.

Affirmation: I am fully present when I am with my children.

Feel Your Feelings

Feel your feelings; they are a natural part of this life experience. The important thing is to feel them cleanly and express them purely. Do not act upon your feelings in a destructive and hurtful manner, neither toward another nor toward yourself. When you are hurt or mad, simply say so. You can say it with a great deal of vehemence and energy that is without attack or blame.

See that each hour's feelings and thoughts and actions are pure and true; then your life will be, also.

—Henry Ward Beecher

Just as importantly, when you are joyous and happy, enjoy it without guilt or shame; just don't require others to be in the same place. When you are determined, go for it without running over anyone else. And when you feel like playing, invite the whole world to play with you!

Reflection: Which feelings am I most able and willing to feel and share? Which ones do I avoid or express inappropriately?

Affirmation: I allow my feelings to wash over me like waves on a beach. I enjoy surfing them, without avoidance or drowning.

The Headless Chicken Routine

When you are in a tough place, do you ever feel like the proverbial headless chicken running around in circles, asking other people what they think you should be doing? Is it because you feel someone else knows what is best for you? What's in your thinking that puts more faith in another's viewpoint about your life than your own? What do you need to be telling yourself so that another's perspective has more relevance than your own in your world?

Other people's opinion of you does not have to become your reality.
—Les Brown

You are the only one who has been part of every one of your life experiences and decisions. You know what is going on, inside and out. No one is going to know you better than you know yourself. Appreciate all you are aware of about yourself … it will lead you to your Divine connection. Yes, you are interested in what others have to say, but don't give your power away by thinking their view of your life is more valuable than yours. The amount of wisdom available to guide your life is in proportion to your conscious awareness of the presence of God within.

Reflection: What happens when you follow what other people think you should be doing with your life because you value their opinion more than yours?

Affirmation: I trust my inner direction!

The Donkey Ride

An old man, a boy, and a donkey were going to town. The boy rode on the donkey, the old man walked. As they went along, they passed some people who remarked that it was a shame the old man was walking and the boy was riding. The man and boy thought maybe the critics were right, so they changed positions.

Later, they passed some people who remarked, "What a shame. He makes that little boy walk." They then decided they both would walk! Soon they passed some more people who thought they were stupid to walk when they had a decent donkey to ride. So they both rode the donkey. After some time, they passed some people who shamed them by saying how awful it was to put such a load on a poor donkey.

Don't pay any attention to the critics—don't even ignore them.
—Samuel Goldwyn

The boy and man said these people were probably right, so they decided to carry the donkey. As they crossed the bridge, they lost their grip on the animal, and the donkey fell into the river and drowned.

The moral of the story? If you try to please everyone, you might as well kiss your ass good-bye.

Reflection: Where have you taken a "fall" because you were attempting to please other people?

Affirmation: I honor my inner knowing!

Whose Station Are You Listening to?

Have you ever walked into a restaurant and noticed there was a TV on or gone into someone's home and the stereo was playing? The stations that were dialed in might have been pleasant or not, but the fact is that they were being broadcast, and you had to choose to dial in to a different frequency, or you would be a receiver to someone else's choice.

The world is constantly sending its messages of concern, so you must pick your empowerment channels rather than unconsciously becoming manipulated into reacting to the broadcast of others. You are never out of reception to the Divine Frequency. It is always available for you to tune in, no matter where you are. As others make their listening and viewing choices, you, too, are always at choice about where you turn your dial for conversations and images.

Short as life is, we make it still shorter by the careless waste of time.
—Victor Hugo

Reflection: Notice what sounds and images are being broadcast around you.

Affirmation: I am dialed in to the Divine Frequency!

June 21
Celebrating Their Success

One of the best ways to increase your joy and prosperity is to celebrate the good that other people are receiving. Being truly joyful for another expands your mental equivalent and creates a strong attractor in your own consciousness. Every time you can genuinely celebrate someone else's success, you are adding the feeling and the image you hold about success in your own mind.

You need to be aware of what others are doing, applaud their efforts, acknowledge their successes, and encourage them in their pursuits. When we all help one another, everybody wins.
—Jim Stovall

When you get lost in comparisons, become envious, or are simply unable to celebrate someone else's good, you contract your own mental equivalent, and this closes the door in your own mind to your greater good. You can feel the sense of contraction this creates, rather than the expansion that celebrating, with real joy, creates.

Reflection: How can you celebrate someone's good fortune with them today? Where are you holding back your joy regarding someone else's good?

Affirmation: I joyfully celebrate the success and prosperity of others.

Claiming Good

Why do bad things happen to good people? This ancient question is one of life's mysteries. We can never really know the answer to "why." You may not know why something is happening the way it is, but one thing you can know for sure ... Good will come of it. How do you know Good will come of it? You know it, because you demand it.

Look back over your life and see how many times something happened that you thought was bad at the time, but actually is part of what brings you to being who and where you are today. Notice when something "bad" turned out to be a bless-

We refuse to believe that evil has any reality of its own; its only claim to existence is the one our belief gives to it.
—Ernest Holmes

ing in disguise. Now, make this claim on the Universe. Demand to make Good out of what is going on right now, even if you don't know or can't imagine what that Good might be. YOU don't have to know. The Law of Life itself must make it so.

Reflection: List "bad" things that have happened in your life that turned out to be all right in some way or even became a gift in your life.

Affirmation: I claim that Good must come of this situation. I demand it of the Universe, and I trust that it is so, even if I can't see it right now.

Setbacks Are Setups

June 23

Setbacks Are Setups

Spiritual growth is not based on how many classes you've taken or how many years you've engaged in spiritual practices. Nor is it based on the number of advanced trainings you've been involved in facilitating and degrees you've got hanging on your wall.

Rather, spiritual growth is a sense of harmony in your human affairs with no great emotional roller coaster or fluctuation in facing the human condition. This kind of harmony is not based on outcome or income. It is the natural, spiritual state. Our spiritual identity is not based on changing, correcting, or manifesting anything in this world of form. All discord is a belief that you have a life separate from God. Harmony is. Not will be or can be—it is.

Wherever you are is the entry point.
—Kabir

Reflection: Where in your life would you like to step up to higher ground? Step on top of the setback to get you higher so you can see the expanded options from your experience.

Affirmation: Spirit lifts me ever higher!

Nondebatable

Getting a child out of bed and ready for school can be a battle of the wills. This child has known the morning routine for years, yet seems to resist the inevitable. Emotions can take over with threats and force, or you can come from a nondebatable perspective. Either way, the kid is going to school. Which choice leaves you feeling better about the early morning encounter?

When life seems to continuously resist your perspective, do you allow your emotions to pull you down to childish behavior, or do you maintain an unwavering, emotionally detached assurance of the outcome? Your child eventually responds and, when

Even though your kids will consistently do the exact opposite of what you're telling them to do, you have to keep loving them just as much.
—Bill Cosby

you look back, somehow you've gotten him through school. Your world will respond and, when you look back, you may wonder how you ever got through it, but you did! You can journey with upset or neutrality when faced with life's resistance—the choice is yours, not the resister's.

Reflection: Where in life do you seem to be giving your power away to what seems to be resisting you? Can you move back to a place of emotional neutrality while seeing the result?

Affirmation: I stand unwavering in the Truth!

Setbacks Are Setups

Complaint

Pay attention to what you are paying attention to. Do you tend to point out what's not working, what needs to be corrected, or someone's faults or flaws? If this is all you are noticing, then you are missing what's working, how much someone is doing, or how perfectly something could work out if you're not getting in the way. What you pay attention to becomes the magnet for your life. The very things you don't want or like become the mold for what you are creating.

You can become blind by seeing each day as a similar one. Each day is a different one, each day brings a miracle of its own. It's just a matter of paying attention to this miracle.
—Paulo Coelho

Pay attention to, focus on, and speak about what is working, no matter how small. Notice how things work out. Speak about the best in people and how much they do actually give and do.

Watch how your life begins to grow in a more positive direction instead of re-creating more of what you don't want.

Reflection: What is my favorite litany of complaint? What could I focus on instead?

Affirmation: I turn my attention to what is working. I notice the positive. I speak what I like and want into being.

From the Expanded Vista

For the mystic, it's about the constant conscious contact with the Infinite. When a less-than-pleasant dynamic arises in life, can you remember to touch the Infinite and trust that this union will provide all that is necessary?

It's easy to get caught up thinking, "I know what's best here and how everything is supposed to turn out" … then outlining the orders to the universe as to how to fix things. A healthier approach is to courageously pause, turn within, and listen for a higher guidance to show a way beyond the present, engaged human perspective.

By fighting for the impossible, one begins to make it possible.
—Oscar Arias

Allow your perspective and proclamations to come from an expanded vista and your resolutions from revelations.

Reflection: Where in my life would it be good to pause and listen for a higher perspective in a difficult situation?

Affirmation: I am a positive contributor to life!

A Complaint-Free Zone

Become part of creating a complaint-free world. Complaining about the weather, taxes, children, or freeway drivers simply focuses your attention on what you don't like. Every time you start to complain, find something else to praise instead. It will change everything!

As selfishness and complaint pervert and
cloud the mind, so love with its joy clears and
sharpens the vision.
　　—Helen Keller

Reflection: List your favorite things to complain about. Pick three that you will never complain about again. Then add three more.

Affirmation: I live in a complaint-free zone in my mind, in my thoughts, and in my speech.

Inner Speech

The way in which you speak to yourself about yourself, your life, and the events around you will shape the way you see them and how you will respond. The things you say over and over again to yourself in your head—things like "I'm tired," "I'm too busy," or "I don't have enough money for that" —become affirmations that your subconscious mind accepts as real. Noticing and changing your habitual self-talk is one of the most powerful spiritual practices you can do in your life.

Start speaking to yourself about the good, positive, and beautiful things that are going on. Speak to yourself in the same loving and supportive way as you would to a friend. This way, you are speaking those things you want to experience into your subconscious mind, which then shapes into your reality.

The inner speech, your thoughts, can cause you to be rich or poor, loved or unloved, happy or unhappy, attractive or unattractive, powerful or weak.

—Ralph Charell

Reflection: What is the nature of your habitual self-talk? What do you talk to yourself about? How do you talk to yourself?

Affirmation: I speak loving, positive, and spiritually grounded words to myself about myself and my life.

Time for an Exorcism

Enough of Not Enough—The "Nots"

Are you tired of struggling? When have you had enough of the "nots"—not good enough, not worthy enough, not intelligent enough, not good looking enough, not prosperous enough, and the list goes on and on. If that is not enough, there is the collective consciousness that many people live in, which believes there's not enough to go around, not enough time, or not enough resources. These are just a few of the debilitating thoughts that are ready to catch a ride in your thinking and put on the brakes to your good. They will steer you into a life of fearful living from scarcity, while the truth is that you live in an abundant universe where you are the channel for its expression.

The mind is its own place, and in itself, can make heaven of Hell, and a hell of Heaven.
—John Milton

Step beyond the hoax of your limiting story into the soul's vision of what's possible. It is right for you to live in a Divinely sustained expanding expression of good! Ease and effectiveness are your natural states of expression. When you know there is enough to source your journey, then nothing other than your story can keep you from joyous living.

Reflection: Make a list of your "enough of not enoughs" and write the expanded new story. What does your new world look like without those constricting factors putting on the brakes?

Affirmation: I live in a Divinely sustained expanding expression of good!

Time for an Exorcism

How much of your life has been organized around fear? It doesn't matter where you got those fears … society, parents, actual experiences, or a carry-over from a previous life. The challenge arises when you give your voice of reason the power to pull you in a different direction than your intuition is telling you. How often are you disloyal to your soul's voice just to defend your fear?

When something has power and influence over your actions, it's as if you've been psychically possessed. Well then, it's time for an exorcism. Fear can hold you captive, and healing and freedom cannot take place as long as you are under its spell. Guidance for your healing is always available. But if you need to know the reason why something happened to you, you could remain stuck in your head. You take the misfortune you experience in the outside world and allow the resources of the inside world to transform. By this practice, you'll come to know what's in you is greater than what's in this world, and you'll watch those fears dissolve.

If we let things terrify us, life will not be worth living.
—Seneca, Epistles

Reflection: Journal about what fears are directing your life.

Affirmation: I am responsive to my intuition!

July

Living Creatively

Creative Flow

There is more than enough creativity, joy, abundance, and life to go around. Trust in the Infinite Supply and Abundance of the Universe! You cannot run out of ideas or creative solutions because you live in an Infinite Reality. Remember that there is always something more. This expands your pipeline and opens the channels.

The whole course of things goes to teach us faith. We need only obey. There is guidance for each of us, and by lowly listening we shall hear the right word.... Place yourself in the middle of the stream of power and wisdom which flows into you as life, place yourself in the full center of that flood, then you are without effort impelled to truth, to right, and a perfect contentment.

—Ralph Waldo Emerson

Fear and worry come from a belief in scarcity and lack, as if all the new or good ideas have already been thought, and all the creative options have already been tried. This scarcity mentality contracts and restricts the flow. Know you stand in the midst of the stream of life, even if you can't see it or feel it. Your powerful, positive mental attitude of trust will make the difference!

Reflection: Where is your creativity constricted? How can you place yourself in the middle of the abundant flow of life?

Affirmation: I trust in the abundantly creative flow of Life that moves through me right now.

From Analysis to Action

Therapy may assist you to identify your blocks. You'd be a lot happier just getting over them or going around them. A lot of creativity can come from using your pain to produce. Alchemy doesn't just look at what's at hand and analyze it; it uses what's there and transforms it into gold. Take your wounds and blocks as fuel to create, write, produce music, paint, dance, or whatever your creative modality is to bring forth the masterpieces of your soul.

Therapy aims at making us normal. Art aims at expressing our originality.
—Julia Cameron

But remember, don't make producing a masterpiece or needing transformation your goal, but rather keep creative expression as your purpose. This is when healing happens. Your creative expression moves you from judgment and analysis to action. Exercising your soul's creativity gets you out of your funk and back into life's flow by getting you over or around the blocks.

Reflection: Take the feeling from a blockage in your world, and take those emotions and pour them freely through a creative expression of your choice.

Affirmation: I am a creative outlet for life to flow!

Patience with the Process

Patience is a virtue
Possess it if you can
Seldom in a woman
And never in a man!

This anonymous poem speaks volumes about how our culture experiences patience. In this instant gratification world, you may discover that you want things to change as instantly as you can press a button and get an entirely new web page to buy from. Unfortunately, while there is no time in God, it is often actually necessary for something to grow in this space/time continuum.

Be patient toward all that is unsolved in your heart and try to love the questions themselves. Do not now seek the answers, which cannot be given you because you would not be able to live them. And the point is to live everything. Live the questions.

—Rainer Maria Rilke

Patience with the unfolding process is a part of being Present. Your change and healing may not be instantaneous, but that doesn't mean it isn't happening. Delay is not denial, just the molecules of the Universe rearranging themselves for your good. Look for small signs along the way. EXPECT things to shift and serendipitous events to take place. One day, you'll awaken to see that the change has already arrived!

Reflection: Are you patient with the process?

Affirmation: I am patient with myself and with others. I am patient with the process of growth, and I relax into the unfolding of Life.

Rights and Privileges

Rights are absolute; they are not negotiable. Privileges are granted and can be taken away as quickly as they were given. Most of modern history shows those in charge ... the ones who had the wealth and power ... held the rights and granted the privileges.

Our Founding Fathers thought they would reverse this concept with a new democracy where the people would guide themselves. Instead of the government and businesses having the rights and passing on privileges to the people, the people would hold the rights and grant the privileges to the government and businesses. If those rights are violated, We the People, who grant the privileges, have the freedom and the rights to withdraw them.

We hold these truths to be self-evident, that all men are created equal, that they are endowed by their Creator with certain unalienable Rights, that among these are Life, Liberty, and the pursuit of Happiness.

—The Declaration of Independence July 4, 1776

My God! How little do my countrymen know what precious blessings they are in possession of, and which no other people on earth enjoy!

—Thomas Jefferson

Reflection: Where in your world have you abdicated your rights to something you feel is bigger and more powerful than you? How can you reclaim your unalienable right of freedom today?

Affirmation: I reclaim the authority in my life!

Natural Curiosity of Your Soul

There is so much more in life for you to enjoy than you can imagine. Your spirit came into this world as an explorer. As a child you were curious, as an adolescent you were rebellious, and as a young adult you were willing to risk it all. Then something happened to you and your flirting with disaster! Somewhere along the line, you started to need to know the outcome before going down the path. You wanted to know how deep the pool was before jumping in. The person who liked to push the envelope started getting pushed aside by the person who wanted to know how it would turn out before beginning.

It is not down on any map; true places never are.

—Herman Melville

Two roads diverged in a wood, and I—
I took the one less traveled by,
And that has made all the difference.

—Robert Frost

At what point did you reel yourself back in and say it's time to play it safe and get serious? Have you traded the excitement of the unknown for comfort and security? Has your calculating mind stopped you from taking a step that is based on trusting something greater inside you that knows a better outcome than your thinking? Stop the mature expression of oppression, and say yes again to the natural curiosity of your soul.

Reflection: What adventure is calling you at this time that you are saying no to? What good might come if you said yes?

Affirmation: I say yes to life's adventures!

Creativity and Your gift

Creating your life comes from who you are and the gift you have to give to the world. Don't worry so much about what form it will take—will it be this job or should you write that book? Focus, rather, on who you are and what your gift is.

Now begin to look for all the ways you are already giving your gift. These are the seeds of your creative adventure. Build on the things that come so naturally to you. Be the gift, and your creativity will flow effortlessly from your center. The form your creativity takes will be a natural outgrowth of your inner light.

If you would create something, you must be something.

—Johann Wolfgang von Goethe

Reflection: Are you fixated on the form through which you think your creativity should express? Where are you already being creative?

Affirmation: I allow my creativity to flow from my innermost being. I let the form it will take emerge naturally from who I am.

July 7
Lessons in Creativity

Being creative does not only include artistic endeavors. You bring creativity to all aspects of your life every time you use your imagination to create a new way of seeing, being, or doing something. Every time you try something new or think outside the box, you are being creative.

The biggest trick to being creative is not to worry about mistakes or perfection. Too often, you hold yourself back because you don't yet know how to do the new thing perfectly. Or you're not sure if you really know how to think outside the box. Just start somewhere. As you practice, you can get better at it.

Every artist was first an amateur.
—Ralph Waldo Emerson

Reflection: Is your perfectionism or unwillingness to feel awkward or make mistakes running your life? Where could you use more creativity in your life?

Affirmation: I am a creative being. I think outside of the box. I allow myself to try new things.

The Creative Urge

Inspiration and ideas come from everywhere. Everything that catches your awareness is attempting to tell you something. Your creative urge doesn't care where you are; it's always wanting to infuse you with desire. What matters is to give it an outlet. Your creative expression is an act of faith. You must give it passage from the abstract into form by trusting what's coming through you.

When there is no motion, it's only a dream and remains in the realm of possibility. You don't need to know how an adventure ends before you begin it, nor do you have to know where your creative urge is going to take you before you begin.

The great Creator loves artists and is waiting as a lover waits to respond to our love when we offer it.
—Julia Cameron

Like all great artists, there is the desire to reach a dimension not yet conveyed. This genius state of illumination cannot be reached on command, but rather you must make yourself available for its guidance and revelation. Make yourself receptive to the creative urge, and you will find the time and energy for what you love. You will attract all that is necessary for its expression through you.

Reflection: What creative expression do you love that you are not doing? Create some space now in your life and get to it.

Affirmation: I now give space to my creative urge!

Ramadan

Ramadan is the month for deepening one's spiritual connection. During Ramadan, the believer seeks Allah's grace and forgiveness. This is the month for renewing one's commitment and reestablishing one's relationship with the Creator. It is observed during the ninth month of the Islamic calendar, believed to be the month the Qur'an began to be revealed. One of the five pillars of Islam is fasting during Ramadan. During the daylight of this month, one is to have greater spiritual practices. It is believed that fasting from food, drink, and sexual activities helps redirect the heart away from earthly desires to a greater closeness with God. Spirit is with those who have space for the Divine.

Allah is with those who restrain themselves.
—Qur'an

"Salat," the five daily prayers, is a great way for reconnecting with Spirit throughout the day. Spirituality is not about isolating yourself from the world; it's more about integrating your spiritual awareness into your daily life. If you can fast from the enticing demands of your world to remember God first in all things always, you reclaim your connection with the Divine Power. Your soul will be blessed, and your actions in the world will be generous.

Reflection: What earthly desires take your awareness off God? For the next month, reclaim your power and fast from those activities and at least five times in a twenty-four-hour period, stop and remember your Higher Power.

Affirmation: My soul stamina strengthens!

Creating Yourself

Isn't Life amazing? Here you are, surrounded by a planet that feeds you, friends that love you, and a life that's yours for the making. What are you creating with this marvelous life of yours? Are you creating busyness, unhappiness, or boredom? Or are you creating connection, creative expression, meaningful activity, and hope?

Your life is as amazing as you make it. Stop believing in your own lack of creativity. You are as creative as the Universe because the Macrocosm is reflected in you, the microcosm. All the creative nature of Life is available to you, right now! What do you want to create?

It is better to create than to learn! Creating is the essence of life.
—Julius Caesar

Life isn't about finding yourself. Life is about creating yourself.
—George Bernard Shaw

Reflection: Do you believe in your ability to create the life of your dreams? What's holding you back?

Affirmation: I now create the fulfilling, meaningful, loving, and expressive life of my dreams. My life is amazing!

Infinite Imagination

Soul's Urge

Feelings of inadequacy and emptiness can be a real downer, yet they are more common in people than often thought. It's one reason the hero's journey has been popular since recorded history—from the Mesopotamian king Gilgamesh, to Ulysses in his wanderings, to King Arthur's search, to the vision quest of the indigenous. There is something in you that wants to confront and triumph over your fears and doubts and master the earthly forces, freeing yourself to be your potential fully expressed.

Pure logic is the ruin of the spirit.
—Antoine de Saint-Exupéry

You've got your logical side, whose job it is to keep you comfortable in the familiar, and your intuitive urgings enticing you to explore greater possibilities. When you don't honor your soul's urge, you put yourself on a collision course leading to a crash. This ordeal will be a catalyst for change that you might not otherwise have made to open the door to discover you have what it takes to live a fuller expression of joyous living. You can get there through the drama of a crash or choose to listen to your soul's urgings and be guided to your destiny. Either way, it works … the approach is your choice.

Reflection: Where has drama been a catalyst for a change for the better that you otherwise would not have made? What earlier signs did you have letting you know it was time for a shift that you did not heed?

Affirmation: I now say "yes" to my soul's urgings!

Comparison

Never compare yourself to anyone else. Your gift is unique and precious. No one creates, thinks, feels, or sees the world just like you do. You can always find someone who you think is better at something than you are. Do not try to be just like them. Allow them to inspire you to possibility, not imitation.

You can always find someone who isn't as good as you are. Thus, you can, at any moment, feel both superior and inferior, neither of which is true. You are a precious, unique, one-of-a-kind, never-to-be-repeated incarnation of Life Itself—just like everyone else. See it in yourself. See it in others.

Comparison is the death of joy.
    —Michael Gott

Remember this, you are absolutely unique, just like everyone else.
    —Margaret Mead

Reflection: Where do I compare myself to others? What opportunity or possibility is this blocking in my life?

Affirmation: I am a unique and precious expression of Life. I am exactly who I am. My gift to life is mine to give.

Infinite Imagination

July 13
The Ride of Your Life

Have you ever found your rational mind telling you how it is supposed to be rather than experiencing how it is actually unfolding? To participate in your own life, you have to be present. Many people are called into life not because of the joy but because of the pain. When you can let go of what you want, you can receive what is really yours, which will be greater than your plan.

Lost yesterday, somewhere between sunrise and sunset, two golden hours, each set with sixty diamond minutes. No reward is offered for they are gone forever.
—Horace Mann

It's time to stop holding back your potential and move beyond what you know. Can you trust your soul to take you on the ride of your life through life? Stop being the brakeman and applying the friction, and allow yourself to see the wonder of life in this very moment. You miss your life when you are not present.

Reflection: What if your greatest joy was available to you right in this very moment, but you were preoccupied, thinking that the present was supposed to look different, and you were missing it? How could you become more available to joyous living now?

Affirmation: I am available to the joy of this moment!

Infinite Imagination

One of the most amazing things about being a human being is that you can imagine something that you've never seen or experienced before. Kennedy imagined us going to the moon. Edison imagined that there must be a better way to make light than with fire. Neither of these things had ever been done before, so it was through the power of imagination that the field of our human experience was expanded by these and so many other inventions and ideas.

The power of imagination makes us infinite.
—John Muir

What is so amazing is that you can imagine anything, everything, way beyond what you are currently experiencing. This expands your life into the realm of possibility, which is endless. You live in an infinite Universe, so there must be endless possibilities.

Reflection: Where does your life need to be expanded by imagining something different from the way it currently is?

Affirmation: I live in a limitless Universe. I effortlessly imagine all sorts of possibilities. My whole life expands.

Beyond Your Wildest Dreams

Do you remember your most magnificent childhood dream and the possibilities that lay before you and what you were here to do? It has great value to be able to return to this kind of connection with Source that placed the dream inside you. All that is necessary to bring the Vision from the abstract realm into form is for you to return to the belief frequency of being.

Who looks outside, dreams; who looks inside, awakes.

—Carl Jung

Returning to the visioning flow of life will neutralize the constrictive locks you've allowed yourself to enter. By doing the routines and obligations of your life, you may have forgotten what the excitement of possibilities felt like as you saw yourself living from your heart's passion. The Life that infused you can never be less of life. It is Infinite and therefore only awaits your invitation to give you your vision that is beyond your wildest dreams.

Reflection: What was your most favorable childhood dream? Enter into that again and play in the energy of that possibility again. What is your heart longing for now? Bring that childhood energetic belief into your current vision.

Affirmation: My vision of heart moves from the abstract to the real!

The Attitude of Inspiration

Being creative may start with an idea, but then it moves into implementation. This is often the place where it fizzles out because of a lack of discipline, drive, and willingness to stick to it.

"You can do it!" "Attitude is everything." "Believe you can, and you can." These are not simply empty words. This is a powerful formula for the alchemy of consciousness that causes you to succeed. This is the discipline required of you to do what you want and to create the life and success you desire. Yes, you CAN do it! Just start, and then stick to it.

Genius is 1 percent inspiration and 99 percent perspiration.
—Thomas Edison

Reflection: Am I easily discouraged, and do I give up? What attitude do I have toward my goals and dreams?

Affirmation: Yes I Can! Spirit supports me! I am consistent, committed, and diligent in moving toward my dreams and goals.

Recurring Yearnings

Addictions really get in the way! If your awareness is filled with desire for the same vices repeatedly, you are getting frozen in time. Rather than having a mind free to take hold of a new idea, when it wants to take hold of a drink, a joint, or a tub of ice cream, there may be an issue. The stories of denial can be deceiving and convincing: "It loosens me up. I'm more creative. It puts me in the flow." When followed by, "Just a little more to keep the feel-good feeling going," what follows is not Divine intoxication but a fog that slows you down.

Just because you got the monkey off your back doesn't mean the circus has left town.
—George Carlin

It takes a humbleness to honestly look at your patterns to see if your desires for more sex, love, money, drugs, gambling, attention, or any one of a number of other reoccurring yearnings has become the dominating theme of your thinking. In the afternoons, are you thinking about your visions or your cravings?

Reflection: Is there a recurring craving that is disproportionately dominating your thoughts and actions? Do you live in denial about this yearning and don't really want to acknowledge it? What do you need to do to dissipate this energetic sucker?

Affirmation: I am free!

It's Their Reality

There's some scary information out there in the world that I could perpetuate by mentioning it here. The doomsday prophets are plentiful with their Armageddon statistics. The sad part is this is their true world of fear in which these individuals have chosen to live. They'll tell you, "It's not a choice—it's reality. Just look at the facts."

Then there are those who naturally see Good everywhere. The world they have chosen to live in is filled with Light and Good, and they can't be convinced otherwise. It's their reality, and they have the evidence to prove it. Neither can understand the perception of the other.

You shall know the Truth and the Truth shall set you free.
—The Bible (John 8:32)

The mystical aim is to behold Spirit in all things. The mystic's desire is to move into a higher state of consciousness at will and not be caught in the gravitational pull of duality. If Spirit is Infinite, then logically there cannot be God and something else. As you accept this spiritual status, you'll be free of the torment of fear, which means you'll be dropping the negative perspectives you are holding on to, thus allowing the Infinite to guide your thoughts and life to a higher perception of Truth. If you don't want to live by the collective beliefs of a fearful society with its documented reason to fear, you must choose your alignment of thought: be governed by Truth or led by fear.

Reflection: Where are you being led by fear? What would you imagine to be the Truth if you moved to a higher state of consciousness?

Affirmation: My life is filled with abundant Good!

The Alchemy of Awe

Inevitable Changes

The only permanent thing in this world is change. Spirit may be absolute and unchanging, but the physical world in which you live is constantly changing. Change is as inevitable as the seasons. Rather than clinging to what is or trying to avoid what's coming, learn to welcome change.

Seek to embrace the chaos and uncertainly that come with releasing the familiar and moving into something new. This creates opportunity and possibility rather than resistance and despair. When change is inevitable, flow with it; this way you will see the new opportunity in front of you, rather than being stuck gazing longingly at the one that is now going away. Allow yourself to be changed and moved. This keeps you sane and healthy, ready to open the next new door.

When one door of happiness closes, another opens; but often we look so long at the closed door that we do not see the one which has opened for us.

—Helen Keller

Reflection: Where am I resisting change in my life? What am I not willing to let go of?

Affirmation: As this door closes, a new one is opening. I turn my attention from what was, and I am completely available to what is and what is coming!

Ask for Help

Rugged individualism, spiritual pride, or a need to do it yourself may be causing your load to be heavier than it needs to be. Don't be afraid to ask for help. There is nothing unspiritual about being caught in your human experience and needing help to get things straight. Remember how good it feels when you can help someone else? Open up and let someone do that for you!

That's why Spirit created friends and community ... so you can celebrate with each other when things are great and lift each other up when things are not. Don't wait until you are happy to be around others or to get involved in mutual support. Find a prayer partner, get a sangha group. Reach out! Do it today and discover how much easier it becomes to carry your load along the way!

It's not the load that breaks you down; it's the way you carry it.
—Lena Horne

Reflection: Where could you ask for help or let someone else support you? What are you willing to do to reach out?

Affirmation: I am strong enough to ask for help. I invite others to support me with the same ease with which I support others.

The Alchemy of Awe

The Alchemy of Awe

Alchemy is about turning base metals into gold or transforming the mortal body into life everlasting. It is changing the basics into the golden experience. Awe is an emotion that's been compared to wonder. Usually it is inspired by objects considered more overwhelming than the observer ... like huge waves, majestic mountains, or the vastness of the cosmos.

You are an Alchemist; make gold of that.
—William Shakespeare

One is in awe when catching a glimpse or having an experience of the Infinite. With this vision, there will be a shift. Life never fits back into the constraints of the previous container of consciousness. When in awe, you are Grace-filled. You have been given the cherished and mystical alchemic ingredient.

Whether your life turns golden or morphs in another direction, it is in the hands of the alchemist. You have been entrusted with the "philosophers' stone." You can crumble with the burden or use it wisely to create the heavenly experience. Everything it touches has the potential to turn to gold. Are you ready for your world to be so bright?

Reflection: Where have you misused your insights? What have you turned to "gold"?

Affirmation: My life is golden!

Monotony to Magnificence

Sitting on a white sand beach, watching the sun rise over the turquoise-colored bay while the fish are jumping with joy to greet the new day, it's easy to see the Divine at play. With the lush, green jungle along the water's edge filled with the sound of monkeys howling and birds singing, and the jungle's fresh fragrances lifting to the morning's warmth, you'll know there are a lot of different opportunities of experience waiting for you to choose where you are going to play this day.

The real voyage of discovery consists not in seeking new landscapes, but in having new eyes.

—Marcel Proust

Stepping into a new environment, you have fresh eyes and see many different paths for your day. Sometimes in life you become so accustomed to where you live that you don't notice the sun's rays touching your view or remember to look around and see all that the Divine has planted in your neighborhood for you to explore. Life is meant for joyous living, and you are the point that transforms monotony to magnificence.

Reflection: Where have you gotten into a routine and forgotten to notice the Divine at play? Where can you schedule a moment in your day to see with fresh eyes?

Affirmation: I greet the dawn of this new day with fresh sight!

Nourishing Rain

When you were a kid, did you ever run outside to stand in the warm pouring rain? We did! We'd throw back our heads with mouths wide open and catch the raindrops on our faces and tongues. We'd create whole dam systems in the rivulets that ran beside the road. I remember feeling absolutely nourished and washed clean by those summer rains.

Rain is grace; rain is the sky condescending to the earth; without rain, there would be no life.
—John Updike

You are nourished by the gentle presence of Life, just as the earth is nourished by the rain. Spirit is forever showering you with life, Love is always radiating into your life, and Light is forever illuminating your way. Stand open in the "rain" of Life's bounty and allow yourself to receive the blessings of this downpour of Love, Joy, Wholeness, and Peace. Let it wash your mind and heart clean of the past. Open your heart and mind wide to take it all in.

Reflection: Are you open to the nourishing rain of the Presence? Where are you holding up an umbrella?

Affirmation: I allow Spirit to wash over me, nourishing and fulfilling all my needs. My light and love overflow and nourish others.

Heaven on Earth

How often do you strive to transcend your life and your problems into a spiritually enlightened state? Yet the Master Teacher reminds us that the Kingdom of Heaven is not some place or time—it is "at hand," it is "within."

The whole point is to live the Kingdom of Heaven right here on Earth! Not to seek to leave the human for the spiritual world, but to bring Spirit right here, to Earth, to every human situation and experience. You are in the Kingdom of Heaven when you know "the Christ Consciousness that You Are," and you let it be in charge of your life. This brings you into alignment with the forces of the Universe and bestows peace, joy, bliss, and contentment to your very being. And isn't that the definition of Heaven?

The Kingdom of Heaven is within.
—Jesus of Nazareth

Reflection: When do you try to "run away" to Heaven and leave your earthly experience of the world behind? How can you bring Spirit right there, into that situation?

Affirmation: I reveal the Kingdom of Heaven right here and right now. I am a bringer of Light and Love, Presence and Peace. I bring Heaven to Earth.

Go for It

Caught Looking

Have you ever been around a group of people in a restaurant or other crowded space and felt someone staring at you, and you turned and saw that he was? Or maybe you were looking at someone when he turned around and caught his eyes with yours? There is some kind of conduit or something moving in the unseen space that is as real and definite as your other five senses. Just because it can't be seen doesn't mean it's not real.

When you change the way you look at the things, the things you look at change.
—Wayne Dyer

Have some fun and experiment with this. Add some emotions or feelings to your psychic tap, and see what kind of response you get. Expand your distance to see how far away you can touch. Think of some friends who are not even around, and check in with them to see if they thought about you for some unknown reason at just the same time you were opening your heart to them.

Obviously your contribution to this invisible field is real! Imagine … if you consciously chose to make deposits of love, generosity, appreciation, and joy, what a significant energetic sea you'd be swimming in.

Reflection: The big question is, what are you adding to this collective field? What would you like to dissolve? What new good do you want to bring to your invisible environment?

Affirmation: I am a positive contributor to the energetic field around me!

Why Is Not a Useful Question

"Why me?" or "Why do I keep ending up with this place/job/relationship/ thought?" are not useful questions. You are here out of habit. The Law is simply creating for you a mirror of what you believe, expect, or accept. Asking why is like trying to brush the hair of your reflection in the mirror.

The question is never "Why?" The more useful question is "Now What?" "Now what" invites you to think about what you want instead. This is creating a new future rather than simply repeating the past. Then you must keep re-choosing that new thought/ act/word/being over and over again, until it becomes your new habit.

We need not ask why these things are so. There can be no reason given as to why the Truth is true. We do not create laws and principles, but discover and make use of them.

—Ernest Holmes

Reflection: Where are you stuck on the question "Why?" How would it change if you asked "Now what?" instead?

Affirmation: I no longer look to the why of the past. I focus on the what of my future.

Go for It

Willing Servant

The Law of Cause and Effect is a stern taskmaster but a willing servant. The causes you have set in motion have been playing out in your life. God isn't punishing you. There are simply consequences to the inner, subconscious stories about life that you have come to believe. Over and over again, the Law is showing you what is stored there, without variation or relief.

The Karmic Law is not kismet. It is not fate but cause and effect. It is a taskmaster to the unwise; a servant to the wise.

—Ernest Holmes

The good news, however, is that you can set a new cause in motion. You can create new ideas and generate new beliefs that the Law will just as willingly and truthfully manifest in your life. By truly changing your mind/heart/beliefs about something, you can cocreate a new reality. Use the Law; don't be used by it!

Reflection: Is there any area of life where you rail against fate or the way things are? What belief is operating that the Law is using to create?

Affirmation: The Law is my willing servant. I consciously cocreate my life by setting a new cause in motion.

Go for It

When young with nothing to lose, you went for it—whatever it was. There was a blind strength of believing in yourself. You were able to hear guidance and feel possibilities. You knew your dream and potential. You were led from within and stepped into synchronistic, Divinely inspired, unfolding outer events. With little to lose, you would say, "I am doing this," and others would say, "Yes." You found support, and those who didn't support you gave you greater determination. There was a larger vision calling you. It became an important part of your life. Your genius was stirring, looking to bring forth form to the call from within.

Nature never did betray the heart that loved her.
—William Wordsworth

Whatever you can do or dream you can, begin it. Boldness has genius, power and magic in it.
—Johann Wolfgang von Goethe

The beginnings of any undertaking may be exposing you to criticism from others. Your belief in what you see must be stronger than the doubters before you. Your creative expression wants to expand, yet when it meets with resistance, the emotionally immature custodian of the vision finds it's easier to contract to where it is safe. If you choose the comfort of approval, the boldness you once had softens, the early strength gives way to safety, and the once clear voice becomes a distant memory.

Reflection: When have you abdicated your vision in order to have comfort and approval? What did it cost you?

Affirmation: I am going for my vision!

Happy Dreaming

Your dreams are you speaking with yourself. They come from your subjective with images that have been created or allowed through and by you. There is great value in taking a moment before getting out of bed to see what messages you are attempting to convey to your conscious mind. Every image and aspect has some kind of significance because you, as producer, have put it in the movie of your mind.

There are those who say they can't remember their dreams. A trick to trigger the morning memory is to go out and buy yourself a Montblanc pen and a fancy journal and place it next to your bed. With that kind of investment, you'll be amazed at how some lingering images from your astral experience will be there to be captured on paper. The more you are consistent in writing down the little you've got, the more you'll remember the next morning for adding to your expanding journal. Just for fun, after your dream ask yourself, "What could this mean to me?"

A dream that is not interpreted is like a letter which is not read.
—The Talmud

Reflection: Put a pen and paper next to your bed tonight. When you go to sleep, tell yourself you will remember your dream. Then, first thing in the morning, write it down, including any significance or insight it might have for you.

Affirmation: I remember my dreams and know their significance!

I Am Great

Fear, criticism, envy … all come from not knowing one's inherent greatness. When you don't remember your Wholeness, it will keep you feeling small and unimportant. These kinds of feelings will close you down to the magnificence of who you truly are. These self-images are contrary to the Truth of who you are, which is Spirit expressing. If you choose to convey who you are and bring forth your distinctive and irreplaceable soul expression, you'll be in the groove of joyous living.

When driven by fear, mistakes are created, poor choices are made, illness is felt and hospitals are needed. So give up judging what you think is the right and acceptable way to be; let your hair down and feel good about who you are. Healing will happen in your life in the appropriate places when you feel unconditionally good about yourself. Your job is to love yourself and know you are a perfect expression of God, here to share that with the world.

I am the Greatest!
—Muhammad Ali

Reflection: Where do you feel less than perfect, magnificent, or wonderful about yourself? Close your eyes and feel the ever-loving arms of the Divine embracing you, rocking you. Sense the feeling from the revelation that comes from knowing the incredible radiance that is God expressing as you.

Affirmation: I know my greatness and honor others' greatness!

Go for It

One Heart

Whatever the challenge or problem you may be facing, there is only one cause—a sense of separation from Source. If you find yourself in a dangerous situation, yes, remove yourself from the condition, but it's not up to you to change the outer picture. Don't look at it with your human eyes, but close those eyes to the conditions of the world, and open your spiritual eyes and behold with the Divine Perspective. You'll be guided from within.

The foolish man seeks happiness in the distance, the wise grows it under his feet.
—James Oppenheim

As you look into the heart rather than the mishaps of those around you, you'll find a healing force that is naturally released. Don't attempt to reach out and heal another; only within your own consciousness do you need to sense the Truth. When you do this kind of knowing, it's through the connectedness of all Life that there will be a responsiveness within the One Heart, the Heart of God. Your conscious oneness with Spirit livens your oneness with all, because all are part of the whole.

Reflection: Your conscious awareness of Spirit is necessary for healing. Where in your life are you feeling a sense of separation from Source?

Affirmation: I am consciously aware of my life as God's expression!

August

Living a Relaxed Life

August 1
Lazy Days of Summer

Remember what it was like—those long, lazy days of summer when you didn't have anything to do? You were faced with endless hours of games, boredom that made you creative, and a slow and easy pace. It is important to find times like these as adults. They renew, rejuvenate, and enliven your whole life.

Being is the other side of doing. Being means you are simply enjoying, savoring, the present moment without the need to accomplish anything. This doesn't necessarily mean you are inactive. It just means your activity has no purpose or end result, no busyness or goal to it. Find a few ways you can simply be—with yourself, with a few friends or family, with nature, with Spirit, and enjoy a few hazy, lazy days of summer!

A perfect summer day is when the sun is shining, the breeze is blowing, the birds are singing, and the lawn mower is broken.
—James Dent

Reflection: What is your favorite way to simply be? How can you have more time to be?

Affirmation: I experience the joy of being. I simply am present and allow myself to enjoy whatever is.

Silence

When you give up being motivated by fear, a new kind of silence will fill your mind. When you stop talking, it doesn't mean there is silence, it just means you stopped talking. The chatter going on inside your head can be deafeningly loud and all consuming, leaving no open space for graceful revelations to fill. When you come to know silence, you can be with others and still carry an aura of calm. Even in the midst of confusion, you remain clear and connected.

Silence is more musical than any song.
—Christina Rossetti

Take the iPod out of your ears, leave the cell phone behind, step outside, and take a silent walk communing with nature. Find a quiet place with no computers, TV, music or outside distraction, and take an inner walk into the silence, giving your mind and body a rest. The more you relish the gifts of silence, the more you'll make it a priority in your life.

Reflection: Take some time in the silence today.

Affirmation: I find the time to make silence a priority.

Sabbath Time

The Sabbath is set aside to take a complete break from the ordinary demands of life. Regularly set a day aside to turn off your phone, email, and Facebook. Turn off the TV, news, and Internet. Stop trying to complete what's in your inbox or on your to-do list. Take a day and let yourself get bored. This reconnects you with a slower rhythm and helps you find your own pace again. This recenters you in yourself and in your own life.

Sabbath requires surrender. If we only stop when we are finished with all our work, we will never stop, because our work is never completely done. With every accomplishment, there arises a new responsibility.... Sabbath dissolves the artificial urgency of our days, because it liberates us from the need to be finished.

—Wayne Muller

Reflection: How can you create a regular Sabbath time in your life?

Affirmation: I take time to reconnect with my life by slowing down and unplugging from all electronic devices.

Stopping the Wild Ride

There is a well-told story of a guy riding a horse at a full run through a town as if he knew where he was going and he was going there fast. As he raced by, one of the onlookers yelled out, "Where are you going?" to which the rider yelled back, "I don't know, ask the horse."

Sometimes in life, your thoughts, emotions, habits, and life's situations can begin to start running in different directions and you don't know where they are taking you. It's as if you are holding on for dear life on an out-of-control wild ride, hoping it will end soon. To rein in the wild gallop through life, first breathe, bringing your mindful awareness to those out-of-control places, and bring it to a stop in consciousness. Deeply know there is nothing that can drive your world other than what you give the reins to ... so take them back.

He who controls others may be powerful, but he who has mastered himself is mightier still.
—Lao Tzu

Reflection: Sit down and stop your wild gallop through life by breathing into each situation where it feels to be moving too swiftly for you. Slow it down in your awareness and regain your composure; take the reins and redirect it to the pace of your choosing.

Affirmation: I take the time to make sure I am going in the direction of my soul's choosing!

Jumper Cables

When the battery is dead in your car, you have a couple of choices—you can pull out your jumper cables or call someone to bring theirs to "jump" your car. To hear your car turn over from the energy boost is such a relief and good feeling. Sometimes all the car needs is a good charge to get it going.

Prayer can be like those jumper cables … it can bring the necessary boost to get you going again. Sometimes life can be so draining; you feel you don't have the energy to keep going. This is the time to hook up to the Divine Energy source through prayer. You can connect yourself, or, when you can't seem to find what it takes to make the link, you can always call on a Spiritual Practitioner to share his or her gift of prayer. Either way, don't forget to charge up when you are depleted.

Prayer is the key of the morning and the bolt of the evening.
—Mahatma Gandhi

In prayer, it is better to have a heart without words than words without a heart.
—Mahatma Gandhi

Reflection: It's your responsibility to take care of the vehicle your soul is traveling in through this earth plane journey. So, when you are feeling depleted … no need to go through life feeling drained … remember to get the "jump start" with prayer so you can be charged up and good to go again.

Affirmation: I remember prayer is always a good "jump start" to the day!

Sneak Off with Yourself

Texts, tweets, email, faxes, cell phones, radios, TV, advertisements … throw in career, family, friends, and a few new acquaintances, and it's no wonder you might feel a bit overwhelmed and a little stressed in your attempt to keep up with life. Did you notice that none of those were about honoring your inner self? It's the part of you that is nourished by downtime and quiet inner reflection. The recharging aspect of you needs time to reflect, read, meditate, and enjoy bubble baths, naps, writing, playing, and creating. Yet, too often, the nourishing behaviors for your soul are the ones that get pushed to the bottom of the to-do list.

I think women are natural caretakers. They take care of everybody. They take care of their husbands and their kids and their dogs, and don't spend a lot of time just sitting back and taking time out.

—Reese Witherspoon

You can always push the off button in your world—the one that tells the world you are not available right now and you'll get back to it when you get a chance. Remember what it was like to hear yourself think, create, and feel from the abstract realm, not having all your thoughts be about what's going on in your physical world? Just as if you had a secret lover, you might need to sneak off to have some private time with yourself. When you honor having your downtime, others will, too. You will also have so much more to bring to them and to the demands of your life.

Reflection: What can you do to create a space in your day just to be with yourself and not the demands of the day—and will you do it?

Affirmation: I take time to be with me each day!

Currents of Adventure

Talking to captains or sailors while watching boats gently bob up and down as they are moored safely inside the protective bay, I find they all have stories of their adventures at sea to freely share. Just outside the cove are the currents of adventure waiting for them to re-enter. But in the meantime, it's time for rest, security, and restocking.

The spiritual journey is individual, highly personal. It can't be organized or regulated. It isn't true that everyone should follow one path. Listen to your own truth.

—Ram Dass

Being able to find a safe harbor to reorient and ready yourself is extremely valuable. To be in a heightened state of awareness is powerful and exciting, but to never come down can be depleting. Life will always be waiting for you to reenter its currents of adventure. You must replenish and strengthen yourself with nourishment of the soul by stepping out of the currents of your activities. Catch your breath, let your guard down, and reorient your course by checking your inner map to make sure you are still moving on your life's direction. Refuel, do the repairs, adjust, clean up, renew, and then set sail—life's adventures are waiting.

Reflection: When it was your time in life to rest, how did you not rest and what price did you pay? Where is your next cove so you know your next rest is on the horizon?

Affirmation: I surrender to my rest!

Spending Time

Taking time, killing time, wasting time, never having enough time ... How often do you describe your experience of time in one of these ways? In using these words, you perpetuate that feeling, and therefore you are actually creating exactly that experience for yourself.

How would you rather be spending your time? Enjoying it, savoring it, filling it? What kind of time would you like to have—creative time, play time, nap time? Are you paying attention to your subjective time, meal time, and bed time? It takes all kinds of time to make a day. And it's all happening in the eternal Here and Now!

Time is free, but it's priceless. You can't own it, but you can use it. You can't keep it, but you can spend it. Once you've lost it, you can never get it back.

—Harvey Mackay

Reflection: How do you describe your experience of time? What kinds of time are you creating? Do you want to create?

Affirmation: I have all the time I need. I enjoy my time. My time is always well-spent.

There Will Be a Splash

Expanding Time

When doing yoga, there is a magical moment between postures when you breathe and center yourself for the next Asana. In this brief space, time expands and there is a replenishing, calming, and energizing for the next posture. It's in this gap between actions that you get to choose how you approach the next activity. Whether energized or exhausted, it's up to you.

We must learn to keep ourselves awake by an infinite expectation of the dawn.
—Henry David Thoreau

In the day-to-day busyness, if you pay attention, you'll notice there is a moment where one activity ends before the next one begins. No matter how busy your life is, there is still a space between each action. Bring your attention and breathe into this space, and choose to calm your mind before having it race off to your next obligation. You'll find time expands, your body relaxes, and your approach to whatever is at hand won't be clouded with the carryover from what was.

Reflection: Practice breathing and centering between activities.

Affirmation: I remember there is a moment to breathe between my activities.

Making Time

Are you on your own priority list? Making time for the things that are important to you means you are creating the life you choose to live. When all your time is devoted to your work or to the television, someone else is in charge of the way you spend your days.

Put time into your day for those things that matter in the life you want to live. Schedule a date with your partner. Plan your exercise and meditation times into your calendar. Set aside a day just for creativity or for working on your dream. Don't just wait for it to happen. Make an appointment with yourself. You will be happier, healthier, and wealthier because you made time for you!

Don't count every hour in the day, make every hour in the day count.
—Unknown

Reflection: When are you making time for you? How could you schedule time for things that are important to you?

Affirmation: I easily make time for myself because I know I am worth it.

There Will Be a Splash

There Will Be a Splash

My son Trevor and I had been enjoying canoeing on our lake one fall afternoon in Montana. Canoes are far more tipsy in the water than flat-bottomed boats, but we had developed a good routine of getting in and out of the canoe from the dock without too much rocking and rolling. But no matter how good your practice might be, the next time you do it you have to get it right. The laws of balance and the gravitational pull don't remember the last time. Their operations are always in the now. One cold fall afternoon, Trevor felt he could jump in with no regard for balance, and the next thing we both knew, the canoe was rolling over and we were both rapidly swimming for the dock in the ice-cold lake. Being the responsible and dripping wet dad, I got to fish the canoe out of the water while Trevor stripped off his wet clothes and ran naked and screaming through the woods, heading for the warmth of home.

We are not troubled by things, but by the opinions which we have of things.
—Epictetus

You can't fool the balance of nature, and you can't fool the balance in your life. One of the top desires I hear in counseling is how much people want balance back in their world. When one side is overburdened for too long, there will be a splash—you will roll, it's the law. You can consciously choose to bring your life back into equilibrium, or nature will help you by dumping you. It's true at the individual level, the corporate level, and the national level. There is no large or small when dealing with the universal principles of Truth.

Reflection: Where do you feel your world is tipsy and out of balance? What can you do to reallocate the load?

Affirmation: I live my life from Balance!

World Saved in a Half Hour

People have become so accustomed to watching a TV drama and having the most intense situations resolve themselves within an hour. If you want a faster version, you could always watch a sitcom where you can have a blown-out-of-proportion problem resolve itself within a half hour while laughing all the way. Wasting your time on mindless entertainment has its value in removing you from the demands of your life. The challenge is when you forget it might take a bit longer to resolve some of the issues in your world.

Life is rich with its experiences. You are given an amazing array of situations to stretch and grow you on

Life loves to be taken by the lapel and told: "I am with you, kid. Let's go."

—Maya Angelou

your soul's journey. But don't get overly frustrated if your life challenges aren't resolved in an hour. Your reality is different from reality TV. Of course you would like to find a way out of the problem, but thinking something is wrong because it takes time is misleading. Be patient in your becoming.

Reflection: Where do you need to exercise some patience in the unfolding of one of your life's challenges?

Affirmation: I have all that it takes to resolve my challenges in perfect timing!

There Will Be a Splash

The Centering Breath

Learn to breathe your stress away. In yoga, it's called that centering breath. Take a moment, and simply breathe. Take one deep, conscious breath. Then take another one. You can take as many of these as you need. Notice how the breath takes you deep into the center of your being. Simply breathe.

This centering breath makes all the difference, and takes no time at all. You can do it anywhere, anytime, and in any situation. As you do this more and more often, it'll take only one breath to bring you back to center. Breathing is free. Moments are free. Then, you are free!

To insure good health: eat lightly, breathe deeply, live moderately, cultivate cheerfulness, and maintain an interest in life.
—William Londen

Reflection: Do you remember to breathe?

Affirmation: I take a centering breath. I breathe in Spirit and breathe out everything else.

Spiritual Drano

Have you ever felt stuck in life, where the challenges just didn't seem to go away, where one more small aggravation seemed to get blown out of proportion and added to the mess? You saw the back-up coming; you knew you were cramming too much into your world. You thought you could just stuff more garbage down the drain of consciousness without having to deal with it, and somehow it would miraculously disappear.

You can shovel only so much crud down the disposal pipes of consciousness before something sticks and stinks. When the garbage of your life stops disappearing and comes back into your world, you have to

The quality of the imagination is to flow and not to freeze.
—Ralph Waldo Emerson

clean it up. When this happens, it is time for some spiritual Drano. You need to open the flow again. Your affirmations are like a plunger … with your assertive determination, you can push the clog away. Your prayers are more like pouring some clog-dissolving power so the blockage is dislodged. You could try some forgiveness, which would be similar to getting a wrench and taking the pipe off where the jam is and removing it. The meditative approach is to stop adding to the challenge and wait for the natural forces to do their handiwork. You have a lot of tools to keep those spiritual pipes flowing, so take notice when the junk of your world is not being eliminated as swiftly as you'd like, and get into action sooner than later with the spiritual Drano.

Reflection: Where are things backing up in your world?

Affirmation: Life continues to flow through me!

Energy Boosters

Do you feel valued because you work so hard? Do you feel the need to convey to people how many hours you put into work, how full your schedule is, and how exhausted you feel? Is there some strange sense that the more burned-out you are, the greater your value? Does it seem there isn't enough time to play in your life? There is no happy ending to this cycle other than a crash. Your creativity withers when your life force is squeezed out. You can sacrifice your life and body, but there will always be the demand for more. Looking for validation for overachieving is a sure way to fry your internal circuitry.

We must be willing to get rid of the life we've planned, so as to have the life that is waiting for us.

—Joseph Campbell

Joyous living is being full of energy, a conduit for the life-affirming expression of Wholeness. When your inner state is one of happiness, there is a sense of belonging. This is what manifests in your ability to contribute at work and with family, friends, and new acquaintances. You will find time to play, rest, exercise, meditate, and be creative, all of which become energy boosters looking for outlets through you.

Reflection: Do you tell people how much you work more than you tell them how much you play? What is it you are cutting out of your life that you would like to be doing, but you are working yourself too hard?

Affirmation: I have the time to do what I love!

Sightings of the Divine

Keep your eyes peeled for sightings of the Divine! These may show up as "coincidences" or serendipitous happenings. You may see the Divine in someone's joyous laughter or a special gleam in his eyes. Notice beauty that moves you. Pay attention to possibility as it presents itself to you. Especially look for things that uplift and expand your heart and your soul.

The easiest way to catch a sighting of the Divine is in those moments of connection when you are with someone, and you know you are meeting heart to heart, or when you experience oneness communing with nature. You may often be looking directly into the heart of God! Pay attention. Don't miss it!

How often in my trivial conversation with my neighbors that someone higher in each of us overlooks this by-play, and Jove nods to Jove from behind each of us.
—Ralph Waldo Emerson

Reflection: When and where do you catch glimpses of the Divine?

Affirmation: I pay attention to all the ways that Spirit shows up in my life—through people, circumstances, and all of life.

Love and Laughter

Laughter is the best medicine—for the body, mind, and spirit. Norman Cousins, diagnosed with a terminal illness, decided to watch nothing but laugh-out-loud funny movies. This was his medicine, and it cured him. Laughter releases healing chemicals and relaxes different parts of your physical, emotional, and mental being.

All you need in the world is love and laughter. That's all anybody needs. To have love in one hand and laughter in the other.
—August Wilson

Invite all sorts of laughter into your life. Giggle, chortle, guffaw, belly laugh, and laugh so hard the tears are streaming down your face. Even sharing a simple smile lightens the load.

Reflection: How much laughter is there in your life? What kinds of things can you invite in to enjoy more laughter?

Affirmation: I laugh out loud easily and often. I walk around with a smile on my face.

Life Is Your Playground

Life is your playground! The very nature of the Universe is like Play-Doh. Quantum science shows how the interaction of observation and intention literally shapes the physical reality. In the same way, your life is shaped by the "hands" of your attitudes and beliefs.

What this means is that nothing is permanently the way it is. Everything can be reshaped. You can take any part of your life and roll it back up into a ball, and begin again. You can renew yourself with a positive attitude, expecting a good outcome for whatever you try. Like a game, you can change the rules or start over again. Just start playing!

You are led through your lifetime by the inner learning creature, the playful spiritual being that is your real self. Don't turn away from possible futures before you're certain you don't have anything to learn from them. You're always free to change your mind and choose a different future, or a different past.

—Richard Bach

Reflection: What area of your life would be enhanced by a more playful approach? Where are you taking yourself way too seriously?

Affirmation: I playfully engage with my life. I take my life in my own hands and create it however I choose!

Life Is Your Playground

Foolishness Is Good for the Soul

Mix a little foolishness with your prudence: it's good to be silly at the right moment. *(Misce stultitiam consiliis brevem; dulce est desipere in loco.* Horace*)*

Play is as important as laughter. Silliness lightens the load.   Do something simply because you enjoy it, without any thought of accomplishment or return.

When you act out of present moment
awareness, whatever you do becomes imbued
with a sense of quality, care, and love—even
the most simple action.
   —Eckhart Tolle

Reflection: Are you playing enough in your life? Create something here that is playful and silly.

Affirmation: I am secure and confident enough in myself to be silly and playful!

The Omnipresent Sanctuary

Life is like a heartbeat with its ups and downs. Sometimes the highs can be exhilarating and the lows excruciating. This is not a bad thing, because if your life was a flat line you'd be dead. What is interesting to note and be aware of is that part of you that is observing your journey—the awareness itself.

The observer, that aspect of you who is just watching and noticing, has not been impacted by the experiences. With all your life's tussling and wrestling, no matter how excruciating, your observing self was never affected—it just noticed what your earth self was going through. Imagine this undisturbed omnipresent sanctuary you'd have if you learned to go there in your time of pain. There is a place in you that has never been violated by this world and is always available to you.

There is a place in you that has never been violated.

—Ernest Holmes

Reflection: Find a quiet place to sit and allow some unresolved emotions from past experiences that still have life in you to float into your present screen of observation. Notice the awareness of you observing the situation that impacted your earth self but not the observing self. Realize you are more than the experience or the experiencer, and feel the release of emotional energy this awareness brings.

Affirmation: I am aware of my awareness!

Nothing but the Truth

Have you ever not fully spoken the truth to someone? The truth is so powerful that it is often withheld or not fully disclosed. Do you do this because you don't want to hurt someone or make him feel uneasy? Or is it that you don't want to feel the discomfort? Are you a safe place for the full truth to be shared, or are you defensive and abrasive in your retaliation with your perspective?

Honest disagreement is often a good sign of progress.
—Mahatma Gandhi

Are you able to see beyond your perspective and interpretation to "nothing but the truth"? Which of your perspectives are you maintaining that may not be the full story yet keep you in a place of discomfort? Trust the truth to direct you to resolution and healing.

Reflection: Think of a person or situation where you haven't been fully truthful and reflect upon the questions above.

Affirmation: I trust the truth!

Eater of Impurities

There is a Native American shamanic practice that has been referred to as the "eater of impurities." This is when one of the spiritual elders sits with an individual and has him bring to mind something he wishes no one to know about … something that has been parasitically alive within the darkness of his awareness. This action or concern would be eating away on his inner world, making it difficult to be fully present in the physical world. The spiritual elder would instruct the tormented one to bring his fear into view. When the shaman could sense the rising real fear of the consuming darkness, he would then tell the person to give it to him. The darkness was brought into the light and absorbed.

When you are in doubt, be still and wait:
When doubt no longer exists for you, then go
forward with courage.
So long as mists envelop you, be still;
be still until the sunlight pours through and
dispels the mists—as it surely will.
Then act with courage.
—Ponca Chief White Eagle

These days, society has its therapists, the churches have their confessionals, and it's not uncommon during preparing for death for individuals to desire to purge their misdoings. The secret to being the "eater of impurities" is to have a big heart and know there is nothing that needs to be forgiven. Being and releasing unconditional love creates a trusting atmosphere that allows you to be freed from your fears and be healed.

Reflection: Is there an area of concern lurking in the dark recesses of your mind that you would like to have exorcised from your subjective field of thought? Try this ancient practice with a trusted spiritual friend and see what happens.

Affirmation: I surrender any past mistakes to the light of my love!

Inside-Out Living

There is an ancient fable that says that when the gods decided to create man and make him divine, they wished to hide his divinity in some place that would be difficult for him to discover. And so they held a consultation in which one of the gods said, "Let us hide man's divinity in the air." But another replied, "No, someday he will create a machine and fly through the air and discover his divinity." Yet another god suggested that man's divinity should be hidden at the bottom of the sea. While another said, "No, we have given man such power and such an imagination that someday he will make a machine that will penetrate the depths of the ocean." So after much discussion, they all agreed that the best place to hide man's divinity, the place where he would be least likely to look for it, would be deep within himself. "Deep within," they said, "for he will always be looking outside himself. And he will never think that he already has the thing he is looking for." And so they hid his divinity at the very center of his being and left him to discover it.

Tears of joy are like the summer rain drops pierced by sunbeams.
—Hosea Ballou

The real problem is not whether machines think, but whether men do.
—B. F. Skinner

Each man carries within him the soul of a poet who died young
—Antoine de Saint-Exupery

Outside-in living is the product of our consumer society—always looking "out there" for something to make you happy. Inside-out living is the product of Spiritual connection—always looking within for the happiness that is present in your life, right now!

Reflection: Are you living from the inside-out or the outside-in?

Affirmation: I live FROM the truth of my being. I love FROM love and joy, peace and wholeness.

Against Nothing

Are you for something or against something? Too often, when you are against something you are actually lending your energy to the very thing you don't want to have happen. Being for Peace rather than against war focuses all your attention and intention on the end result you want to experience.

The same thing applies when you think about whether you are moving toward your dreams or moving away from something that you want to avoid. Running *to* something is always taking you to a better place while running away *from* something just causes you to re-create the unhealed experience someplace else. Being for and moving toward are both positive, expansive actions. Being against and seeking to avoid are both contracting, negative actions.

Find me one person who is for something and against nothing, who is redeemed enough not to condemn others out of the burden of his soul, and I will find another savior, another Jesus, and an exalted human being.
—Ernest Holmes

Reflection: Where are you against something, and how can you change it to be for something instead? Is there someplace in your life where you are running from rather than running to?

Affirmation: I am for everything that supports life—my life and all life. I move toward my dreams, letting them expand me!

Societal Impressions

It's easy to get caught up in self-evaluation of images you see outside yourself. Do I match up to these societal impressions or not? Am I as good or am I less than? Your higher self is calling to you to wake up to who you truly are. Use this lifetime to bring forth the gifts of your spirit. Embrace the invitation for joyous living by being true to yourself and letting go of the comparisons.

Imitation is suicide.
—Ralph Waldo Emerson

How will you spend this particular life span? Where are you going to be focusing your attention … on others or on expressing who you are and what you are to do? Your ancestors gave a lot in order for you to come into this world. Are you honoring their legacy by being your true self?

Reflection: How has comparison sidetracked you from who you truly are? Where are you holding back your true self?

Affirmation: No more comparisons—I share my true self with the world!

Seeing Spirit's Presence

Do not be afraid of the negativity in the world or in someone else. You do not want to become superstitious or afraid. Each time you are confronted with negativity, whether it is in the news, on TV, or from the mouth of a friend, it is a call to prayer. Rather than becoming worried, fearful, or angry, move into the centered space within that you know and feel every time you go into meditation or prayer.

Pray for peace, healing, justice, and right action. Speak your word of truth that Spirit is present and everything will turn out for good. You will be a benevolent presence to everyone, including yourself, and to Life itself.

It is easy in the world to live after the world's opinion; it is easy in solitude to live after our own; but the great man is he who in the midst of the crowd keeps with perfect sweetness the independence of solitude.

—Ralph Waldo Emerson

Reflection: What do you do when confronted with negativity? How could you come from a place of Truth?

Affirmation: I speak for the Presence and Power of Spirit in any seemingly negative situation for the Good of all.

Brush It Off

Have you ever been sitting around a bonfire at night, listening to the crackling of the fire, when an ash popped from the wood or a spark just danced up in the smoke? Then, to your sudden surprise, it landed on you? Without thought, you quickly slapped that combustible ember as fast as you could before you went up in a blaze of glory. Maybe not quite as dramatic as that, but instinctively you dealt with it.

The last of the human freedoms is to choose one's attitude in any given set of circumstances.
—Viktor Frankl

A lot of negative thoughts that you didn't create are floating around out there and somehow have landed in your thoughts. It's no big deal, unless you don't brush them off. After they catch your attention, if you don't brush them off but allow them to smolder in your consciousness and stoke them with your fear, the destructive thoughts will burn and blaze a path of destruction through your life. There are a lot of negative images and thoughts popping up in the world that don't belong to you. When some land in your field of awareness, it doesn't mean you created them or they belong to you. Honor your instinctive urge for joyous living and brush them off, and enjoy the star-filled sky calling for your attention with the soul-enticing images of infinite possibilities.

Reflection: What negative sparks that need to be brushed off have popped into your reality? Visualize yourself brushing them away.

Affirmation: I brush off any negativity that has caught my attention!

Temptations

Don't think for a moment that once you get some enlightenment the temptations of this world go away. Remember the story of Jesus in the desert being tempted to use his self-mastery for wealth? Buddha was continuously dealing with Mara, Peter denied his association with the Truth, and the stories go on from the days of old. Then there are fallen gurus of today, and you don't have to look far from your own life to see the temptations you have faced. There are not only enticements of the flesh but also of the ego to be glorified by what you can do and get through showing off your spiritual connection.

Temptation is the fire that brings up the scum of the heart.
—William Shakespeare

When you come into the Truth and healing occurs in your finances or health, it could be easy not to return to the practices that got you there, making no further attempt to deepen your connection. It takes time to walk with God, and, when you forgo that for the ways of this world, the price you pay after spiritual illumination is higher than those who have never known. For those who have much, much is expected. When you have experienced the ease and grace of conscious alignment with the Source, every step away from this is more painful because you know how good it is to be in the illumined flow.

Reflection: What is tempting you right now in your life? What kind of discomfort would be created in your world if you gave in to earthly persuasions?

Affirmation: I live from the allure of Spirit!

Societal Impression

August 29

Contribute

Depression and suicide are epidemic today in all ages—young, middle-aged, and elderly people. Sometimes people are overwhelmed by the pace of their lives or simply unable to cope with changes and loss. Yet there is nothing too big, too hard, or too much for the Infinite Divine Reality. Spirit is bigger, deeper, wider, richer, and more full than you can possibly imagine.

The attitudes of praise and thanksgiving are salutary. They not only lighten the consciousness, lifting it out of sadness and depression; they elevate consciousness to a point of acceptance.
—Ernest Holmes

Do not despair. There is always hope. Even if you do not have, or cannot get, everything you want, you have something to be grateful for. No matter how low you might feel, you have something to give. You can give your love, your song, your time, your creativity. You can be grateful for the air to breathe and the sunshine and rain. Giving and Gratitude are what make life meaningful.

Reflection: What one thing can you contribute today? What are you grateful for?

Affirmation: I am filled with the presence of Love and Hope, for Spirit can handle anything! Nothing is too big for God!

Your Gift to God

Your life is God's gift to you. What you do with it? That's your gift to God. It's simply not enough to know that Spirit is the indwelling presence in your life. You must act on that fact as if you believed it to be true.

You are constantly cocreating your life with the Universe. Stuff happens (that's the Universe!) and, then, you get to decide what to do and how to respond. The more creatively you can respond, the less stuck you are. Even out of the negative stuff, you can create possibility.

"Faith without works" is mere belief in a theory, without having proved it to be true. Its opposite, "active faith," is knowing from direct experience that a theory can be proved.
—Ernest Holmes

Reflection: Where are you not acting on your faith? What "move your feet" actions do you need to take?

Affirmation: I confidently step out on my faith and cocreate a joyous life in partnership with the Divine.

Societal Impression

Be Yourself

Be yourself! Do not try to be like anyone else. Do not waste your time trying to be something you are not. Trying to be something other than who you are creates an inner discord that is harmful to yourself. The tension you feel gets communicated to those around you, no matter how hard you try to pretend.

You are a priceless gift to the world! Your unique qualities and talents are your special gifts. You are free to express yourself in the ways you choose: ways that bring more love, joy, light, and hope to you and to the world.

Envy is ignorance, imitation is suicide...To be yourself in a world that is constantly trying to make you something else is the greatest accomplishment.

—Ralph Waldo Emerson

Reflection: How are you trying fit in? Where are you trying to be something you're not?

Affirmation: I am wholly and completely myself. I like who I am. I am a gift to the world!

September

Living Your Lessons

The Teeter-Totter

You may think balance looks like having all your ducks in a row, everything lined up perfectly and going smoothly, without anything ever changing. That may actually be making your life more static.

Balance is actually like playing with your friend on the teeter-totter. The fun is in the winging back and forth without crashing to the ground. Balance is the ability to move easily from one end of the teeter-totter of life to the other. It is knowing what part of the rhythm of ebb and flow is required. It's not trying to keep the teeter-totter level. That will only stress you out more. Learn to move with the flow, gently balancing things out over time.

Happiness is not a matter of intensity but of balance, order, rhythm, and harmony.
—Thomas Merton

Reflection: Where are you trying to get your life to be absolutely level and holding it static? How can you enjoy riding the rhythm a bit more?

Affirmation: I embrace the rhythm of my life. I know when to push and when to pull back, when to direct and when to receive, when to assert and when to allow. I am in perfect balance.

The Pause Button

On the seventh day, even God took a break. It's the space between the notes that make the magic of music. In the intensity of a game's final minute, the coach calls a time-out to realign. There is a part of one's being that wants to handle it all and is afraid to stop for fear something will catch up. Your soul needs you to hit the "pause button" from time to time, or it will crash to get the rest it needs.

There must be a space for the Infinite to replenish. The quieter you become, the more you see, feel, and hear. Creative expression occurs through the realization of the other dimensions of your consciousness. It

Take rest, a field that has rested yields a valuable crop.

—Ovid

becomes so real that it no longer lies outside of you, but is an emerging force of new strength and knowing. You no longer will be attempting to reach it, but rather the pause brings it forth. Your new desire is to share or express it because you are refilled, replenished, and now overflowing. You, once again, are the instrument of Spirit's expression.

Reflection: Where in your life do you need to hit the "pause button" so you can be refilled?

Affirmation: I honor my space of rest!

Prayer

Prayer is the way your soul praises Life and remembers your place in the Universe. Prayer is a way to cocreate with the infinite Presence and Power, joining your heart with God's, your will with Life, and your dreams with the Future. Prayer aligns you with Truth and allows you to bring that Truth into being. Pray every day.

Prayer is nothing but a mental attitude.
Prayer is nothing you eat, nothing you smell,
nothing you taste, nothing you feel, but you
cannot pray without thinking. Every word
is an audible expression of a thought, and
therefore, the ultimate essence of prayer is your
thought. . . . It is nothing but a simple and
direct, positive believing, a mental attitude.
—Ernest Holmes

Reflection: How is your prayer life?

Affirmation: I pray every day from the presence of Spirit within for the truth to be revealed in my life.

The God Myth

What kind of God do you need to make your world work? Is your God logical, orderly, reasonable in Its rewards of good actions and punishing of bad based on your value system through the Law of Cause and Effect? Or is your God spontaneous, unstructured, making you nervous in Its unpredictability?

Unable to trust God, people have constructed a system where God plays rationally. This closes down the space for Divine intervention and Grace if Spirit has to operate by your decree. Is your God-myth based on a rational realm at the cost of surrendering that which goes beyond all your judgmental fears?

We have come from God, and inevitably the myths woven by us, though they contain error, will also reflect a splintered fragment of the true light, the eternal truth that is with God.
—J.R.R. Tolkien

Reflection: How have you constructed your God? Or is this topic too sacred to honestly look at? Is it possible that your reasoning mind has too much power over you, and it has constructed a God so you can know the rules but has eliminated the space for faith? Or do you have rules ... unless an Outside Force wants to supersede them with what It wants?

Affirmation: I let go of my God-expectations and open to that which is even greater!

September 5
Seaweed

One day, an indigenous chieftain was down by the ocean, snacking on some seaweed, enjoying his alone time in the noonday sun, when, in a blaze of glory, the heavens opened up to reveal its secrets. He was elevated to a new state of being, exuding Peace and Love. He knew there was no beginning and no end and somehow saw that all were connected in the One Great Spirit. When he returned to his clan to share his tale, people saw his countenance shine in such a way that crowds gathered around to hear him speak.

Understand that the right to choose your own path is a sacred privilege. Use it.
—Oprah Winfrey

Upon waking the next morning, the chieftain found his community empty. Wondering what had happened, he looked for his clan everywhere he could think of, but they were nowhere to be found. So, he thought he'd head back to the beach where, to his great surprise, he came upon his whole clan eating seaweed down by the ocean.

It's easy to get caught up in the method and forget it's about the Spirit. People become devoted and fixated on the approach, losing sight that it's about the illumination. Leave the seaweed for the chieftain … that was his path. When you are not attempting to replicate someone else's journey but are receptive to your own unique revelation, it can be revealed to you anywhere at any time.

Reflection: At what unique place have you had a flash of spiritual insight that caught you by surprise? What were those revelations?

Affirmation: I am open to Spirit's revelations anywhere, anytime!

Is It Really True?

Take control of your self-talk; you need to actually hear what it says. You can be so used to the way you talk to yourself that you don't even realize you can be aware of it. Start by noticing that you can notice your self-talk.

Now, ask yourself what is the harshest, meanest thing you say to yourself? Look at it clear-eyed and ask yourself, "Is this really true?" Don't ignore it. Every time you hear yourself say it, ask yourself, "Is this really true?" Is this true about my deepest, highest Self? Of course it's not! Remind yourself of that over and over again, until you can laugh at the absurdity of this thing you say to yourself. Then, watch the real you emerge!

Every waking moment, we talk to ourselves about the things we experience. Our self-talk, the thoughts we communicate to ourselves, in turn control the way we feel and act.

—John Lembo

Reflection: What habitual things do you say to yourself that are simply not spiritually true? What is true about you?

Affirmation: I speak lovingly and with kindness to myself. I speak only words of affirmation and spiritual truth.

September 7
Parroting

There's a story about a sailor who gave up smoking his pipe because his parrot developed a chronic and consistent cough. The sailor felt bad that it might be from the smoke of his pipe, and he was responsible for the lung problem in his best buddy, so he took him to the bird vet when he came ashore. After the examination, the doctor informed the bird's owner that there was no sign of respiratory issues; the bird was just parroting back his owner's cough.

Every great dream begins with a dreamer. Always remember, you have within you the strength, the patience, and the passion to reach for the stars to change the world.
—Harriet Tubman

Life is a reflection and mirrors back to you your behaviors and beliefs. It's easy to think what you see in your world is separate from you. Your world will not be reformed from the outside. You cannot change what you see by wiping the smudge off the mirror. If you pay attention to what your world is telling you, it can give you a clear snapshot of what is truly going on in the creative factor of your belief system. When you see something in your world you'd like changed, for some reason it seems easier to go to a manipulator of the world of form. Yet the only way for real change to happen is to go to the cause of the image, which is within yourself, and listen to the true revealer of the greater possibility for life.

Reflection: Where in your life are you attempting to change your world by adjusting what's in front of you rather than what's inside of you?

Affirmation: I am able to see my world as a reflection of my beliefs!

Trained Thought

Train your thoughts to dwell on Spiritual Truth. Discipline your mind to be guided by Spiritual Principles. This is how you train your thoughts. All the various practices of meditation are designed to give you control of your mind, so that you may be the author of the thoughts you think rather than having your monkey mind chatter away without you. Disciplining your mind is the process of choosing your thoughts, rather than having them choose you.

Since you know that your thoughts become the beliefs that create your life experience, trained thoughts can be used to create new belief. As you train your thoughts,

Trained thought is more powerful than untrained thought.
—Ernest Holmes

you discover the power that consciously chosen thoughts have to create through the power of the Law. Affirmations and affirmative prayer are ways in which you consciously use trained thought to create the life of your dreams.

Reflection: Are your thoughts well trained? Are you disciplining your mind?

Affirmation: I consciously train my thoughts to dwell on Spiritual Truths and Principles.

The Word of Power

Your word is very powerful. It is the very word of creation, especially those words that you believe to be true. Pay attention to the words you use, including those phrases you habitually say, even when you don't really mean them. Pay attention to how you describe your life, another person, or the situation. The words or phrases you choose reveal what you really believe in your subjective mind, that you may not even be aware of.

Moses said that the word of life, the word of power is your own mouth. The ancient Upanishads, the Vedas, the Bhagavad-Gita taught these things.
—Ernest Holmes

Sometimes you are simply not careful to say what you mean or how you speak. You may tend toward exaggerations or words that are emotionally loaded. You may like catch phrases or sarcastic remarks that you think will make you cool or popular. Are they what you want to manifest in your life? Is it really what you mean to say about another person? Always speak as if God were listening, because the Law of the Universe IS always listening!

Reflection: What do you believe about the power of your word? What words do you most habitually say?

Affirmation: I am careful with my words. I speak only words of power and truth.

That's Too Bad ...

Many years back, little Zack was on the bow of a boat when a pompous intellectual snob wanting to show him up asked him what he knew about astronomy, to which he replied, "Nothing." The erudite guy said, "That's too bad. You've wasted much of your life because captains of ships can navigate the globe with that kind of knowledge." Then he asked him if he knew about meteorology to which Zack replied, "I don't know what meteorology is." To this the intellectual said, "That's too bad. You've wasted much of your life, because the sea captains are able to catch the winds and move with great speeds across the waters with that knowledge. Well, what about oceanography? You've got to know something about that," asked the intimidator. "No, no, no, I don't," answered Zack. "That's too bad. You've wasted much of your life because with this knowledge you can catch currents, find food, get into safe harbor," the academician told him.

People only see what they are prepared to see.
—Ralph Waldo Emerson

Sometime later, little Zack was making his way back to the stern of the boat when he came across his pompous questioner and stopped and asked him, "Do you know how to swim?" to which the guy replied, "No, I've been busy learning about all these important things." To which Zack replied, "That's too bad. You've wasted all your life because the boat is sinking."

Our intellectual capacity is a beautiful gift of life, but it is important to have balance with the physical realm we live in. It's essential to get out of your head and open your heart to the world you walk in. Otherwise it is easy to miss out on some simple signs that will help you in joyous living.

Reflection: Where am I not being kind to life? Where am I not paying attention to the world around me?

Affirmation: I am in touch with my surroundings!

September 11
Positive Attitude

It's much easier to deal with challenges when you stay centered and calm. This doesn't mean you don't act. It means you don't react. Reaction comes from a negative emotion like anger, resistance, fear, or uncertainty. These are the attitudes that cause the whole situation to get even worse.

Having a calm and centered attitude means you act out of your desire to create something different in the situation. Rather than going with the problem, you become part of the solution. This makes your actions much more powerful, and definitely more useful.

The only thing we can do is play on the one string we have, and that is our attitude. I am convinced that life is 10% what happens to me and 90% of how I react to it. And so it is with you... we are in charge of our Attitudes.
—Chuck Swindoll

Reflection: What situation in your life are you reacting to? What attitude would be more helpful?

Affirmation: I engage every challenge with a positive attitude, knowing there's always a solution.

Your Slide Projector

Imagine your life like a slide show. Spirit provides the power and the light and the projector. You provide the slides. Whatever slide you put in, whether it's painted all black so no light can shine through or beautifully crafted with multiple colors and hues, that's what you'll see on the screen of your life.

You create your reality by the lens and filters through which you look at life—the lens of your expectations and the filters of your beliefs and emotions. What is your lens focused on—the story of your victimhood or of your possibilities? Are your filters clear, perceptive, and open, or are they clouded with judgment, disappointment, or fear? Spiritual practices cleanse your filters and refocus your lens.

Love and fear represent two different lenses through which to view the world. Which I choose to use will determine what I think I see.
—Marianne Williamson

Reflection: What slides are you putting in your projector? Do you like what you see?

Affirmation: I clean the lens of my perception of anger, judgment, and projection. I see with the filter of love.

Rise in Consciousness

You have a body and you have a mind, and they are instruments given to you to journey through this world. Who you are has authority over your mind and body. They are yours to use, as are your arms and legs, in their response to the direction you give them. To experience healing, you rise in consciousness above the influence of word and thought to communion with Spirit Itself.

Loving ourselves is the miracle cure we are all looking for.

—Louise Hay

When a life issue presents its position to you, do not surrender to empowering it by attempting to know the truth about the problem. It is imperative you realize there is no truth about the challenge ... there is only Truth about Truth. How you rise in consciousness is to forget what you heard about your body of affairs and allow your awareness to realize the Divine Truth. Reclaim your dominion over your runaway mind.

Reflection: Where am I attempting to know the truth of a problem rather than just knowing the spiritual Truth?

Affirmation: I am seeing the Divine Truth in all of my life situations!

Look for the Good

Imagine a black dot on a white board. Are you focused on the dot or on the white board itself? This is the most fundamental of all spiritual principles. Looking for the good and praising it means, over and over again, turning your mind from judgment, gossip, arrogance, or fear. Every time you are confronted with a challenge, look for some good in it. Declare some good that will come out of it. Even in your ordinary conversation, focus on telling the stories that highlight what is working and how great life is. Find ways to praise and compliment those around you.

Look for the Good, and praise It!
—Ernest Holmes

In any situation, in every situation, there is good to be found and declared, even if it's only relative to something that could be worse. You don't have to know what that good is or will be. You just have to know that it is always there, just like the sun is shining, no matter how dark the clouds or severe the storm.

Reflection: What good can you find in the challenging situation you are now, or have recently been, facing? What good can you praise in the people around you?

Affirmation: Everywhere I look, I see the Good and I praise it!

Test of Trust

Driving to the Lodge of La Paz Waterfall near the base of Paos Volcano in the rainforest of Costa Rica for the first time can be a test of trust. You'll be told that once you start up the mountain to just follow the signs for an hour. The challenge arises when you don't see signs for an extended period of time, not that you really need them other than to give you peace of mind. The reason, you soon learn, is that they have only put signs at crucial junctures in the road. You keep going until you come to an arrow that tells you to turn. Otherwise you proceed in the direction you were headed. It doesn't matter if you've run out of asphalt and find yourself on a one-lane pot-holed dirt road hugging the side of the mountain with endless chasms on the other side, and you can't really see because you are in a thick rainy cloud, barely able to see the ground in front of you. You continue in the direction the last blue arrow pointed. You trust you'll receive new information to turn on a need-to-know basis.

Everything in your life is there as a vehicle for your transformation. Use it!
—Ram Dass

Continued reassurance and comfort that you are headed down the right road in life would be nice. Sometimes you have to trust that awareness of when and where you need to make adjustments will come on a need-to-know basis. Spirit has gone ahead, and the Divine signs have been posted in the appropriate intersections of your life. You just need to follow them, because they are there.

Reflection: Where in your life are you getting anxious about not having recent signage for direction in your life? Did you miss the turn, or do you just need to trust a bit longer?

Affirmation: I trust I'll know when I need to know!

Flexibility

Standing your ground and speaking your truth are an important part of spiritually maturing. Sometimes it is just as important to let go. Being flexible and open allows you to embrace life with all its challenges without the resistance or struggle that causes unnecessary pain.

Practice bending like a willow in the breeze. Try flowing like water around the rocks in a river. Be the wind, as it moves easily through the branches. Use any image that helps you stay flexible and open. This puts you in alignment with the natural state of the Universe.

Some of us think holding on makes us strong, but sometimes it is letting go.
—Herman Hesse

Reflection: Where are you holding on where you could be letting go? Where could being more flexible make you stronger?

Affirmation: I am flexible and open. I flow and bend easily with the winds of change. I allow life to unfold.

Test of Trust

The Young Father

Thich Nhat Hanh tells the story . . .

A young widower, who loved his five-year-old son very much, was away on business, and bandits came, burned down his whole village, and took his son away. When the man returned, he saw the ruins, and panicked. He took the charred corpse of a child to be his son, and he began to pull his hair and beat his chest, crying uncontrollably. He organized a cremation ceremony, collected the ashes and put them in a very beautiful velvet bag. Working, sleeping, eating, he always carried the bag of ashes with him.

The only thing worse than being blind is having sight but no vision.
—Helen Keller

One day, his real son escaped from the robbers and found his way home. He arrived at his father's new cottage at midnight and knocked at the door. The young father asked, "Who is there?" The child answered, "It's me, Papa. Open the door. It's your son." In his agitated state of mind the father thought that some mischievous boy was making fun of him, and he shouted at the child to go away and cried. The boy knocked again and again, but the father refused to let him in. Some time passed, and finally the child left. From that time on, father and son never saw one another.

Reflection: Is there an area in your life where you hold a pain so near and dear that when the healing that you love comes knocking, your door is locked so tight you can't let it into your life?

Affirmation: There is always space in my life for greater good!

Life Prepares You

Life prepares you for your spiritual path, and all you experience today has its place of value in your tomorrows. It's sometimes tough to think you know what is best when you don't even begin to know what your tomorrow holds. Trusting what's before you is perfect preparation for your life's coming attractions.

Relaxing into Divine guidance in your spiritual evolution plays a big part in experiencing ease and joy. Fighting and resisting what you are going through anyway will close you to the personal soul gifts at hand. Somehow they all come together as one. In retrospect, you'll finally see and understand, on this dimension, what was only hinted at prior to its happening.

And while I stood there
I saw more than I can tell
And I understood more than I saw;
For I was seeing in a sacred manner
the shapes of things in spirit,
and the shape of all shapes of all things
as they must live together like one being.

—Black Elk

Reflection: What event in your life made no sense at the time, and, in retrospect, you realize its gift prepared you for being more present and available for a later event in your world? With this in mind, what is going on in your life that you are finding difficult to grasp, and what shift could happen if you didn't have to understand it, but chose to trust that its value would be revealed?

Affirmation: I know today's events make me stronger for tomorrow's!

Test of Trust

September 19
Compassion and Connection

Life is interdependent. We need each other in more ways than we can imagine. Every life is dependent on every other life for sustenance and growth. Give yourself to others. And let them give to you.

Do not isolate yourself from others. When life is challenging, you may feel the need to withdraw or protect yourself. But from whom or what? You may feel shame, regret, or defeat. But this is unnecessary. This is the time to reach out. The hand you seek is Spirit's hand incarnated in a friend or loved one. They cannot fix it for you, but you do not have to face it alone.

The whole idea of compassion is based on a keen awareness of the interdependence of all these living beings, which are all part of one another, and all involved in one another.
—Thomas Merton

Reflection: Do you let others care for you as easily as you care for others? Are you compassionate about your interdependence?

Affirmation: I easily reach out to others. I am effortlessly there for others.

It can be an interesting perspective to observe your thought process when you get summoned to do your civic duty to serve as a juror. Do you dread it, get excited about it, or is it just a neutral date on your calendar? Does your mind start making up excuses as to why you don't want to or can't? Do you get excited about being part of a trial that will give another person a fair process? Sitting in the jury lounge of a courthouse, waiting to be called to be questioned to see if you are a match for the jury box, will bring up all sorts of beliefs from your subjective you may not be consciously aware of, but which are operating in your life.

> *I consider trial by jury as the only anchor yet imagined by man by which a government can be held to the principles of its Constitution.*
> —Thomas Jefferson

Whether you feel it is right to sit in judgment of another human being or you feel this is what keeps our government accountable so no one person can operate outside of the justice is all part of your internal process. To some extent, the trial helps keep people from taking the law into their own hands, putting violence on the streets and returning to the days of the Wild West. Trusting the collective perspective of a dozen peers to see beyond who has the best lawyer to hearing the truth gives all the opportunity to live in a fair and just society.

Reflection: Where in your life do you feel the collective wisdom of a group of your friends can help you gain a clear perspective on a controversial issue?

Affirmation: I am able to understand the collective perspective in an unclear position in my life!

World Peace Day

Discover how those annoying people or the ones you are mad at are tempting you not to love them. They may actually be doing something you don't like, and you can certainly say what you don't like or would like to have different. That is about you, not about them. Notice, however, all the inner-dialogue that you create around them, and the story you tell about who they are and their motivation. That's the part that is a reflection of you.

You must recognize that all people belong to the same kingdom.
—Ernest Holmes

Every person or situation that causes you discomfort is an opportunity for healing! Find out what is being triggered within you or what you are inviting yourself to grow into. You want to act and speak from love and connection, not out of reaction. Practice being and behaving toward that person the way you want to be.

Reflection: Who in your life is tempting you not to love them? What story (not the facts) are you telling about them? What does this say about you?

Affirmation: I approach each person with the eyes and heart of love, seeing the God presence that they are.

From Awareness to Action

You might know that the plastic bottles from bottled water are not good for our environment, or gas-guzzling cars are not the wisest choice for the planet we live on, or consuming lots of sugars and fats isn't the healthiest thing you can do for your body. Yet you just keep on doing it anyway, even though you know these kinds of activities are detrimental. How come convenience and self-interest trump what you know is best? No one operates on the planet in isolation. Even if your friends aren't doing it, it's imperative to all of us that you open your eyes as a global citizen.

The biggest problem in the world could have been solved when it was small.
—Lao Tzu

When all people have hope and take some kind of minor action toward the future, it blesses us all! When your self-indulgence is replaced by a respect for humanity, you will be effecting a planetary turnaround that will benefit all people of today and tomorrow. You can be a model of compassionate awareness moved to action through small personal choices that make a difference. You don't have to take on the big conglomerates of the world, unless that's your calling. When enough people shift their awareness to action, there will be a collective shift in the human awareness, and then some previous actions will no longer be acceptable. There will then be space for unimaginable answers to the human dilemma to surface. Awareness can no longer just stand by and watch self destruction; awareness must move to action to make a difference.

Reflection: What are the small steps for conscious living you know about and haven't taken that you are now willing to take to make a positive difference for your body and planet?

Affirmation: I move from awareness to action!

September 23

Gifts of Service

It's not enough just to be about your own spiritual growth and personal well-being. You live in the midst of all creation, which is expressing life through all beings everywhere. The Universe can take Love and Care only so far. After that, it needs for love to be expressed and to take action.

You are the hands and voice and heart of Spirit. Your gift of service is one of the ways Life helps, supports, and nurtures Life. Through your gifts, talents, willingness, and time, you are Love in Action, the Bounty of God made manifest. Let Spirit's Love flow through your service.

Being good is commendable, but only when it is combined with doing good is it useful.
—Unknown

Reflection: Where are you being the hand, voice, or heart of God for others? What service gives you the most joy?

Affirmation: I am the way Love manifests in the world. I give my love and my service joyfully and freely.

The Emperor's New Clothes

Remember Hans Christian Anderson's iconic tale, "The Emperor's New Clothes"? The emperor paid a large sum of money to the two weavers for some invisible clothes that only the worthy supposedly could see. As the emperor paraded down the street, everyone was caught in the hypnotic trance, unwilling to look stupid by admitting he could not see what the experts were telling him to see, until a child said, "But he doesn't have anything on at all."

Society will often cover its self-deceiving actions with pretentiousness and collective denials implying you are ignorant, unpatriotic, or just unwise if you don't see the value of what is being told to you. The farce is supposedly invisible to the unworthy, when in reality it doesn't exist at all. The falsehood, propaganda, and spin will create an expanding collective hypnotic trance where people are ostracized for not believing it, until the voice of innocence and common sense pierces the insanity of the deception. The gentle whisper of truth by the one can grow into a roar of the many. Then you just might see the deceptor end his parade with more flamboyance than ever and a show of arrogance to save as much face as possible, knowing he's been exposed.

"But he doesn't have anything on at all!" said a small child.

Reflection: Have you ever gone along with something that didn't sound right just because you didn't want to make waves?

Affirmation: I speak the Truth where I see it!

Resistance Is Futile

Get out of Your Mind and into Your Life

When I planted a peach tree in my garden, I didn't tell it how many branches to grow or how much fruit to bear. All I did was hold the vision of the most beautiful peach tree flourishing in my yard.

We can get so caught up outlining and micromanaging things that we end up in our heads and out of our lives. When you speak your prayers, attempt to leave the "how-tos" up to God and stay in your heart. You'll find the results far more enjoyable.

What we are looking for are leaders at every level who can energize, excite, and inspire rather than enervate, depress, and control.

—Jack Welch

Reflection: Where am I getting too controlling in attempting to outline things for God?

Affirmation: I love my life!

Insanity

Do you think that if you will just work harder, try again, and keep at it, things will change? If you are getting the same results in relationships, work, health, and other areas of your life, something actually has to be done differently. For things to be different, things have to be different!

So what has to change? Change your thought about it. Change your belief about it. Change the way you engage. Change how you act, what you say, or what you do. Yes, you may be uncomfortable, but for things to change, something has to CHANGE! That something is You!

Definition of Insanity—"doing the same thing over and over again, expecting different results!"
—Albert Einstein

Reflection: Where are you stuck trying to do the same thing over and over but not getting any different results?

Affirmation: I am willing to change—my ideas, thoughts, words, and actions.

Resistance Is Futile

Torment

Have you ever found yourself tormented by some of your past actions, the kind of self-expression you might not be the most proud of? In those quiet times alone, do you find your thoughts or memories of your blunders won't leave you alone? Do they create a felt sense of anxiousness or shame from the pictures of your behavior dancing through your awareness? Do they have you feeling split off from who you know yourself to be by the excruciating anguish of your behavior?

The torture of a bad conscience is the hell of a living soul.
—John Calvin

To save yourself from your inner agony, you must reconnect with the values that can bring you back to a more respectable view of who you truly are. It's self-kindness and a return to trust that will help you learn from your human mistakes. Try some compassion and understanding for yourself rather than the ruthless approach of self-abuse. If coming back into integrity with what you value is your desire, stop giving yourself a hard time while you are struggling to get back into alignment. Growth in this world of form can be hard, and some soul-stirring shakeups are part of the transformational process. So notice, learn from your mistakes, and try some self-respect while you clean up the messes you can, and release yourself from the ones that are now past.

Reflection: What thoughts torment you in the early dark of the morning … the ones you can't stop beating yourself up for? Try some compassion and understanding so you can learn more about your soul's process, and return to living your true values.

Affirmation: I am learning and growing from my mistakes!

Resistance Is Futile

Remember "Resistance is futile!" from the Borg in *Star Trek*? What about "What you resist, persists"? Resistance is simply our unwillingness to look at or deal with something. It is futile, because as long as you resist something, you are actually actively holding it in place.

When you resist or push against something, you end up staying focused upon, and constantly thinking about, the very thing you don't like or want. Since you know that what you focus on grows, this means you are growing the very thing you are resistant to. Stop resisting it! Let it go by you like a martial arts master; pay attention to

Resistance is thought transformed into feeling. Change the thought that creates the resistance, and there is no more resistance.
—Robert Conklin

something else—something positive, uplifting, powerful; or simply allow the change to take place.

Reflection: Where are you in resistance in your life?

Affirmation: I allow things to be what they are. I allow change to take place. I allow my life to flow effortlessly.

The Journey

Every time you get "there," there will be another one to strive for. Life is about the journey, not so much about the destination. How are you enjoying and living your journey? Are you waiting for something to happen? Are you so anxious to get to the next stop that you are missing where you are? Do you feel frustrated with today's part of the journey because you're not there yet?

A Journey of a thousand miles begins with a single step.
　　—Lao Tzu

Try treating it like a vacation. Plan for wonderful experiences! Be willing to take unexpected side trips. Explore the road less traveled. Take time to rest in your moments of joy and celebration. Notice how far you've come. Savor each moment for what it is.

Reflection: What brings you joy about being on the journey? What parts of the journey do you love?

Affirmation: I savor and enjoy every moment of the journey of my life. I move forward confidently, enjoying the twists and turns along the way.

Don't Quit

To get to the top of the mountain, the trail may be twisty and steep. Many a mountain climber has turned back just short of the top, missing the breath-taking view and powerful sense of accomplishment, because she gave up too soon.

Sometimes faith is simply an unshakable persistence toward your desired goal. Don't take no for an answer! Don't let yourself be sidetracked because the first or even second thing doesn't work out. Don't give up because it takes time. Hold fast and firm. The Law of the Universe must respond, even if it has to rearrange the entire Universe and all the molecules in it to do so!

Nothing in this world can take the place of persistence.... The slogan "press on" has solved and always will solve the problems of the human race.

—Calvin Coolidge

Reflection: How are you at persistently stepping out in faith? Do you need to build your "don't quit" muscle?

Affirmation: I am determined and persistent in the pursuit of my dreams. I trust Spirit is making them possible.

Resistance Is Futile

October

Living Abundantly

October 1-8
Resting in the Abundant Ocean

October 9-14
Vow of Prosperity

October 15-23
Prime the Pump

October 24-31
Your Worthiness Quotient

October 1

The Tipping Point

You live in a field of consciousness called "the Morphogenetic Field" or simply "the Field" by scientists, the "Collective Unconscious" by psychologists, and simply "Consciousness" by spiritual and evolutionary leaders. The extraordinary thing about this field of consciousness is that what is known anywhere in the field is instantly known everywhere in it. As a collection of new ideas, beliefs, or behaviors reaches critical mass, the whole energy or vibration of the field changes.

The tipping point is that magic moment when an idea, trend, or social behavior crosses a threshold, tips, and spreads like wildfire.
—Malcolm Gladwell

Personal growth and spiritual maturity are intimately connected with the health and well-being of others and of the planet. You are part of the growing consciousness that is evolving on our planet. Your enlightened thoughts, loving heart, peaceful practices, and life of integrity make a huge difference by being part of the critical mass toward change. Every time you release anger, forgive, or demonstrate a Spirit-filled, abundant life, which you believe everyone deserves, you are adding to the good for all. Do not doubt your impact on the Whole for one minute!

Reflection: What contribution are you making to the field of consciousness and adding to the shift toward greater good for all?

Affirmation: I affirm that my own growth is in service to the growth and health and well-being of all beings everywhere. I am positively adding to the shift in consciousness toward a healed planet.

God Is All, Including Technology

To be one with nature doesn't make technology wrong. Being in the rhythm of your life's flow, you can live in the city or live in the trees. You are an aspect of nature, and it's just as natural for you to create as it is for a bird to build a nest. Whales have their internal GPS, and there is nothing unnatural about you using one either. Our species' creations are an expression of our use of intelligence. The problem is not in the technology but in the hands of the user.

So let go of the issues around the culture's technological advances, and enjoy the gifts of God that have been revealed. Use the key pads like you were playing the piano. Use the different communication modalities to deliver your inspired thoughts, and fly in a plane as if it were a chariot of the gods. Of course you don't want to give your power away to a technological addiction or abuse your time, but like all good things, being in balance with this convenience and blessing of our day can help lead to more joyous living.

Whatever we are waiting for—peace of mind, contentment, grace, the inner awareness of simple abundance—it will surely come to us, but only when we are ready to receive it with an open and grateful heart.

—Sarah Ban Breathnach

Reflection: How can you shift some of your negative perspectives about some of society's advances to see the blessing they can bring as gifts from God?

Affirmation: I see Spirit in technology!

Resting in the Abundant Ocean

I Had It All the Time

If you owned a healthy brokerage account with significant value, but didn't know you had it, what good would it do you? If you were to discover it, you could pay off all your financial responsibilities and move forward with your dream. The financial struggle you'd been attempting to overcome would have just been neutralized. It would no longer be a battle to overcome. This kind of comfort around your finances had always been available to you, but you couldn't experience that until you realized it.

It can only do for you what it can do through you.

—Ernest Holmes

When you attempt to overcome error with truth, you acknowledge a power in error. God is the only Power there is, and when you know this, the battle is done, the controversy is over, and there is nothing left to overcome. All you need do is come to realize this Truth is already available to you, just waiting your discovery of this Divine account. This account or Truth doesn't do anything for you unless you are conscious of it. It's your awareness of the Truth that makes it of value to you. The Truth is always the Truth, whether you know about it or not. It will work for you only in proportion to your awareness of it.

Reflection: What in your life would you like to see neutralized so it is powerless and a nonissue for you?

Affirmation: I know the Truth, and the Truth sets me free!

The Journey to Brilliance

It'd sure be nice to be immediately brilliant at whatever you decided to undertake. Yet there is an unfolding and becoming process. Even the overnight success took years to achieve. You have to begin the process with whatever blunt tools of creativity you might have at your disposal. It can be tough having a big dream and stumbling in the initial stages of development. But the greats in your field had to begin somewhere, and they didn't get to begin at the top, but begin they did. They, too, had to be less-than-production perfect.

If you can't allow yourself to be graceless and a bit clumsy, then you will never move beyond being grace-less and a bit clumsy. It's the journey that is the adventure that creates the hero. Yes, skipping the uncomfortable parts of development would be nice, but it's those moments that give you a new strength, propelling you to a new level. It's those moments of challenge that have you searching in the depths of your soul for a greater way to express your spirit. Once expanded and transformed, you will never fit back into your smaller self. You'll be joyously living your brilliance.

Only those who dare to fail greatly can ever achieve greatly.

—Robert Kennedy

Reflection: What dream do you have that could use a bit more of your patience in the developmental stages? How can you be kinder to yourself during this time?

Affirmation: I am enjoying my journey to brilliance!

What Is Abundance?

Abundance is more than just money, although it certainly includes money. Abundance includes many things, as Edwene Gaines describes—living a healthy, happy, joyous, and fulfilling life with meaningful work, loving relationships, and creative expression. This is actually Spirit's desire to be and express through you. This is the reason you are here: to express and experience a full and rich life.

Is there any part of this that you aren't currently experiencing? Right there is where you apply your spiritual tools and claim it as your good!

Abundance is:

Having a "vitally alive, healthy body"; for the God-being that we are to express through Relationships that are joyous, satisfying, intimate, honest, and nurturing; and work that we love so much it's not work but play. Plus...All the money that we can spend.

—Edwene Gaines

Reflection: What do abundance, success, and prosperity mean to you?

Affirmation: I claim a joyous, healthy, happy, fulfilled, and prosperous life for myself and for everyone.

Resting in the Abundant Ocean

When you approach an enormous cruise ship or aircraft carrier that is larger than a hundred-story high-rise lying on its side, you are dwarfed by its enormity. Yet as you stand on the top deck while you are cruising, looking out over the expansive ocean and sky around you, the ship can all of a sudden feel like a cork bobbing in an infinite ocean. Just as ocean liners float on the sea, you, too, rest on an abundant sea of life. There can be storms from time to time, making it harder to proceed, but no matter what, you are still sitting on the Infinite expanse of the unlimited.

If the doors of perception were cleansed, everything would appear as it is—infinite.
—William Blake

It's easy to forget the wealth that lies below the surface when you get caught up in the enormity of what you are up to. Liberty is not gained by fighting the waves of the world on the surface, but by remembering the secret of what lies below the visible level. As much as you see, which can seem like a lot, it's a drop in the bucket compared to what you are resting upon. When you know what's holding you up is far greater than the squalls on the surface, you can proceed in joyous living with a confidence not based on the size of the scenery.

Reflection: Imagine sitting on a ship in the middle of the ocean and contemplating all the water beneath you. Now see if you can transfer the realization to the sea of immeasurable life you are resting upon and everything that supports you beyond what you visibly see. Can you sense the enormity of the Infinite holding you up?

Affirmation: I am supported by more than I know!

Awakening to Abundant Blessings

So many people think they want more money. What they actually want is to be free to do the things that are important to them—to be free to live the kind of life their hearts desire.

When you awaken to the abundant blessings surrounding you now, the doors get unlocked for the Infinite Good to once again flow. It can look like cash, and it can also look like a lot of other options that free you up to live your dreams. But remember, you have to take on the awakened embodiment of freedom now. No matter what's going on in your life, you still have an attitudinal choice to go confidently in the direction of your dreams of joyous living.

Abundance is not something we acquire. It is something we tune into.
—Wayne Dyer

Reflection: What are you willing to do now to step into your abundant blessings?

Affirmation: I am now moving in the direction of my dreams!

Limitless Infinity

Infinity may be hard to grasp, yet that is the size of the Universe. One way you can begin to imagine infinity is to imagine that you are standing on a beach holding a scoop of sand in your hand. First try counting all the grains of sand in the palm of your hand. Now try to imagine how many handfuls of sand are on this beach, and then imagine all the beaches around you, and all the beaches on the continent, and now all the beaches in world. How many handfuls of sand is that? How many grains of sand? Another word for infinity is limitless.

This is the nature of the whole Universe. You can see infinity in the

To see the world in a grain of sand, and heaven in a wild flower, to hold infinity in the palm of the hand, and eternity in an hour.
—William Blake

blades of grass in your yard and the leaves on your tree. This same infinity, limitlessness, is also true about your life. Release any belief that limits you or others. Court the limitless in your life. Practice Infinity.

Reflection: Where and how can you be more intentional? Claim this vast abundance for yourself and for everyone.

Affirmation: I am an unlimited, limitless Being. This is my true nature and the nature of everyone.

Resting in the Abundant Ocean

Charge It

Credit-card debt is not a healthy thing. When you are low on cash and tell yourself you'll pay it off later, it only sets up a painful later. Paying only the minimum can move you to start playing credit-card roulette, ultimately coming across the bullet. Maxing out one card, then moving to another card and another is a sure path to angst. Then the "miracle" happens—you receive the new pre-approved credit card offer in the mail having no interest for months, only to have the debt come due all too soon. Eventually, paying things off with the equity from the home or investment or retirement is robbing your future, particularly if you start the vicious cycle again.

> *A big part of financial freedom is having your heart and mind free from worry about the what-ifs of life.*
> —Suze Orman

This is not a peaceful habit for traveling through life. How do you stop the worry of debt? You stop debting. Stop writing checks based on the incoming pay check. Pay as you go! Don't beat yourself up for past mistakes, but stop them now. Also, clean up all areas of your life where you have been debting. Have the conversation you have not been fully forthright with, make the change at work you've intended to shift, get clean in your relationships, and stop mortgaging your future … the due date always comes around.

Reflection: Where are you debting, and how can you clean that up?

Affirmation: I am now living in the abundant flow of life!

Someday

It's written that Spirit said through Jesus, "All that I have is yours." He didn't say someday you might get some if you are lucky. He said, "Today you will be with me in paradise." He didn't say anything about having to wait … he said "today." These are clear truth statements of your good—now. Where do you live in self-induced bondage by saying, "Someday I'll be joyously living my dream?" Your Good is available to you now! Stop mortgaging your future when you have been offered your dream today.

How soon "not now" becomes never.
—Martin Luther

If you are tired of being a step behind your Good, always on the verge of the "mother lode" but not quite in sync with its delivery, there is a Divine Presence within you that never leaves you or forsakes you. It supplies you, supports you, and sustains you, but you must be in constant contact with it. Know these Truths about yourself and forget making deals about putting it off to someday, and you'll find every day is delivery day.

Reflection: Where are you telling yourself, "Someday my Good will come," instead of being in paradise today with it? How can you readjust your thinking so you can be in sync with "All that I have is yours"?

Affirmation: I now claim my available Good!

Vow of Prosperity

October 11
Claim Abundance

CLAIM your good! Announce to yourself that you are a child of the Universe; heir to the Kingdom; deserving of all the Life, Joy, and Freedom you can imagine! You do not have to earn your life—simply CLAIM it!

I've continued to recognize the power
individuals have to change virtually anything
and everything in their lives in an instant.
I've learned that the resources we need to turn
our dreams into reality are within us, merely
waiting for the day when we decide to wake up
and claim our birthright.
　—Anthony Robbins

Reflection: What are you claiming today? I have wished that my rabbit come into the livingroom and be part of our family. Today it happened!! She hopped into the livingroom all by herself! My dogs didn't chase her away. To me it was a miracle I've cried and tried so hard to make it happen and then it did! I claim it. My consistancy made it happen. My prayers were answered and now it was mine to witness and now I can rest and feel that it's not impossible. Patients is definitely a virtue!! Danae 10/11/16

Affirmation: As heir to the Divine, infinite Kingdom, I claim all my good!

Path of Blessings

Peace around your abundance comes from the amount of trust you have in Spirit, not the amount of cash you have in the bank. Society points to fear-driven negative possibilities. It's your flow of faith ... not your flow of dollars ... that brings ease to your life and quiets the concerns.

A way to live in the affluent flow is to take charge of your mind and emotions. This moment is filled with the richness of Spirit. If you look in this direction, instead of the soul-depleting direction, you will remain on the path of blessings. The present moment is filled with joy and happiness. You are living in an abundant universe, and there is enough for all!

If you look at what you have in life, you'll always have more. If you look at what you don't have in life, you'll never have enough.
—Oprah Winfrey

Reflection: Do you put more faith in the abundance of the universe or the fear-driven concerns of the world? Do you make excuses substantiating the fear-driven reason, or do you choose to show your trust by living the spiritual truths of abundance? I spent so long spending every time on drugs that it caused me to constantly wanting to buy things, but now I've filled my home with things and now its full and I realize now that I could have been saving money for vacations or emergencies. Now we've been cut off food stamps so I really can't buy extras anymore!! Live and Learn I say!! Leave the past in the rear view mirror and carry on!!
Danai 14/12/14

Affirmation: I am walking the path of Abundant Blessings!

Vow of Prosperity

Do you still believe that it's more spiritual to be poor? Where in your life have you taken and are living by a "vow of poverty"? What beliefs are you still harboring that tell you it's not spiritual to pray for your good or that you can't experience heaven as a wealthy person? These beliefs come from a misreading and limited understanding about spiritual scriptures. Remember that money isn't the root of all evil; it is actually the "LOVE of money that is the root of all evil." It's only when you make money your god that you are putting something in between you and your good.

It is right that we should be successful, for otherwise the Spirit is not expressed. The Divine cannot lack for anything, and we should not lack for anything that makes life worthwhile here on earth.

—Ernest Holmes

See these beliefs for the lies they are! Actually Money is simply God in action, in a form you can see. Remember that Spirit is the Source of your gifts and your good, and your success is the powerful and joyous expression of these gifts given to the world. The more you align yourself with Spirit, the more you are promised Abundance, Joy, and Fulfillment. Claim all of these today!

Reflection: Where in your life have you taken and are living by a "vow of poverty"?

Wow; yeah I haven't vowed for poverty but I'm am living below the poverty line, but I don't look poor. I have more than I need and pretty much everything I want! My life my love my animals I'm rich with Love from them and some family and that's more than I had and I'll never let it go!!

Danai
10-13-16

Affirmation: I take a Vow of Prosperity. I know that Spirit is my Source and my success glorifies the Divine!

Accept Your Good

When you are confronted with good you cannot imagine as possible— a healing, unexpected abundance, or a happy relationship—you have stepped right to the edge of your belief and are now confronted with your unbelief. Here, at this moment, is where your faith ends. Spirit can only give, provide, be, or do this much but no more for you. This becomes the limit to the amount of good you can experience and accept.

If you want to experience and accept more life, greater abundance, and deeper meaning in your life, you have to see/feel yourself as someone who has that. You have to see/feel the Universe providing you with everything you need. Stop saying, "I can't believe it!" and start the practice of imagining and accepting your good. Keep pushing the boundary between your belief and your unbelief. There lies your greatest spiritual work.

We must not only believe, we must know that our belief measures the extent and degree of our blessing. If our belief is limited, only a little can come to us, because that is as we believe. We call this the law of mental equivalents. How much life can any man experience? As much as he can embody.

—Ernest Holmes

Reflection: What's too good to be true? What great good is hard for you to accept?

Affirmation: I accept my good! Nothing is too great for Spirit. I accept my good!

Distribution Value Center

You are a distribution center for the undifferentiated Infinite Life Force. It is directed through every aspect of your thoughts, feelings, beliefs, and emotions. It takes form through your health, relationships, career, finances, and every aspect of the world you live in. Too often, it will take a life crisis to shake you enough to reevaluate your distribution value center.

The ability to perceive or think differently is more important than the knowledge gained.
—David Bohm

Here's a hint to avoid crisis: your spirit starts checking out long before your body and world start breaking down. The yearning of your spirit is stronger than your mind. You will experience healing when you have the courage to connect with your life force and let it gracefully guide you to where you are to be now in your life. It will look like having to give up some of those old distribution directives that no longer support you in joyous living. Through your willingness to be present in your choices today, your new intentions will empower you to step beyond illness and limitation into Wholeness and Abundance.

Reflection: In what area have you stopped evolving because you are on the same automatic distribution of your creative forces as you were years ago? What value centers of yours can use an updating?

Affirmation: I am courageously reexamining the directives of my distribution center.

Circulation

You live in a reciprocal Universe. You breathe in and you breathe out. Without both sides of breathing, you would asphyxiate and die. This Universal Law is stated in so many ways: "What goes around, comes around." Or "What you put out, you get back." This is true with love, time, talent, and treasure. If you want more of anything, you have to get the cycle or the flow started. And just like breathing, you can take in more air if you blow out all the air in your lungs first.

When the law of circulation is retarded, stagnation results. It is only when we allow the Divine current to flow through us, in and out, we really express life. The law of giving and receiving is definite.

—Ernest Holmes

Giving is a way to open the channels for more to come into your life. Giving primes the pump, starts the flow, and gets the whole thing rolling. Giving is gratitude for what you have already received. Giving is the nature of the Universe itself, as it gives life to all of its creations. Give until you feel joyous and free! Then trust the Law of Circulation to return it to you pressed down, shaken together, and running over!

Reflection: Where is the Law of Circulation stagnant in your life? What do you need to start giving?

Affirmation: I joyously and effortlessly give of my love, time, talent, and treasure. The Universe loves giving it back to me, multiplied!

The Affluent Flow

Abundance is being in the flow, while fear creates constriction that cuts the flow down to a drip. Constriction is about "I can't; I shouldn't" and contraction follows. When the constriction is released, your world will expand. Abundance is life moving freely through you. A prosperous life is one of freedom. Life is playful, generous, and generative. Living in abundance and creativity is more a matter of where you are coming from with your consciousness than what the world of your affairs is displaying.

Creeds, ritual, religion, and different theologies are all derived from man's yearning for the vast Reality beyond—and flow in the thousand different forms, fertilizing many fields, calming many communities, refreshing tired people and, at last, carrying people to the ocean of Bliss.
—Sri Sathya Sai Baba

An ease and Grace from within will open your path through your life when you swing from constriction to flow, from fear to frisky. A whole new realm becomes available that's been there and available to you the whole time. It's not about getting out of the way of your troubles; it's more about stepping into your abundant good that is now seeking expression through you. There is nothing but the fullness of God expressing and available to you in this moment. So if you are seeing constriction, you are interrupting the scene in that way, and you are the only one who can reinterpret it for your life.

Reflection: Where would reinterpreting a constricted area of your life open you to the flow of good again?

Affirmation: I am in the affluent flow of good!

It's Their Birthright, Too

Every being is part of the ONE made manifest. In your desire to live an abundant and prosperous life, remember that you do not live alone. All the abundance you deserve as your birthright is equally deserved by everyone. Realize that the rich, meaningful life that you want to create for yourself is what each person seeks to experience in his or her own way.

One of the quickest ways to open channels for your own good is to help others move toward theirs. Generosity, giving, sharing, and supporting others in a healthy and loving manner allows everyone's abundance to increase together. This is a powerful demonstration of your mutual interdependence with everyone else, and it keeps you focused on the mutuality of your greater good and the greater good for every other individual.

Accept your own divinity. Everything is a manifestation of God. When you know that, the power that is LIFE is inside you, you accept your own divinity, and yet you are humble, because you see the same divinity in everyone else.
—Don Miguel Ruiz

Reflection: How are you empowering and supporting others in their creation of abundance? How is this supporting yours?

Affirmation: I am one with all life. I support Abundance as everyone's birthright.

Tithing

Regular committed giving, or tithing, is a profound spiritual practice of gratitude. Tithing comes from a desire to say Thank You for the abundance you have already received. Regularly contributing a significant amount, say 10 percent, is a profound act of faith. YOU are acting like you believe that you will continue receiving your abundance from Spirit as your Source. Regular giving also keeps the channels open and the prosperity flowing. When you tithe to the source of your spiritual good, you are supporting and empowering the very work that has supported and empowered you so much. This is another way of living in the Law of Circulation. Commit to tithing as one of your regular spiritual practices, and watch your faith and prosperity grow!

We should give of ourselves in love and in service to others, in a spirit of generosity and good-fellowship. To refuse to give is to refuse to receive, for everything moves in circles. Real giving is the givingness of the self. A kind word, a thoughtful act, perhaps just a smile, can help lighten the burdens of others.
—Ernest Holmes

Reflection: What beliefs do you have about tithing or regularly contributing to the source of your spiritual good? Are you willing to grow your abundance?

Affirmation: I joyously give, in great gratitude, for the abundance that I have already received.

Priming the Pump

How spiritual can you be if you are in the "I want," "I need," "I gotta get, I gotta make this happen," "I can't afford"? Life is an outpouring—it's a flow, it's movement. The only thing you "gotta" be doing is finding a place where you can give, share, and express the life you are. It's been said, "God so loved the world, he gave." No one outside you can control whether you are going to joyously let life flow through you or not.

Giving is the effect of prosperous thinking. Too many individuals think they will give after value received, forgetting the spiritual truth of how richly blessed they already are. This kind of thinking pulls you down, having you looking for reasons not to be living in the giving consciousness. The law of attraction can't help but honor the game players and support them in shutting off the flow. Prime the pump of life through first giving. It's the golden key that unlocks the floodgates of the Infinite flow of your good.

> *Be an all out—not a hold out.*
> —Norman Vincent Peale

Reflection: Where are you not being as generous as you would like? Give a bit more, and journal what happens inside you and in your outer world of manifestation.

Affirmation: I am joyously unlocking my good by giving!

Faith, Not Fear

When you step out in faith, that means you are stepping outside of your comfort or moving outside of what you know. Moving in faith means you can't actually see how something will happen; you just trust that it will. Often in this process, you will feel fear or doubt. If you move toward those fears, you will see that they simply illuminate the places where you are not living your spiritual beliefs.

It was a high counsel that I once heard given to a young person, "Always do what you are afraid to do."
—Ralph Waldo Emerson

Go put your spiritual truths to the test—live like you really mean them. Love outrageously. Trust innocently. Give fully. Accept openly. Abandon yourself to the joy and pleasure of Life and invite the Infinite to come play with you. Take the "Nestea Plunge" into the heart of your spiritual beliefs and watch how they support you.

Reflection: Where is fear or doubt holding you back? Imagine what it would feel like/be like for you to step out anyway.

Affirmation: I have faith in the spiritual truths that I know, and I am willing to act on them.

Walk in the Midnight Woods

Walking through the mountains alone at night with trees towering above and the full moon shining through, casting all sorts of interesting shadows, can be either a magical or hair-raising experience. It can be spooky listening to the wind rustling through the branches, the wolf's howling, owls screeching, and the mind wondering if a grizzly has got your scent and now desires you for a midnight snack.

If you allow fear to win, it doesn't matter if the howling of the wolves is coming from a ravine over yonder; your fear exponentially expands and will have you convinced the pack is ready to pounce. You start using the power of affirmation in reverse: "They are stalking me; they are stalking me!" Fear will be neutralized only by facing the illusion and walking solo through the midnight woods. You just must experience it until it passes away. You will then be filled with audacity and a bravery that will allow you to enjoy the majestic magic of the moment in God's mountains. Remember, whatever comes up for you is yours to work with and move through. Your choice is a prison of fear or joyous living.

Courage is being scared to death,… and saddling up anyway.
—John Wayne

Reflection: What is your edge of comfort, where discomfort begins? Face it, do it, and push yourself through it.

Affirmation: I courageously walk through my fears!

Eye of the Beholder

Think of the times you have admired or bought a new car. Isn't it amazing how all of a sudden those kinds of cars seem to be everywhere? Or perhaps it's the time you desperately wanted to be in a relationship but were alone. Didn't it feel like all you saw, everywhere you went, were all these happy couples reminding you of your pain of loneliness? These experiences demonstrate that you see through the eyes of your expectations and whatever you are focusing on in your own consciousness.

What you are looking for, you are looking with and looking at.

—Ernest Holmes

They say beauty is in the eye of the beholder. So is joy, truth, love, peace, and every good thing you desire. It is not what you are looking for that counts. It is where you are looking from. The consciousness with which you look is what you will see. Look from the consciousness of love rather than pain, and you will see opportunities for love rather than only things that remind you of the pain of being left out.

Reflection: Where are you looking from?

Affirmation: I am the love I wish to see and the joy I wish to feel. I look from the Truth of Spirit and see only Spirit everywhere I look.

Mystical Flash of the Infinite

The knowledge most people possess is about the material world. When who you are is part of something far greater and more fascinating than what you see, when you catch a flash from something in you who remembers how much more of the multidimensional Infinite you are a part of, it's truly an awe-inspiring realization.

People fall into a trance and see only what they have the capacity to see. So instead of expanding into the brilliance and creative expression of your soul's capability, there is an underlying ache of knowing there could be more than just living in the tightness of the unfolding of your known world. You are an access point of the Infinite. Without you, It is unformed ... it's just part of the infinite possibilities that haven't materialized. When you live in the aliveness of the Infinite, you will be sourced, energized, generous, creative, inspiring, and understanding. Could you imagine what a different kind of world you'd live in if more people were open to the mystical flashes of the Infinite?

The biggest adventure you can take is to live the life of your dreams.
—Oprah Winfrey

What God intended for you goes far beyond anything you can imagine.
—Oprah Winfrey

Reflection: What would the future look like if more people knew the multidimensional possibilities of their being?

Affirmation: I share in my life from the multidimensional possibilities of my being!

The Divine Breaking Through

I have this great plaque in my kitchen that I look at every day: "Pretending to be a normal person day after day is exhausting!" This reminder brings me back to my true self rather than the outer form of who I think I should be or how I should behave.

There is a powerful wildness in your Soul that is the infinite, awesome mystery of Life Itself. Do not seek to be too outwardly, humanly perfect. Rather, seek to perfectly allow your soul to break through the confines of worldly acceptability. Loose the wild mystery of the Divine! Unleash the creativity of your soul! You have been confined in your box of "trying to do it right" for too long.

The oak sleeps in the acorn, the bird waits in the egg, and in the highest vision of the soul, a waking angel stirs.
—James Allen

By means of all created things, without exception, the divine assails us, penetrates us, and molds us. We imagined it as distant and inaccessible, when in fact we live steeped in its burning layers.
—Pierre Teilhard de Chardin

Reflection: When and where are you pretending to be normal? What would it be like to simply be yourself instead?

Affirmation: I am the Divine breaking through into creation as me! I allow my true nature to shine in all I do, say, and think.

Your Soul's Tattoo

Would you allow a blind individual to give you a tattoo? Why would you go through life blindly accepting the imprints of life? The body of your life is as sacred as the body temple your soul inhabits. If you were to have an image embroidered upon your skin, you would choose the artist and image. Every experience you have is a contribution to the emerging picture of your soul, as surely as the ink of a tattoo artist on your skin.

From childhood to the grave, you are inking your soul. Are you selecting the Divine Vision for your life with your aligned thinking and choices, or do you allow the accidents, mishaps, and aging to dictate the colors and impressed image upon your being? Whether the emerging embroidered picture is exquisite or ugly, it is your call!

Once our minds are tattooed with negative thinking, our chances for long-term success diminish.

—John Maxwell

Reflection: Find at least ten minutes of private time to stand in front of a mirror: invite another dimension of awareness to see your energetic body beyond the physical, and see the emerging picture of your soul. What elements do you want to add to this picture?

Affirmation: The image of my soul is Divine!

Your Worthiness Quotient

You are a radiant light, an incarnation of Divine Love, a place where Consciousness is revealing Itself. You are absolutely necessary for the Universe to fully come into being and express itself. That's how much you matter. Since you matter so much to the Universe, you are worthy of all the good the Universe has to shower upon you, so that you may be the light and give your great gifts.

I wish I could show you, When you are lonely or in darkness, The astonishing light of your own being.
—Hafiz

You are worthy of prosperity and abundance! You are worthy of care, consideration, and love. You are worthy of the support of your family, friends, and people everywhere. You are worthy of the support of the Universe itself, just like acorns are supported by the sun, rain, and soil to grow into great and mighty oaks. There isn't anything you have to do to earn this, other than be the best you that you can be. Expect wonderful things and experiences in your life, and accept nothing less. Do your part by being and doing your best.

Reflection: What is your worthiness quotient? What do you think you have to do to "earn" your good?

Affirmation: I am worthy of abundance, love, meaningful work, and healthy relationships. I am worthy just by being me.

More Than You Were Looking For

People are often led to search for the kingdom of God because of some human challenge. There might be a need for wellness, financial security, or a healthier relationship. The physical healing is good, but what is of even greater value is when it moves you to seek to know more about God. When the desire awakens to know Spirit beyond healing, the transformation in your life really takes off.

In your search to know God comes the realization you cannot influence the Infinite, but you become more available to be influenced. In this revelation, you'll understand that all you seek has already been given,

God must become an activity in our consciousness.
—Joel Goldsmith

all your needs have already been met, and nothing has been withheld because it is ever available. The fun part is you become a conduit for the richness of this kingdom to be expressed, and you can't help but want to share it. This is when your words and actions become healing expressions unto the world.

Reflection: What moved you to your serious Spiritual Quest? Did you find that the more you experienced Spirit, the more you desired to experience Spirit? As you came to know the blessing of the spiritual experience more and more, was there a greater desire to share it with others?

Affirmation: I love being used by God!

Ego

The ego, which we commonly associate with the left-brain functions, is an important part of the mental structure you use to navigate this space/time continuum called "life on earth." Your ego helps you classify, categorize, prioritize, and choose. These are all very useful functions. If you didn't have an ego, you'd never keep an appointment, or decide what you want, or have the ambition to make a difference in the world. Your ego is that part of you that knows that you are you as a separate entity and, therefore, in relationship with all the other separate entities around you.

The Ego is an exquisite instrument. Enjoy it, use it—just don't get lost in it.
—Ram Dass

My left brain is doing the best job it can with the information it has to work with. I need to remember, however, that there are enormous gaps between what I know and what I think I know.
—Jill Bolte Taylor

The only time the ego is a problem is when you believe that these constructs and this sense of separation is the REAL you. When you believe that, you now have to protect your "self" from those "others" out there, and you forget that we are all one—"they" are simply "you" expressing in another way. Remembering this helps you use your ego for its best purposes without being used by it.

Reflection: Where is your ego functioning in a healthy manner, keeping you committed and on track? Where in your life is your ego getting in the way?

Affirmation: I use my ego to operate in this space/time continuum. I do not let it use me. I know who I really am.

The Zenith

The midday, midsummer sun is the brightest, hottest fulfillment of its appearance; it is at the zenith of its expression. Its brilliance shines the light to where there was darkness and brings warmth to where there was cold. Enjoy this peak moment for all the good it brings, but the "aware ones" realize the zenith is not everlasting in the natural rhythm of life.

Bask in the joyous living of the abundant time, and prepare for what's to come. Bubbles burst, and this is not bad, it is natural. When it doesn't feel good is when you are indulging a bit too much and forget to pay attention to the signals of the natural rhythms. There is an impermanence to life; enjoy the ride up, and prepare for the ride back down.

From morn
To noon he fell, from noon to dewy eve,—
A summer's day; and with the setting sun
Dropp'd from the Zenith like a falling star.
—John Milton

Reflection: Where in your life have you indulged in a bit too much of a good thing and went past the zenith and came crashing down too fast because you were caught unprepared? Spend some time checking in with the natural rhythms of the many different aspects of your life so you are not caught off guard.

Affirmation: I bring wise awareness to the natural rhythms in all areas of my life!

Adult, Spiritual Eyes

Beliefs are those things we know to be true. Often, this "knowing" came into being through our child's eyes, which observed our young life experience, and our child's mind, which decided something about how to be and how life works. You are now playing those beliefs out in your life—in your body, relationships, health, finances, creativity, and work. Much of your life is being ineffectively run from the beliefs created in your childhood.

The basis of all mental healing is in a change of belief. Since the subjective mind tends to create all beliefs impressed upon it, it follows that in mental healing the whole object is to change the belief.

—Ernest Holmes

Look at your life with your spiritual eyes and your adult mind, and ask yourself what you "know" to be true. These are the things you have come to understand are true about you, and the world, and the nature of life, through your spiritual and personal maturing. If your life isn't fully demonstrating these new ideas, the old beliefs are still operating somewhere, at some level. Now you get to decide which beliefs you want to believe are really true. Those are the ones to keep!

Reflection: What do you "know" to be true that is really just a manifestation of your child's decision? What do you really know to be spiritually true instead?

Affirmation: I release any old beliefs made from my child's mind. I embrace my adult, spiritual ideas and act on them.

November

Living in Gratitude

Stop Your Asking

The mystical life is about beholding Spirit in action in all things. It's having a Divine understanding and realization even as the world around you is gripped in a sense of duality. When you know the Infinite Intelligence, which created and guides the universe, is not going to be influenced to change Its course based upon your desire to alter the order of it all, it becomes easier to stop your asking in prayers.

Misdirected life force is the activity in disease process. Disease has no energy save what it borrows from the life of the organism.
—Kabbalah

When you perceive you are squandering your time in your attempt to influence God, you'll be moved to get quiet. Your prayer will no longer be one of asking but one of being open to hear, feel, and sense the Divine Directive. God will enter your field of awareness, and you will be guided to be an expression of Truth. Then the "me" that was wanting and listening will disappear, and the Presence will manifest Itself as the "I Am." Let your prayers be with your ears, and allow your words to become a reflection of the God realization.

Reflection: Take an issue from your world that has grasped your awareness as being less than Divine, and, rather than having your prayer be one of asking for it to be different, listen to Spirit's realization and guidance about it.

Affirmation: I behold Spirit in action in all things!

Amazing Possibilities

According to aeronautical engineers, the bumble bee shouldn't actually be able to fly. Given its shape and wingspan, it's actually impossible. Yet it does! Someone once said it was impossible for man to run a four-minute mile, until Roger Bannister did it in 1954. Now people routinely run the mile in less than four minutes. It was once believed to be impossible to sail around the world without falling off or fly to the moon. It was even once thought that it was impossible to drive a car over the speed of thirty-five because it would kill the driver. Now these notions of what's impossible seem quaint and funny.

Alice laughed. "There's no use trying," she said. "One can't believe impossible things." "I daresay you haven't had much practice," said the Queen. "When I was your age, I always did it for half-an-hour a day. Why, sometimes I've believed as many as six impossible things before breakfast."
—Lewis Carroll

Life is full of the most amazing possibilities. This is true of your life as well. Open your eyes, your heart, and your willingness—to see what's possibility rather than what can't work, or won't work, or hasn't worked in the past. If you want things to be different than they are, you start with what's possible, then grow into it in reality. Remember, "With God, all things are possible."

Reflection: What do you believe is impossible for you? How can you imagine it to be possible?

Affirmation: With God, all things are possible. I find new ways of thinking about what's possible for me and my life.

The Faith Factor

You can use your faith to terrorize yourself with your thoughts by placing it on the very thing you don't want to experience. Or you can allow your thoughts to be an instrument of Divine Awareness. Isaiah 26:3: "Spirit will keep him in perfect peace whose mind is stayed on thee."

The moment you start to battle with illusion, you've lost the case. Do not react to appearances, otherwise you'll be using your faith to uphold a nonreality. Living in conscious union with God draws to you all that is ever necessary. Make Spirit your goal, and have the faith of Spirit in all things.

When you talk to God, that's prayer. When God talks back, it's schizophrenia.
—Lily Tomlin

Reflection: Don't get caught in frightening images that the media or others want you to have. How can you step away from the whirlpools of negativity that swirl around you? Where can you take better control of what's going into your mind by placing your faith in a higher perspective?

Affirmation: I live my life in Faith!

Fear

Fear is believing that something bad will happen. It is expecting a negative outcome from whatever is being attempted or done. Fear is the faith that one will lose one's job, or home, or love. So often, fear is completely out of proportion with reality. How many people do you know who have actually died of embarrassment or public speaking, yet this is the number-one fear most people have. Another way of looking at fear is "False Evidence Appearing Real." What false evidence?—the evidence of the worldly wisdom based on the news and the market and the past.

But what is fear? Nothing more nor less than the negative use of faith . . . faith misplaced.
—Ernest Holmes

When you find yourself fearful, ask yourself, Is this REALLY true— or is this an assumption? What is the worst possible thing that could happen? Is that likely to happen or actually happening right now? What if what is, simply is what it is? Can you stay completely present in the now moment and not project a negative outcome into the future? Imagine seeing it in a positive, spiritual light. Imagine what the best possible outcome could be. Why not have faith in that instead?

Reflection: Where are you letting your worry about experiencing something you don't want to have happen (another way to describe fear) keep you stuck or from moving forward?

Affirmation: I release fear and negative expectations. I move forward with a positive expectation and faith that it will work out.

Faith and Trust

Whatever is happening, approach it with trust and confidence. The wisdom, power, and strength of the Universe is right where you are, right now. No matter what you need or what is going on, you can rely on the Universe. This is called faith.

Faith is the willingness to move forward, without allowing your doubt and fear to get in the way. Faith is the ability to move toward the "what" without needing to know the "how." Faith is a powerful positive expectation that things will actually somehow work out. If your faith seems a little shaky, remember what you are having faith in. You are relying on the infinite, absolutely supportive, completely intelligent power and presence of the Spirit that really knows "how" to create everything and anything. It creates babies and sequoia trees, hummingbirds and galaxies. Surely it knows "how" to get you from where you are now to where you want to be. Learn to engage in your life with perfect trust and confidence, and have the patience to let it all work out.

Faith is like the radar that sees through the fog.
—Corrie Ten Boom

Faith is the daring of the soul to go farther than it can see.
—William Newton Clark

Faith is taking the first step even when you don't see the whole staircase.
—Martin Luther King Jr.

Reflection: What is calling you to a deeper walk in faith and trust? How can you confidently act more on your faith?

Affirmation: I trust in the Universe and have confidence in the Law. I move forward with complete faith that everything will work out in a positive way.

Radical Responsibility

Spiritual maturity is about living in balance between the various values you hold dear. It is knowing that every spiritual question or truth finally resolves itself into the paradox that all sides are right from a certain point of view. This means there is no one way to act or be all the time. You must be able to move in harmony with seemingly opposite spiritual instructions and know when and how to apply them.

Spiritual maturity is the ability to take radical responsibility for your life while being loving with yourself. This means learning from your mistakes without shame or blame. It means enjoying your successes with-

Maturity means being emotionally and mentally healthy. It is that time when you know when to say yes, when to say no, and when to say WHOOPEE!
—Unknown

out false modesty or pride. It means praising the good in another's life without envy or comparison. Most importantly, it means being who you are with confidence and joy. You can do it. It only takes practice.

Reflection: How comfortable are you in living in the paradoxes of spirituality?

Affirmation: I take responsibility for myself while being compassionate with my imperfections. I live in the paradox of my equally important yes and no.

Rub Elbows with Success

Check your ego at the door! Don't be afraid to surround yourself with people who are more skilled, more conscious, or more mature than you are. This demonstrates your ability to see yourself and others clearly, without comparison. It allows you to experience yourself as confident within your own skills and creates an opening for you to learn and grow. Surrounding yourself with people who are already living the life of your dreams, or who have successfully negotiated something you need to walk through, fills in the gaps in whatever you don't know about where you're going.

If you want to succeed, rub elbows with other successful people.
—Unknown

Another person's level of consciousness can pull you forward, when you really let it, toward that same of level of consciousness in you. These people model for you who you are becoming. You will, of course, take this up in your own completely unique way, but they help you create a great mental equivalent to live into.

Reflection: Am I rubbing elbows with successful, conscious people who are living and modeling the life I want to live?

Affirmation: I surround myself with successful, confident, compassionate, mature, and conscious people. I am becoming one of them.

Know Thyself

Socrates was famous for his line "Know Thyself." So often, this means to know your faults and your darkness so you can heal them. Know your triggers so you can get past them. Know your hidden beliefs so you can change them. Know your strengths so you can play to them. This is all well and good, but do you know who you are?

You are not your thoughts, your feelings, your past, your roles and titles, or your accomplishments. You are not your successes or your failures. You are not your body, your age, your abilities, or your fears. Once you realize this, you are free to

Knowing yourself is the beginning of all wisdom.
—Aristotle

ask yourself the most important question, "Who am I? Who am I really?" Do not try to answer this question with ideas or words. Wait—the answer will be revealed.

Reflection: Ask yourself this questions over and over and over: Who am I?

Affirmation: I AM. That is enough. I am that I am. The only thing unalterable and always true about me is that I am the Divine incarnate as me.

Dead Trees Don't Lose Their Leaves

The Strengthening Winds

Hundred-foot pines dancing in the winter winds, with the mystical music of howling weather ricocheting off the trunks and through the branches with the blistering cold just waiting to penetrate any sign of vulnerability, are a reminder of nature's strength and, at the same time, flexibility. Thin or thick, the towering pines dip, bend, and bow as they give way to the forces of the north winds, only to bounce back strengthened for their reach to the heavens.

The higher you climb the mountain, the harder the wind blows.

—Sam Cummings

What a wonderful encourager of flexibility. The bigger the tree, the greater exposure it has to the arctic blasts. When the tree can bend, it will not break. The most rigid will eventually be snapped by nature's forces. The larger you are in life, the more you will encounter the frigid blasts of others' opinions. When dealing with criticism, move with the blasts. The more flexible and bending you are, the stronger you return for your reach to the heavens and joyous living. The tree knows the wind will eventually die down. So, too, will life's blasts.

Reflection: Where could you use a bit more flexibility in your life?

Affirmation: I find strength in my flexibility!

Dead Trees Don't Lose Their Leaves

In the fall as the leaves are dropping, it's lovely to see the bare bones of the tree emerge. In letting the leaves drop in all their brilliant colors, the proud skeleton on which they hang is revealed. Do you know why some trees don't release their leaves when they've turned brown? It's because they are dead and not actually participating in the release cycle. Isn't it interesting to learn that dead trees don't lose their leaves—they just turn brown and hang on. Live trees easily release their leaves when it's time, making room for next year's budding and new growth.

You leave old habits behind by starting out with the thought, "I release the need for this in my life."

—Wayne Dyer

Are you ready to release and let go? Or are you hanging on long after something has died, and it's just hanging around in your life all dead and brown and shriveled up? Let go of that which has served you in the past but is now old and worn out—whether these are people, things, or beliefs. Release them in the brilliant fire of purging, allowing the cycles of life to take their natural course. Letting go, you are making room for the new.

Reflection: What dead things are you hanging on to? What do you need to release?

Affirmation: I easily release and let go of anything that does not serve my greater love, life, joy, peace, and abundance.

November 11

Veterans Day

The willingness to serve and sacrifice for the common good is a rite of passage that many say yes to. Pause at 11:00 on November 11th to allow your heart to be filled with gratitude for those heroes and "she-roes" who are willing to give up their innocence and lives so we can have a safe and free nation and a world where unalienable human rights are honored.

How important it is for us to recognize and celebrate our heroes and she-roes!
—Maya Angelou

Veterans Day originated as Armistice Day and marked the end of hostilities of World War I that occurred at the 11th hour of the 11th day of the 11th month. In 1954, the honoring moved from only veterans of WWI to include all veterans who served. This day is not only a time to remember those who died in service, but also recognize all those who have served and are now in service. Whether you support war or not, the fact that people have put their families and lives in jeopardy because they believe they are helping to make a better world for you, that is worth opening your heart to.

Reflection: Stop today at 11:00 and open your heart in appreciation of all those who were willing to risk it all for their belief that they were making a better world for us all.

Affirmation: I appreciate those who have gone before me, who have given so much, so I may live in joy!

Nondirect Opposition

You might recall, if you've had children, their requests are sometimes a little beyond what is presently practical. "Mom, can I have a pony?" You can get into all the reasons why that won't work, or you can say, "That would be fun someday," and leave it at that. Or "Dad, can we go to Disneyland?" Rather than a combative "No," "Not now, we'll do that later" will often suffice. When your little one asks for a truck as you are tucking him in for the night, a nice response is, "You can have that in dreamland."

It's crazy how you can get yourself in a mess sometimes and not even be able to think about it with any sense and yet not be able to think about anything else.

—Stanley Kubrick

Children have taught you the dance of nondirect opposition. A child can come up with incalculable desires, and you have had to learn to deal with the requests with benevolence. Your mind can be like the child with its relentless onslaught of desires. If you have learned to treat yourself with the same gentleness you show a child, your mind doesn't go into combat mode to win, but releases and moves on to what's next.

Reflection: How can I be kinder in allowing my mind's ideas to come and go without a battle?

Affirmation: I am allowing my mind's ideas to rise and dissipate naturally.

Dead Trees Don't Lose Their Leaves

Heart-Centered

When you say you are coming from your heart or that something just doesn't feel right, check to make sure you're not actually coming from your emotions. Emotions are generally responses to external stimuli. What you are feeling is what that external stimulus has triggered within you. What gets activated is usually a deep or old pain or experience around which you created some definite beliefs about the world and other people.

A man who is master of himself can end a sorrow as easily as he can invent a pleasure. I don't want to be at the mercy of my emotions. I want to use them, to enjoy them, and to dominate them.

—Oscar Wilde

Coming from your heart is coming from your centered, compassionate, still, and healing place. Your heart is the electromagnetic center of your whole physical being as well as the primary energy center through which you engage with the infinite universal energy. Coming from your heart always feels expansive, never constricted. It seems like it's moving toward love, never away from it. It's about being open to life and not shutting down or closing off.

Reflection: Can you sense and feel the difference between coming from your heart and from your emotions? Where are you usually coming from?

Affirmation: I am centered in my heart. I move into life from my open and loving heart center.

Sleep as Spiritual Practice

Statistics show that most Americans are chronically sleep-deprived. This is due to many factors, including long work hours, taking care of children, staying on the computer or watching TV too long into the evening, or just plain stress. If you get less than six hours of sleep on a daily basis, within a very short time your cognitive and emotional functions become impaired. The longer you run on too little sleep, the worse it gets. It is challenging to be conscious, make good choices, and find the good in situations when you are just too tired. Sleep isn't a luxury; it's as necessary as air, food, and water to our overall well-being.

> *Now I see the secret of making the best person: it is to grow in the open air and to eat and sleep with the earth.*
> —Walt Whitman

This makes sleep the most extremely underrated part of our spiritual health. If you find yourself nodding off or falling asleep in your prayer or meditation time, it is because your body needs more sleep. Rather than trying to meditate, first give your body the sleep it needs. If you find yourself easily emotionally off-center or mentally unable to stay focused, check into your sleep patterns. You may simply need more rest.

Reflection: Are you getting enough sleep and general rest?

Affirmation: I give myself the sleep my body needs. I sleep in peace, and I awake in joy.

Dead Trees Don't Lose Their Leaves

God Is Not a Word

You can think about music all you want; it's not going to make music. You can think about being an athlete for years; it's not going happen unless you get out onto the field. You can say and think words about God, but as long as it remains a mental practice, it's not going to be experienced in your world. You must become that which you envision for it to be a reality in your life.

The most effective way to do it, is to do it.
—Amelia Earhart

God is not a word ... it's an experience. Thinking about Spirit is not Spirit. Spiritual statements are nice for pointing you in a good direction, but they are not Spirit. Don't get lost in giving your power away to books with wonderful words ... you still have to live them. Your true understanding won't come from books; it will be attained only by consciously connecting with the Source and being it. If you want Spirit, be still and let It operate through you, as you.

Reflection: Where in your life do you need to move beyond thought into expression so you can have a real experience rather than a mental one?

Affirmation: I am Spirit expressed!

Divine Circuitry

Have you ever seen one of those phone boxes on the street opened by a phone service person and just marveled at the amount of wiring inside the box? There are so many little wires connected to so many different places, it's amazing to think anyone would know where all that circuitry went to and what it is for. As intricate as the schematic layout is, it doesn't do any good unless someone is utilizing the system.

As complex as the wiring is for the phone system, your elaborate circuitry ... your human wiring system ... far exceeds the phone company's. The Grand Creator has you wired for healing and transformation, communication and intimacy, love and abundance, to name just a few. You haven't even begun to experience all you are capable of; just like the wiring on the streets, however, it does you no good unless you use it.

The value of an idea lies in using it.
—Thomas Edison

Reflection: Sit quietly, go within, and divinely Google the instruction manual to your Divine circuitry and discover aspects of your capabilities you haven't even begun to know you could do.

Affirmation: I discover I am wired for greater good than I ever knew!

Your Movie Script

Your Movie Script

Knowing that you create your own reality is one thing, but what about when you are confronted with someone in your life that you don't remember actually wanting, choosing, or creating? Perhaps it's a difficult boss, a disgruntled client, or a whiny friend. Do you have to take responsibility for creating them, too?

Think of it like we are all actors playing in the movie of life. Everyone gets to write his or her own script, but then get other people to play the parts. Those folks are also writing their own scripts. When two scripts fall into alignment, we get to play in each other's movie.

People come into your life for a reason, a season or a lifetime.
—Unknown

Sometimes people are playing a role in our movie—we attracted them to live out our beliefs about life. Sometimes we are playing parts in their movies. Usually, it's some portion of both. Determining which part is yours and which is theirs helps you do the healing work that is here for you to do and not take personally the part which is theirs to heal.

Contemplate: Whom have you attracted to play out a part of your story? Where are you playing out a part in someone else's story?

Affirmation: I take responsibility for the script I write and the part I play in my own and other people's lives. I allow them to take responsibility for the parts that are theirs.

Outside the Everyday

There is a reality outside your everyday responsibilities. There is more to life than your job, goals, or fulfilling your treasure board of pasted magazine pictures. Your meditation practices can sometimes challenge what you had previously thought was so important. This can be very disconcerting when you had been clear on your direction in this world. Yet the silencing of the chattering mind and entering a vibration of love and joy can be very addicting.

Reality is merely an illusion, albeit a very persistent one.
—Albert Einstein

Part of what you get to do in this life, after you have felt the freedom and adjusted your trajectory, is walk through your world with a compassionate heart. You become the calming presence in meetings and

There are no facts, only interpretations.
—Friedrich Nietzsche

hook-ups. You understand how transient your life is, which makes it even more precious. You will no longer want to waste your time with that which is irrelevant to your soul.

Reflection: What does that reality outside your everyday responsibilities feel like? What areas of your life no longer match up with your spiritual unfoldment?

Affirmation: I am a calming presence!

Grief and Loss

Holidays can be wonderful, and they can be challenging. Some of the challenges may have to do with people who are no longer present in your life due to distance, drifting apart, divorce, or death. It is important to acknowledge the sense of loss that is generally more palpable around the holidays. By acknowledging it, you make room for all the great memories and loving times to surface as well. Being present with your grief, whether it's sharp and new, or faded and soft, makes you compassionate and emotionally available to the wonderful people who are in your life right now!

Because God is never cruel, there is a reason for all things. We must know the pain of loss; because if we never knew it, we would have no compassion for others, and we would become monsters of self-regard, creatures of unalloyed self-interest. The terrible pain of loss teaches humility to our prideful kind, has the power to soften uncaring hearts, to make a better person of a good one.

—Dean Koontz

Reflection: What losses are you grieving? Whom do you miss in your life?

Affirmation: I allow the tears of my love to wash clean my grieving heart. I am present to the beauty and joy of every moment with those I love.

Try Kindness

It's one thing for His Holiness to claim kindness as his religion, but what about those of us walking around here at sea level and driving the freeways? I then remind myself of the path he had to endure to be able to make that statement … one where he had to witness the attempted genocide of his culture and the theft of his country.

When I remember this, his compassionate declaration then resonates a lot deeper in me as a practice to emulate.

My religion is simple; my religion is kindness.
—The Dalai Lama

Reflection: What unforgiven issue from your life are you really ready to be done with?

Affirmation: I open my heart to great possibilities!

Your Movie Script

Mirror, Mirror

How much of what you complain about in another person is actually a projection of what you yourself do? When someone really gets your goat and you have a lot of judgment about what he is doing, it may be time to stop and ask yourself, "How is this person's behavior a reflection of my own?" We often project onto another our own suppressed or unconscious feelings and beliefs.

And why worry about a speck in your friend's eye when you have a log in your own?
—Matthew

Thus if we tend toward arrogance, but don't want to admit it, we may find ourselves immensely irritated by the arrogant people in our life.

Spiritual maturity seeks to understand what is triggered within you that produces the feelings of blame, shame, anger, or withdrawal. You begin to see that this person is simply mirroring yourself back to you. Seeing yourself clearly allows you to admit and own a way of believing or behaving, which then allows you to change it. In turn, this allows you to see the other person more clearly, and with more loving eyes.

Contemplate: Find someone in your life who is really irritating you, then ask yourself, "When have I acted in this same manner?" You may be projecting your own stuff onto that other person.

Affirmation: I look clearly at myself and others with loving eyes and an open heart.

The Banquet Table

There is so much wonder, love, and joy in life. The banquet of life is lavishly prepared, and it is waiting for you. Every moment, Spirit is showering you with life, and everything you need is available to you. Do not stand at the banquet table of life starving, thinking you do not deserve or aren't worthy of what is already yours.

Go to the table with a good-size plate and take what you want. You may go back to the table as often as you like. Simply leave what you don't need or want or whatever you don't like. You are not required to take anything but whatever is enough for you

You only live once, but if you do it right, once is enough.
—Mae West

to experience a rich, fulfilled, and meaningful life. You can have as much as you can truly see yourself experiencing. You can have as much as you can accept. It is all there for your enjoyment.

Reflection: What part of the banquet of life are you not enjoying and accepting as yours?

Affirmation: I stand at the banquet table of life and accept all that is mine to enjoy. I deserve all the good Spirit has to offer.

Your Movie Script

Enough

Sometimes enough just doesn't feel like enough. Often it seems to mean barely enough or some form of limitation. Another way to really experience your abundance and gratitude, however, is to feel *enough* as that satiated feeling you get at the end of a great meal, when you push back from the table and say, "Mmmm, I've had enough!" This doesn't mean that tomorrow you can't go back to the table and have more. It just means that if you ate more right now, you'd actually become painfully uncomfortable.

Gratitude unlocks the fullness of life. It turns what we have into enough, and more. It turns denial into acceptance, chaos into order, confusion to clarity....Gratitude makes sense of our past, brings peace for today, and creates a vision for tomorrow.

—Melody Beattie

Enough is the state of being satisfied with what you have right now—not resigned or that you can't have as much as you want. But once you get it, it's actually enough. Encourage yourself to explore what satisfies you. What is enough? What brings you contentment and a feeling of being fulfilled? Anything beyond that is "more than enough," which usually leaves you groaningly full, in pain, or in debt. Enjoy having enough.

Reflection: How do you know when you have "enough"? What satisfies you and makes you feel fulfilled?

Affirmation: I have enough love, joy, peace, and abundance in my life for me to be completely fulfilled and satisfied.

Prayer of Gratitude

Gratitude is the most powerful way to increase your blessings. Gratitude focuses your attention on what you have already received, which increases because of your attention to it. Remember, what we pay attention to, grows. Gratitude for knowing that you have already received something in consciousness is the most powerful way to attract it into your life. Having that "already having received" feeling means the Universal Law must now bring that about.

Now, being grateful for your good is easy. Being grateful for the Good you know Spirit is showering you with is also pretty easy to learn. It's also important to learn to be grateful for those who irritate you, situations that trigger you, and things that you wish were different. Each one is teaching you something. Being grateful for the situation invites you to be grateful for what you are becoming aware of, which leads you to be grateful for the new truth you actually know. Living in gratitude for the new truth is what then causes that to grow instead of more of what triggered you. Always seek the deeper spiritual truth, and be grateful for everything that has helped it to emerge.

> *If the only prayer you ever prayed was "Thank you," it would be enough.*
> —Meister Eckhart

Reflection: What events or people have you had trouble being grateful for? Practice gratitude for them. What learning or deeper spiritual truth is revealed?

Affirmation: I am grateful for everything in my life. I am grateful for the good that supports and the lessons that enlighten me.

Life Is Good

There is a key to turning your life around: appreciation and gratitude.

When you feel life closing in on you, a tightness taking over your thoughts and body, it's time to know beyond appearance that life is good and start looking around and saying, "Thank you, God!" Gratitude lifts your vision from the valley of despair to the realization "God owns the cattle on a thousand hills, the wealth in every mine."

Give thanks to the Lord, for He is good. His love endures forever.
—Psalm 107:1

When you hold back in concern that by helping another you may be somehow taking from yourself, you are only holding yourself back. You are claiming the limitation in a life that is Infinite. God's Good is not received in your bank account; it is received in your consciousness. And when you have embraced the Good that is already yours, it doesn't take long for it to convert into all the appropriate areas of your life. God's Grace is sufficient.

Reflection: Feeling tight in any area of your life? Look around you for the Good in your life, and get claiming, "Life is good!"

Affirmation: God's Grace is sufficient. My life is good!

The Big Table

When you were younger, did you ever have to sit at the kids' table during family gatherings … the one that was set aside for the little folks? Then the big day (or the new generation of kids) arrived, and you were promoted to the adult table! It felt good to finally be a part of the grown-up world.

You've been invited to the adult banquet of life. You have all the offerings presented to you that are offered to the world. You have had the opportunity to mature into the wise choosing of that which makes you feel good rather than sick. All the world has been made available to you. Are you still mentally and emotionally at the kiddies' table, wishing you had what was over there? You are a mature adult who no longer needs supervision. You have been given an infinite amount of choices. Choose wisely because the parental supervision was gone a long time ago, and there is no one else in your world to blame for what you are choosing from the banquet of your life.

Anyone who lives within their means suffers from a lack of imaginations.
—Oscar Wilde

Reflection: When did you realize you were at the big table in life … and would receive the ramifications of your choosing … and there was no longer anyone to blame for your life choices?

Affirmation: I choose what I like and what enriches my soul from the banquet of life!

Prayer of Gratitude

Praise and Celebrate

Fall is traditionally a time to celebrate the harvest. The fruits and vegetables are taken in to be stored for the lean winter months. It's a time of bounty and a wonderful time of celebration.

This is the time to see the fruit of your own labor for this past year. Your harvest is the result of the spiritual growth, inner personal work, and outer achievements you've accomplished. Take a moment to stop and see how far you've come. Look back at your intentions. Notice your progress. Catalogue your results. Celebrate every step, every breakthrough, every result! Even the little ones, the not so obvious ones, and the inner ones no one sees. You have been working diligently and now is the time to enjoy the fruit of your labor.

> *The more you praise and celebrate your life, the more there is in life to celebrate.*
> —Oprah Winfrey

Reflection: What have you accomplished? What are you harvesting in your life as a result of your inner growth?

Affirmation: I joyfully celebrate the fruit of my own personal and spiritual growth. I am grateful for every accomplishment and forward step.

Gratitude, the Sweetener of Life

Gratitude is like adding sweetener to your life. Being grateful is the ability to turn anything into a blessing. By focusing your attention on the good, you are directing a proliferating energy. Energy flows where attention goes. Where your awareness is becomes the reality you choose to play in. Gratitude will lift you from the clutches of concern to joyous living. You become joyously excited about the possibilities that lie before you.

When you are truly grateful, you are nourished. Wherever you place your appreciation will grow in value to you. Gratitude allows you to live in a rich and abundant universe. The

The most important thing is to enjoy your life— to be happy—it's all that matters.
—Audrey Hepburn

greater your ability to appreciate what has been given, the greater your ability to expand your good. As soon as you open to the pleasure of the present, you deepen your connection to all the good that life is now offering you.

Reflection: Make a list filled with all that you are grateful for in your life. Set it down, let it fill your heart, and from that fullness write some more gratitudes.

Affirmation: I am grateful!

Prayer of Gratitude

November 29
Time to Connect

When traveling in a happy third-world country, there is no Black Friday following Thanksgiving or Cyber Monday. What kind of idol worship has people making a sacred midnight pilgrimage to camp out in the cold at a department store? Does your love for your loved ones really want them to submit themselves to that kind of materialistic hysteria? If the marketing genius and dollars put into creating the hysteria and need were redirected to remind us the gifts that people are in our life, the world would be transformed.

How wonderful it is that nobody need wait a single moment before starting to improve the world.
—Anne Frank

In slower-paced cultures, people seem to have time to connect, talk, and lend a helping hand. There is joy around being together, not based on "stuff." There are laughter, smiles, and non-sensual touching. People see each other as gifts in the moment and in their life without attempting to change them into someone they are not. People are honored and loved for who they are and not for what they've got and give. So make Black Friday brighter—slip out of the cyber realm and return to the human realm.

Reflection: Take a stroll to the beach, or park, or some community gathering place, and take the time to have a conversation with someone you don't know (and not just because s/he is cute).

Affirmation: I am enjoying taking time connecting with people!

Holiday Blues

Being a humbug around the holidays may simply be a protection mechanism you have developed because of your personal experiences with the holidays when you were younger. You may not have great memories of family holidays. You may not have had great experiences with gifts, or traditions, or even the presence of life. Yet these past experiences do not have to dictate your current reality. Remember, you are always at choice.

You can choose not to become sucked into the dreariness or disappointment of the past. You can choose not to re-create the experiences of your childhood. You can

It is you who are choosing, in any moment, to be happy or choosing to be sad, or choosing to be angry, or forgiving, or enlightened, or whatever. You are choosing.

—Neale Donald Walsch

choose, instead, to have your life and your holiday experience however you want it to be, right now. You can see it differently by exploring traditions that interest you, finding rituals that are meaningful for you, and discovering the presence of love. You can choose whom you spend time with and how much time you spend with them. Choose to create some joyous holiday time, now!

Reflection: How do you engage with the holidays? How would you like to experience them?

Affirmation: I release my feelings about past holidays. I create new traditions and rituals that bring meaning to my life today.

Prayer of Gratitude

December

Living in the Light

The Summer of Winter

Now is the time to set aside your final tithe or gifts for the year. You have been well nourished by life this whole past year in many different ways. Take time to be grateful for all the good you have received, all the precious life you have lived. Make your declaration of abundance by willingly giving of that abundance. It's like storing seeds over winter so you can plant them again in the spring..

During Winter it is Summer underneath the surface of the earth. And it is this Summer under the surface of the earth in Winter time that enables the roots of the plants to thrive.
—Alicia Hamberg

What's happening in the quiet of winter? The roots are growing deeper into the Earth. This quiet and deepening is so necessary for the bursting forth of new life in the spring. Without it, nothing would have the energy needed to create the profusion of joy and color that starts with the first blooms of the season. Take some time to enjoy this quiet season. Let yourself become more grounded. Reach more deeply inside. Feel your energy anchoring you deep into the Earth. It is from these depths that your growth springs. This creates the springboard for greater good in the coming year!

Reflection: How can you create and enjoy moments of a quiet winter within yourself?

Affirmation: I create fallow time in which my roots run more deeply, and I become more grounded in Great Spirit and Mother Earth.

Two Dimensions of Consciousness

Beyond the world of form, there are two dimensions of consciousness: the mental and the spiritual. When first consciously becoming aware of the spiritual exploration and the responsiveness of the world of form to thought, it's easy to think that the ability to direct the material universe is spiritual. Learning the mental science of mind over matter can be very engaging, because it is something greater than being at the effect of the material world. Most people will stop there and call it heaven.

When you enter the spiritual realm, there is nothing to overcome; there is only God, Wholeness, Completeness. There is only One Power, and it's not a Power over anything—it is the only life there is. To enter this field of awareness, healing happens because there is no otherness, nothing to overcome. You are that place where it is revealed in real and relevant ways.

If I prayed for something, it would mean I have a desire, an end, an objective in life that I am seeking. But I have nothing to pray for. I have only this minute to live, this minute in which I must be fulfilled by the Spirit.
—Joel Goldsmith

It's very simple to know what dimension you are truly playing in. The mental realm has two powers—good and not so good (that which you want to overcome)—whereas in the spiritual kingdom, there is only the Divine Realization and nothing to overcome.

Reflection: Can you notice areas in your life where you are attempting to overcome the negative with Good rather than just know the Good of the situation?

Affirmation: I see and feel only Spirit in the hot spots of my life!

December 3
Creating with Your Word

"Be impeccable with your word" (the first of the Four Agreements by Don Miguel Ruiz) reminds us that our word is the most powerful creative instrument we own. Your word is the paintbrush of your life. The words you use reveal what you really believe. The things you talk about become the Cause of your life's experience. The stories you tell about yourself narrate your life into being.

The word gives form to the unformed. The greater the consciousness behind the word, the more power it will have.
—Ernest Holmes

What kinds of colors and brushes are you using to create your life through the power of your words? You create one kind of life with stories of gossip and judgment, comparison and exaggerations. Every time you speak, you can either paint your life with spiritual truths or with the same old lies you tell about yourself—things like "I'm never enough" or "I'm not worthy" or simply "I can't do it." Every conversation, every personal sharing, every phone call, text, or email gives you an opportunity to work on the canvas of your life. You can use the brush of beauty and love, colored by striking statements of faith to absolutely form and create a beautiful rendition of the life you choose.

Reflection: Do you say what you mean and speak with integrity? What words are most often on your painter's palette?

Affirmation: I speak words of truth and love. I am careful with my words, for they have power. I speak only that which I choose to experience or create.

Beyond Articulation

Imagine someone telling you about a magical garden with its enchanting fragrances that are otherworldly. It doesn't matter how descriptive he may be in his details of the scents of the beautiful blooms, he can never come close to capturing the subtle scents of the bouquet. You must enter the garden if you are to know the transportative qualities of the intoxicating aroma of these God-created essences.

There is a realm beyond articulation. To enter, you must surrender the need to describe it, which runs contrary to the controlling mind. Yet healing and transformation require that you relinquish the need for explanation. Allow that which defies reason to push you beyond the grasp of reason. As the mystical sojourner, your spirit will naturally wander into its homecoming of the nurturing wholeness of your being. You will be uplifted by Grace, empowered by Vision, and revitalized by Life Itself. When you return from God's Garden, there will have been no photo ops, no journaling or even words to describe, just a lingering fragrance on your healed soul that will defy description.

I only went out for a walk, and finally concluded to stay out till sundown, for going out, I found, was really going in.
—John Muir

Reflection: Attempt to describe your favorite fragrance to someone without comparing it to another scent. Then sit and see if you can bring the remembrance of this essence back into your field of awareness.

Affirmation: I travel in realms beyond description!

The Fulcrum

Connect with your Center and you connect with the Source of All. You are a portal to the Divine. You are the place where the infinite meets the finite, where consciousness becomes aware. Your being is the fulcrum where Spirit meets matter and human meets Divine. This still point within is the Center that is everywhere, and a unique expression of it is right here, as you.

Incarnated within each one of us is not only a divine Spark, not only an incarnation of the living Spirit of the Cosmos, but a unique presentation of the Cosmic Whole.
—Ernest Holmes

Breathe into the stillness, into your Center. Breathe into the Divine Reality of your Being. This is the truth of who you are. You are not anything you have, a role you play, or an experience you can say about yourself. You are the Infinite incarnate, so you have all of Life present, right where you are. Now you know you are never alone.

Reflection: What do you find when you breathe into the center of your being?

Affirmation: I am centered within, and there I find the Center of All.

Caring for and Nurturing Yourself

You cannot keep giving and making a difference in the world from an empty cup. You cannot love another if you are not caring toward yourself. You cannot find true compassion for others if you are not compassionate with your own soul and physical body. The Master Teacher reminded us to "Love your neighbor as yourself." The word "as" is so very critical. "As" functions there as an equal sign, turning the statement into an mathematical equation of symmetry and equality. You could just as easily say "Love yourself as your neighbor." It doesn't say love your neighbor more than yourself, nor love yourself more than your neighbor.

Growing into your future with health and grace and beauty doesn't have to take all your time. It rather requires a dedication to caring for yourself as if you were rare and precious, which you are, and regarding all life around you as equally so, which it is.

—Victoria Moran

Curling up in front of the fire with a good book and a cup of tea is one of many wonderful ways to love and nurture yourself. Taking the time to simply "be," in the midst of the busyness of your life, is an important antidote to stress that you may be feeling. Simply sit, relax, enjoy, and savor the moment. Feel yourself become rejuvenated!

Reflection: What are you doing for self-care and to nurture yourself?

Affirmation: I nurture and care for myself. I love and approve of myself.

December 7

Pearl Harbor Day

Growing up, I wondered how and why my dad's generation all seemed to remember December 7, Pearl Harbor Day. In his speech to Congress, President Franklin D. Roosevelt described the bombing of Pearl Harbor as "a date which will live in infamy." As a child, I'd listen to guys tell their war stories from World War II, thinking everyone lived to tell since I didn't know anyone who didn't live to tell. Then we had our 9/11 with its images blazed into this generation's consciousness, and I understood the heartache of loss and an official start of war. Now I know how my dad remembered the date ... a day the world changed.

You can be sure that the American spirit will prevail over this tragedy.
—Colin Powell

The emotional turmoil and pain of sending our brothers and sisters, sons and daughters, off to a foreign land, some never to return and no one returning with the same innocence we sent him or her off with, is heart-wrenching. The sacrifice that would be asked, the families that would be ruined, and the negative financial impact of an economy that would hurt all the people of a nation, is more devastating than could ever be conveyed by history books. Yet the inspiration of those who are willing to give their lives for the universal vision of a world that works for everyone, where joyous living is what prevails for one human family, will continue to inspire and uplift the human spirit from the darkest of times to the brightest of possibilities.

Reflection: Take a moment this day to open your heart to add your love to those points in history whose call through time is one of pain.

Affirmation: I bring love to where there is heartache!

Prepare Yourself

Advent is the time of preparation. It is a time of anticipation for the birth of the incarnation of the Divine. Along with preparing for the family, gifts, and feasts, prepare for the incarnation of the Christ Consciousness within you. You want to be ready to reveal that the Prince of Peace is within you. Prepare by spending some time in the quiet, listening to your inner guidance, and be willing to let Spirit in.

Preparing yourself for the feasting, the family, and the fun of the festivities can be so fraught with stress that making a place for peace to enter is completely forgotten. It is important that your preparations don't make it difficult for you to enjoy this coming celebration. You want to enjoy…to be "In Joy." What good is all the preparation if you do not enjoy your holiday time? Relax; you are doing all you can.

Take time to be aware that in the very midst of our busy preparations for the celebration of Christ's birth in ancient Bethlehem, Christ is reborn in the Bethlehems of our homes and daily lives. Take time, slow down, be still, be awake to the Divine Mystery that looks so common and so ordinary yet is wondrously present.

—Edward Hayes

Reflection: With what spirit am I preparing for the holidays?

Affirmation: I take time to prepare a place for the Christ Consciousness of Peace to awaken within me.

December 9
Divine Grace Percolating

When you get called into a deeper relationship with God and you say, "Show me!" a light is turned on in you that will shine for the rest of your life. You become the place where heaven touches down. Your edge to win the mortal race of acquisition lessens. There is a growing desire to be of service and to be more generous; you find time to care and understand.

> *You have to grow from the inside out. None can teach you, none can make you spiritual. There is no other teacher but your own soul.*
> —Swami Vivekananda

Your rational mind doesn't quite get it, but gives way to the emergence of your soul's expression. You feel the Divine Grace percolating into your awareness. You'll notice a change in the quality of your attitude, infused with more compassion and kindness. You may not be able to express all the shifting going on, but you do notice the desire to live more consciously attuned to these soul qualities.

Reflection: How is your desire to live more consciously attuned to your soul qualities emerging in your everyday life?

Affirmation: God now percolates through me!

How do you define success? Not what you see in the media or how your family describes success. Define success for yourself. Is it financial and business success or fabulous wealth? Is it having peace of mind or a family you love? Perhaps success to you is growing a garden or raising a child. However you define success, it is a goal worthy of your time and effort.

Remind yourself as you strive for success always to do your best. Every day that you do your best, it is always good enough. Your best at this moment is the best you can do at this particular time. Perhaps it's not great. Perhaps later you even see how you could have done it differently or better. Do not become overly concerned

Finish every day and be done with it. You have done what you could; some blunders and absurdities no doubt crept in; forget them as soon as you can. Tomorrow is a new day; you shall begin it serenely and with too high a spirit to be encumbered with your old nonsense.
—Ralph Waldo Emerson

about this. If you could have done it differently, you would have. So let it be. If you have given it your best, then it simply has to be good enough, because it is the best you could have done.

Reflection: Can you see how you have done and are doing your best?

Affirmation: What I do is good enough. My best is the best I can do. It is always good enough.

Wake Up

Have you ever watched a hypnotist entertain a crowd? He finds the most receptive individual in the house and gives him a suggestion, and that person sees what has been suggested to him. Imagine if he were told to see a giraffe? All of a sudden, he would have concern that this giraffe would run into things or people in the room, or whatever it was about the giraffe that came to his imagination. Now, to get rid of the giraffe, this individual would want somebody to remove it from the room. Yet the truth is, all he would have to do is wake up from the illusion.

This whole of creation is essentially subjective, and the dream is the theater where the dreamer is at once: scene, actor, prompter, stage manager, audience, and critic.
—Carl Gustav Jung

In life, one gets caught in a hypnotic trance, then attempts to remove the illusions … like wanting someone to get rid of the giraffe. All you have to do is wake up and see it's not there. Yet people give their power away every day to headlines, doctors, and bank statements, thinking this is the truth. It's time to wake up from the constriction of the societal hypnotic trance and realize nothing needs to be removed from your life; it's all been suggested to you, and you've believed it as the truth. It is an illusion. Clear your perception of the mirage, and be prepared to see the integrity of Spirit as your life.

Reflection: What mirage has captivated your attention, creating discomfort in your world? What would waking up look like if your world were all of sudden to get cleaned up and brightened up?

Affirmation: I now wake up to my happier, healthier, prosperous, and brighter life!

Don't Take It Personally

A powerful spiritual practice is not to take anything personally. How often do you assume that what's been said or done is aimed at you, in a negative way? Usually, this is simply a projection of what you actually think about yourself! Stop your self-criticism and judgment, and you will take things much less personally.

Taking things personally may also mean that some deep, unconscious inner belief, based on an old hurt, has been activated. Somehow this current event sounds, feels, or seems exactly like what happened before. At that time, usually as a young child, you made a decision about how to protect yourself from how life is or how people are. This belief has now been activated through this current situation, and you have taken it personally. Learning not to take things personally reduces the impact these old beliefs have on you, until they finally fade away altogether.

> *Don't take anything personally.*
> —Don Miguel Ruiz

Reflection: When and how do you most often take things personally? What is being triggered in you?

Affirmation: I choose not to take this personally. I choose to respond from a calm, centered, spiritually grounded place of love and truth.

Defending the Self-Image

No longer needing to defend the self-image or the imagined self, you'll free your life up to be lived as it was intended to be. You become free to go where your ego would not have let you go. You are lifted to a higher realm of possibilities that are not earthbound. The shackles are unlocked, and you are freed into a finer frequency of being, a place beyond mind. You will see the world from a different perspective.

At any moment, you have a choice that either leads you closer to your spirit or further away from it.

—Thich Nhat Hanh

Imagine seeing your world through the eyes of your Divine Self, and your awareness becomes the connection between eternity and this world you are playing in. Grace becomes the bridge that unites you to a joyous trust in living beyond worries or ambition. You become the channel through which God is expressed in your sphere of influence.

Reflection: What self-image is keeping you earthbound?

Affirmation: I am the channel through which God is expressed!

Relax into the Flow

This can be a very hectic and stressful time of year. Lots to do, people to see, places to go, presents to buy. The holidays tend to be a microcosm of how the rest of your life is going. Whatever isn't working, wherever you feel lonely, overwhelmed, or in lack and limitation, all can get magnified, if you let them.

You can practice bringing your spiritual vision and intention to the party instead. Use this time as if you were at an intensive spiritual training. Practice relaxing into the bustle of the holidays. This is great training for living a centered, spirit-filled life. Let the noise and lights, lines and music, wash over you like the sound of the

When every situation which life can offer is turned to the profit of spiritual growth, no situation can really be a bad one.
—Paul Brunton

surf. This is as powerful as any mindfulness or meditation practice for staying in the moment and not getting hooked on anything that's going on around you. Practice nonresistance, simply allowing the malls to be crowded, or the family to be trying, or your feelings to be whatever they are. This is great practice for going with the flow and staying present in the moment.

Reflection: Where are you allowing life to push you off-center? What practices could support your spiritual training right now?

Affirmation: I bring my spiritual vision and practices to every situation. I use all of my everyday life as a spiritual training ground.

Seeing with God's Eyes

Seeing with God's Eyes

Spirit sees you as infinitely precious and worthy. You are, after all, an incarnation of Itself, expressing and experiencing life as YOU. Spirit always wants the highest and best for you, and sees you having it. Do you? So often, you don't ask for what you want, because you don't see yourself having or deserving it.

Imagine seeing yourself, your life, and everyone around you through the eyes of Love. Love always wants what's best for someone. Love sees that everyone is worthy of love and joy and great happiness. Love is the way God sees. Start seeing yourself through the eyes of love. Now think about what you want to ask for. You don't need anything to make you feel better because you already have all the love you need. Now ask for what you want that will help you be more, express more, give more, love more, and experience more of the life you deserve.

You can't ask for what you want unless you know what it is. A lot of people don't know what they want or they want much less than they deserve. First, you have figure out what you want. Second, you have to decide that you deserve it. Third, you have to believe you can get it. And, fourth, you have to have the guts to ask for it.

—Barbara De Angelis

Reflection: Is it okay for you to ask for what you want for Christmas or in any area of your life? What would it be like if you saw yourself and others as God sees?

Affirmation: I see myself and others through the eyes of Love, as worthy, deserving, and joyful beings. I easily ask for what I want.

Beached

From time to time, whales and dolphins somehow end up beaching themselves. Why do they do it? Only they know what drives them on this suicide mission. As people come from all over to save them, a little water splashed on their drying skin is refreshing, helpful, and nice, but a little moisture is not going to turn their lives around. The only thing that will save them is to get them back into the water. There is no alternative.

In your life, you hear all sorts of nice spiritual phrases and well-meaning words that may be inspiring and refreshing. There are doctrines and creeds others will encourage you to adhere to. But the one thing that turns your world around is returning to the Source of life itself. There is no other substitute. The key to a spiritual life is Spirit Itself, not the words about it.

There's a world of difference between truth and facts. Facts can obscure the truth.
—Maya Angelou

We live but a fraction of our lives.
—Henry David Thoreau

Reflection: Where do you feel beached in your life? Rather than just some encouraging words that keep you going through your parched times, stop making excuses and get up and get back into your Source.

Affirmation: I get up and get back into living in the Source of my life!

Seeing with God's Eyes

From Ordinary to Extraordinary

Have you ever been around a child who has lots of little toys? Often you find yourself stepping on the toys or picking them up and throwing them on his or her pile of stuff just to get a room cleaned up. They seem to just pile up over the years. What is fascinating is how a child can pick up one of these inanimate objects and bring it to life. An ordinary Hot Wheels car from a bucket of hundreds can come to be special in the magical hands of a child. A doll from the bottom of a stack can all of a sudden become a best friend.

Passion rebuilds the world for the youth. It makes all things alive and significant.
—Ralph Waldo Emerson

Through the eyes of a child, the ordinary can become extraordinary. Getting so caught up in life, forgetting to see with the power of love, your piles could be adding up. One of the wonderful gifts of the holiday season is that it can stop you in your tracks, reminding you to see life once more with the eyes of God. Those eyes will once again enliven what seems to have lost life. Allow yourself to be a child again, and be the place where joy and passion bring life to where you are.

Reflection: What do you have piling up that is missing your eyes of love? Spend some time bringing life back to what is near and dear to your heart.

Affirmation: I am the life of Spirit wherever I am!

Remembering

Losing a loved one is terribly painful, and no one can ever replace him or her. The grief must be experienced for you to be free to move about life again. You have to be willing to put more than your toe into the pain to check out if you want to go in. You must be willing to surrender and jump into the abyss, not knowing where it will lead or how long it will take. Then be willing to do it again and again.

Acting as if you've dealt with the scarring of your soul, when in truth you never moved beyond the expectations of the head to the reality of the heart, will only come get you later in life. It's valuable to speak your loved one's name from time to time and remember his or her gift to you and how much more you have to bring to life because of the time shared.

> *Death leaves a heartache no one can heal, love leaves a memory no one can steal.*
> —from a headstone in Ireland

Reflection: What warm memories of a loved one haven't you let touch your heart lately? Go ahead, speak his/her name and open up and remember the love.

Affirmation: I am remembering love that has touched my life!

Seeing with God's Eyes

Happiness

Imagine surrendering to that which makes you happy. If your good doesn't lead to excessive greed that leads to frustration and disappointment or bring harm to anyone, what's keeping you from living a life that has you feeling good? Why wouldn't you say yes to happiness? Doesn't that feel like an appropriate gauge to use as a directional for your life?

Thousand of candles can be lighted from a single candle, and the life of the candle will not be shortened. Happiness never decreases by being shared.
—Buddha

It has been said that happy people are self-centered; it's actually the unhappy folks who are thinking about themselves and their issues and are focused on what's not working in their world. Those who are happy are actually enhancing their environment. They are creative, generous, and fun. Their qualities show flexibility in precarious times.

A bit of pleasure is fine, but too much of a good thing is too much. When you are left with a feeling of wanting more, rather than feeling satisfied, there is potential for an issue. True happiness goes beyond seeking physical pleasure, because it's long-lasting. Happiness dissolves anxiety, uplifts discouragement, restores health, and entices others to enter a higher frequency of Spirit. It leads to freedom and joyous living.

Reflection: Think about something that would make you feel good and ask yourself, "Will this bring me mere pleasure or will it bring me a longer lasting happiness?"

Affirmation: I am saying yes to my soul's directionals for long-lasting happiness!

Clear as Glass

Too long, people have lived with a sense of separation from God. People were taught that Spirit is something outside of themselves. To believe in oneness, you have to give up twoness. Yet getting caught up in your humanness creates questions about your Oneness with God, because you know Spirit doesn't do struggle. All that any struggle will tell you is, in this instant, you have a sense of disconnect from Source; it doesn't mean you are not one with Spirit.

I and the Father are One. Be like a window pane—the sun shines through it, but the pane is not the sun. A dirty window with its obstructions might create some questions on

He that sees me sees Him that sent me.
—John 12:45

the brightness of the day, but it will never impact the sun. You can create obstructions to the flow of Spirit by creating questions about Its brightness, but you will never impact the Infinite Potential. Become as clear as glass on a sunny day, and you allow your world to see God shining as you!

Reflection: Go clean the windows to your soul so Spirit can shine brighter in your world.

Affirmation: Those who see me see Spirit shining through me!

Subatomic Light

Winter Solstice

There have been celebrations around the winter solstice since people began watching the sky. Man has lived in touch with the rhythm of the cycles of life since we first walked this earth. The realization that the darkest of times has ended and the light of possibilities is returning has always been worth celebrating. The winter solstice for the northern hemisphere happens exactly when the axial tilt of Earth's North Pole is farthest away from the sun. It is the shortest day and longest night of the year, when the sun's maximum elevation in the sky is the lowest. It's interesting to note that Julius Caesar in 46 BCE declared December 25 as the date of the winter solstice for Europe when it is usually between December 21 and 23.

When we talk about settling the world's problems, we're barking up the wrong tree. The world is perfect. It's a mess. It has always been a mess. We are not going to change it. Our job is to straighten out our own lives.
—Joseph Campbell

Meditation upon an astronomical event has a way of opening your soul to the ritualistic happening stored in the collective subconscious of those who have gone before you. The realization that the ebb of difficulty has reached its lowest point and is now turning brings the potential of leaving anxiety behind. If all the light were to return in a flash, you would be blinded, which is why enlightenment is a gradual unfoldment and becoming. When you come to trust that the challenge or mess you've found yourself in has begun to straighten itself out, you just might find yourself wanting to light a candle and celebrate.

Reflection: What do you want to let go of, in the outgoing tide, so you can celebrate the return of your good into the now-available space?

Affirmation: I celebrate the return of my greater good!

Subatomic Light

At the subatomic level, everything is made of light. These packets of light are constantly winking in and out of existence. What causes them to keep winking back into existence in the place they were before? Habit, expectation, observation, in other words, consciousness. Change any of these aspects of consciousness—change your expectations, your habits, or what you are paying attention to—and things wink back into existence in a new place. This is the basis for healing, growth, and transformation.

The more I see, the less I know for sure.
—John Lennon

Every atom in your body is made up of packets of energy that are photons of light. The higher the vibration at which you are resonating, the healthier and more whole you are, and the brighter you shine! The brighter you shine, the more you glow! This allows you to be a bringer of Light, a healing presence, into any situation or circumstance. YOU are the Light of the World! Really! Go ahead—SHINE!

Reflection: Where could you be shining your light and be a healing and benevolent presence?

Affirmation: I am made of light and energy. I focus my consciousness on wholeness and peace. I shine the light of love everywhere.

The Gift of Love

Love is the impulse behind all of creation. Love is the desire of Spirit to give itself completely and fully into creation, so that It may become every created thing and express all of Its joy and experience all of Its presence. A definition of Love is "Spirit's self-givingness of Itself into creation." Every time you give yourself to something or someonem you are being Love in Action.

Love is always bestowed as a gift, freely, willingly and without expectation. We don't love to be loved, we love to love....What love we've given, we shall have forever. What love we fail to give, will be lost for all eternity.
—Leo Buscaglia

This means that spiritual maturity must inevitably take you beyond your own care and healing. This is only one-half of life and will take you only so far in your personal growth or your spiritual connection. The other half of life is experienced in and through your relationships with others. Every time you extend yourself beyond your own life, giving of yourself in love, in service, in care and compassion, you are expressing more of the Divine Reality. Every time you give yourself to a cause or a community, a relationship or any living being, you are stretched and grown in entirely new ways. When you are love in action, your love multiplies and grows, for you and as a blessing to those around you.

Reflection: Do you give love to be loved? When does giving of yourself take you out of your own small or limited experience?

Affirmation: I freely and joyously give myself with Love to Life, to creation, to others. I let my love out, and it is a blessing to all.

Beyond Sense and Reason

You can't take heaven by storm ... there is no way you can force yourself into the mystical realm. As you dance between the dimensions of self-awareness and unity, you just might get seduced into surrendering to the space beyond sense and reason. When this happens, your sense of self can dissolve into the radiance of the whole where the Grace and Love of God moves as you. This transcendent gift is ecstasy.

Returning from this point in the timeless, you might be surprised at how brief in time this expanded realization was, yet things seem different. From such a heightened state, you may expect to receive the healing of your choice only to find you still have the same issues to deal with. You didn't want the mystical experience ... you wanted the miracle of your choosing. Yet, how you now see your world will have been altered because you have developed an awareness of the Presence everywhere you look, and nothing seems overwhelming any longer.

Love said to me,
there is nothing that is not me.
Be silent.
—Rumi

Reflection: Has your sense of self ever dissolved into the radiance of the Whole?

Affirmation: I joyously dance in the transcendent gift of ecstasy!

The Gold Wrapping Paper

Once upon a time, a man punished his five-year-old daughter for using up the family's only roll of expensive gold wrapping paper before Christmas. Money was tight, so he became even more upset when, on Christmas Eve, he saw that the child had used the expensive gold paper to decorate a large shoebox she had put under the Christmas tree.

Patience in a moment of anger can save a hundred days of pain.
—ancient proverb

Nevertheless, the next morning the little girl, filled with excitement, brought the gift box to her father and said, "This is for you, Daddy!" As he opened the box, the father was embarrassed by his earlier overreaction, now regretting how he had punished her. But when he opened the shoebox, he found it was empty and again his anger flared. "Don't you know, young lady," he said harshly, "when you give someone a present, there's supposed to be something inside the package!" The little girl looked up at him with sad tears rolling from her eyes and whispered, "Daddy, it's not empty. I blew kisses into it until it was all full." The father was crushed. He fell on his knees and put his arms around his precious little girl. He begged her to forgive him for his unnecessary anger. An accident took the life of the child only a short time later. It is told that the father kept this little gold box by his bed for all the years of his life. Whenever he was discouraged or faced difficult problems, he would open the box, take out an imaginary kiss, and remember the love of his beautiful child who had put it there.

Reflection: In a very real sense, each of us as human beings has been given an invisible golden box filled with unconditional love and kisses from our children, family, friends, and God. Open your box and feel the love.

Affirmation: I feel the gift of love from family and friends that transcends time!

What's the News?

During the time of the Kwanzaa, each day is greeted with a Swahili saying, "Habari Gani?"—What's the News? Imagine if you started each morning by checking in with Spirit, and your answer came through the veil of the seven principles of Kwanzaa. Kwanzaa has its origins in the ancient African first fruits of the harvest, which stresses the cooperation, gathering, and sharing of good. Envision your life if you started each day with your first harvest of thought coming directly from God.

This celebration doesn't take you away from the world; rather it brings you right into it. People often forget the richness of their heritage and the gifts of the ancestors. Uniting with all that you are and standing strong in your creative expression allows you to add your unique contribution to the community. Have faith in those first fruits of Divine Thought and feast in gratitude. You are a bountiful blessing and a contributor to life. From the richness of your journey and the fullness of your harvest, the good news is that the path before you is looking bright!

The seven principles of Kwanzaa—unity, self-determination, collective work and responsibility, cooperative economics, purpose, creativity, and faith—teach us that when we come together to strengthen our families and communities and honor the lesson of the past, we can face the future with joy and optimism.
—President Bill Clinton

Reflection: Write your first thoughts, first fruits, of the day for the rest of the year.

Affirmation: The good news about my day is I am blessed by God!

Your Greatness

How would it be if you argued as hard for your greatness as you do for your limitations? Try talking as vehemently about what's going right in your world or about what great things other people are doing as you do when you complain about it. Speak forcefully about your greatness, your ability, your direction, your dreams, and your life, not about the things you think are holding you back.

Our deepest fear is not that we are inadequate. Our deepest fear is that we are powerful beyond measure. It is our light, not our darkness that most frightens us.
—Marianne Williamson

Speaking powerfully about your own light and gifts helps you listen to the future that is calling you! Throw your vision, with power and confidence, like a lasso out into the future to capture it! Then pull yourself toward it with your belief that you can do it. Knowing, speaking, and sharing your greatness helps you unfold your vision, step by step. Since you are now anchored to your future, confidently speaking your future into being, you can be assured that each "next step" will be revealed to you.

Reflection: How does it feel to argue for your greatness and your vision?

The future I envision is a demonstration that I am shining my light reatness today.

Urge to Serve

Service is a generous way to live. It requires you giving of yourself to another or to a situation. Yet it is part of your soul's purpose to live in service. Mahatma Gandhi said, "The best way to find yourself is to lose yourself in the service of others." Sacred service is a spiritual practice because it is love manifested. It looks for nothing in return. You do it because it is who you are ... the hands of God.

To serve is your nature, and you practice sacred service because you have an inner urge to serve. You have so much to give, and there are so many opportunities around you to share who you are. Being in the generous flow of life will bring good feelings, abundance, and healing into your world and those you touch. But that is not why you do it ... it's an offshoot of being an expression of God and making a positive difference in the world.

I slept and dreamt that life was joy. I awoke and saw that life was service. I acted and behold, service was joy.
—Rabindranath Tagore

Reflection: Each day, look around your world to see where you can be of service. It can be small, like letting someone go ahead of you at the checkout counter, or you can pick up some trash, organize a group to clean up an orphanage or your spiritual community, go build wells in a third-world country, or just find a little extra time to give to your children. Large or small, you'll find a soul satisfaction that will energize your spirit.

Affirmation: I love being of service!

December 29

Service as Joy

The best way to stop being obsessed with your own life and concerns is to get involved in something outside of you. Service is one of the greatest gifts of love you can give. It also is a way to shift your focus away from your own problems. Whether it is distributing gifts through a toy drive, helping the homeless, visiting an elderly relative, or caring for abandoned animals, helping others is powerful therapy. There are so many ways to reach outside of your own limited, little world.

I don't know what your destiny will be, but one thing I know: the only ones among you who will be really happy are those who will have sought and found how to serve.
—Albert Schweitzer

During the holidays is a wonderful time to kick-start your focus on service. Being of service is also a powerful spiritual practice. Service reminds you of your connection with all beings and all life. It puts you in right relationship with the world around you, reminding you that every being is part of the whole. Your service is a great act of love and a powerful statement and appreciation of our oneness.

Reflection: How are you serving?

m willing to be of service to others. I make a difference with ng and service bring me great joy.

Release the Past

This past year, you have done good and given love. You have accomplished, created, and enjoyed things. Find every ounce of good, and praise it! Just don't take anything into the New Year that doesn't serve your highest good and your ability to give your gift as a blessing to the world.

This last day of the year, you have come to the "great exhale" at the end! Now is the time to release anything you do not choose to carry with you into this next year. Release resentments, unforgiveness, grudges, and judgments. Release smallness, fear, uncertainty, and worry. Release your worries over things that didn't work out and your embarrassment over times you were unconscious. Release it all with a great exhale!

What you need to know about the past is that no matter what has happened, it has all worked together to bring you to this very moment. And this is the moment you can choose to make everything new. Right now.
—Unknown

Reflection: What have you learned, experienced, discovered, and explored this past year? What are you exhaling and releasing?

Affirmation: I burn away the past in the fire of forgiveness and release. I exhale fear, doubt, resentment, shame, and blame. I move into the new year free and unencumbered.

Urge to Serve

Ouroboros

The ouroboros is an ancient symbol depicting a serpent or dragon swallowing its own tail, representing the perpetual cycles of renewal of life and the eternal return. The end is the beginning. The end of something is the beginning of something else. The completion of one year is the start of a new one. Spring ends and summer begins. You close one door and a new one opens.

The alchemists, who in their own way know more about the nature of the individuation process than we moderns do, expressed this paradox through the symbol of the ouroboros.
—Carl Jung

Life is cyclic. Life concludes to awaken reborn to a new experience. Letting go of what was and not knowing what lies ahead can be scary. You must learn to trust what lies ahead on the other side of the threshold that has been prepared for your soul's unfoldment.

The number nine, through time, has often been referred to symbolically as a representation of attainment and completion. With completion comes a new beginning in the endless cycles of life. With completion comes accomplishment, authority, and power, with an ease and confidence.

Reflection: Can you let go and surrender to your evolutionary expression from the outer walk to your inner journey in this new year?

Affirmation: I trust what awaits me in this new year!